The Idler's Club

Nineteenth-Century and Neo-Victorian Cultures

Series editors: Ruth Heholt and Joanne Ella Parsons

Recent books in the series
Domestic Architecture, Literature and the Sexual Imaginary in Europe, 1850–1930
Aina Marti-Balcells

Assessing Intelligence: The Bildungsroman and the Politics of Human Potential in England, 1860–1910
Sara Lyons

The Idler's Club: Humour and Mass Readership from Jerome K. Jerome to P. G. Wodehouse
Laura Kasson Fiss

Forthcoming
Lost and Revenant Children 1850–1940
Tatiana Kontou

Olive Schreiner and the Politics of Print Culture, 1883–1920
Clare Gill

Michael Field's Revisionary Poetics
Jill Ehnenn

Literary Illusions: Performance Magic and Victorian Literature
Christopher Pittard

Pastoral in Early-Victorian Fiction: Environment and Modernity
Mark Frost

Spectral Embodiments of Child Death in the Long Nineteenth Century
Jen Baker

Women's Activism in the Transatlantic Consumers' Leagues, 1885–1920
Flore Janssen

Life Writing and the Nineteenth-Century Market
Sean Grass

British Writers, Popular Literature and New Media Innovation, 1820–45
Alexis Easley

Oscar Wilde's Aesthetic Plagiarisms
Sandra Leonard

The Idler's Club

Humour and Mass Readership from Jerome K. Jerome to P. G. Wodehouse

Laura Kasson Fiss

EDINBURGH
University Press

Edinburgh University Press is one of the leading university presses in the UK. We publish academic books and journals in our selected subject areas across the humanities and social sciences, combining cutting-edge scholarship with high editorial and production values to produce academic works of lasting importance. For more information visit our website: edinburghuniversitypress.com

Material from Chapter 1 first appeared as 'The Idler's Club: Humor and Sociability in the Age of New Journalism', *Victorian Periodicals Review*, vol. 49, issue 3 (Fall 2016), pp. 415–30. Published by The Johns Hopkins University Press, © 2016 Research Society for Victorian Periodicals.

Edinburgh University Press Ltd
The Tun – Holyrood Road
12(2f) Jackson's Entry
Edinburgh EH8 8PJ

Typeset in 11/13 Adobe Sabon
by Cheshire Typesetting Ltd, Cuddington, Cheshire, and
printed and bound in Great Britain

A CIP record for this book is available from the British Library

ISBN 978 1 4744 9714 5 (hardback)
ISBN 978 1 4744 9716 9 (webready PDF)
ISBN 978 1 4744 9717 6 (epub)

Contents

Illustrations

Figures

Tables

Series Preface

Nineteenth-Century and Neo-Victorian Cultures

Series Editors: Ruth Heholt and Joanne Ella Parsons

This interdisciplinary series provides space for full and detailed scholarly discussions on nineteenth-century and Neo-Victorian cultures. Drawing on radical and cutting-edge research, volumes explore and challenge existing discourses, as well as providing an engaging reassessment of the time period. The series encourages debates about decolonising nineteenth-century cultures, histories, and scholarship, as well as raising questions about diversities. Encompassing art, literature, history, performance, theatre studies, film and TV studies, medical and the wider humanities, *Nineteenth Century and Neo-Victorian Cultures* is dedicated to publishing pioneering research that focuses on the Victorian era in its broadest and most diverse sense.

Acknowledgements

Belonging and exclusivity are perhaps natural themes for a book composed outside of the tenure system. For that reason, I have more people to thank than I can possibly include here: when I could take no support for granted, every expression of support or even interest in this project has felt like a gift.

Being born into the University of North Carolina at Chapel Hill departments of American Studies, English and History, and the larger American Studies community, was like being put down in the club books at birth. Bill and Jean Anne Leuchtenburg, Jennifer Ho, Bill and Marcie Ferris, Jane Thrailkill, Bob Cantwell and Lydia Wegman, among many others, talked with me about clubs and showed me what intellectual fellowship can be.

Vassar College has been the source of much of what's good in my life, including this project, both in my formative undergraduate experience and during my time as Visiting Scholar when the well-stocked library drew me along the novels of Barrie to a novel by Barr. The mentorship and friendship of faculty including Susan Zlotnick, Peter Antelyes, Leslie Dunn, Brian Mann, Lydia Murdoch and the late Michael Pisani has been sustaining, as well as fellow classmates including Gail Goldman, Peter Alfaro and Rebecca Goldstein. The faculty accountability group led by Curtis Dozier provided essential support at the beginning of this project, especially Mita Choudhury.

Many thanks to my dissertation committee at Indiana University: Andrew Miller, Ivan Kreilkamp (who first suggested I write on humour), Joss Marsh and Rae Greiner. Susan Gubar and Peter Bailey provided important feedback early in my progress. My fellow graduate students cohered in various club-like structures, including a writing group. Thanks especially to Heather Love, Julie Kraft, Carrie Sickmann Han, Lauren Simek Prendergast and Maureen Hattrup.

Michigan Technological University supported this research and associated conference presentations through the Humanities Department and College of Sciences and Arts. The Pavlis Honors College, particularly Lorelle Meadows, provided community and opened vistas. Lisa Gordillo, Michelle Jarvie-Eggart, Sarah and Tim Scarlett, Jared Anderson, Mary and Kent Cyr, and Maria Bergstrom are among those who have sustained me and my work on this project. Little Huskies Child Development Center not only cared for our children during key parts of this process, but became another sort of club, with emotional and intellectual engagement – thanks especially to Eva-Marie Hatfield and Nikki Kaufman.

The Research Society for Victorian Periodicals has been an essential organisation for this project, club-like in all the best ways. Patrick Leary, Pickwickian in the best sense, ushered me into this community and has provided essential advice and encouragement, including a kind and helpful peer review. And of course VICTORIA has been a consistent presence, not only helping with enquiries, but also serving as a refreshing reminder of all of the wonderfully esoteric questions researchers are asking. Alexis Easley, Linda Hughes, Laura Vorachek, Kitty Ledbetter and Jim Mussell are among the many RSVPers who have welcomed me and taught me so much about what we do and don't know about periodicals. #SHARPFridays has been a clublike reprieve in the pandemic time, thanks to Marie Léger-St-Jean, Alex Wingate, Colleen Barrett and many others. A member of all these communities, Troy Bassett has been an essential mentor, providing collaboration, support and a thorough and invaluable peer review of the full manuscript.

Libraries are the club premises of any history of the book. Much of my formative reading of Jerome K. Jerome's works took place while guarding an extra desk at Indiana University's Lilly Library, reading copies from auxiliary storage that, to my horror, disintegrated slightly as I read. The Walsall Local History Archive welcomed me as a visitor and cheerfully responded to follow-up queries years later. The New York Public Library provided access to bound volumes of *To-Day* and other period books. The Beinecke Rare Book and Manuscript Library at Yale helped me discover *Home Chimes* and provided scans. The UNC Libraries, especially Wilson, helped me access key texts in print and digitally. Vassar librarians Gretchen Lieb, Deb Bucher, Emily Benton and others have been instrumental. Pretty much all of the library staff at Michigan Technological University have helped with something, from Interlibrary Loan to copyright to book imaging; thanks especially to Erin Matas, David Holden, Jenn Sams, Annelise Doll and John Schneiderhan. For permission to publish extracts, thanks to the Conan Doyle Estate; the Dorothy Sayers Estate, represented by David Higham; and the P. G. Wodehouse Estate, represented by RCW.

Michelle Houston at EUP has understood this book's vision from our first encounter, and I feel so fortunate to have her as an editor. Thanks to Joanne Parsons and Ruth Heholt for improving the book as series editors and to the editorial team, including copyeditor Camilla Rockwood, who kindly saved me from numerous bloopers. All errors that remain are my own.

My parents, John and Joy Kasson, laid the groundwork for this book through early exposure to Victorian humour, and they have offered encouragement and insight at every step of the way. I am so lucky that they are not only wonderful parents but also wonderful academics and writers. I'd like to thank my whole extended family for their support and encouragement: the Fisses, the Rodriguez-Mirandas, and the Kassons (and Kamerlins) both West Coast and transatlantic. My husband, Andy Fiss, has been a sounding board and first audience for much of this material – and he even laughs at my jokes. I dedicate this book to Andy and our children, Sebastian and Toby. I'm glad to be in your club.

Introduction: Imagining Clubland

In the final few pages of the first issue of the *Idler* magazine, dated February 1892, a headpiece introduces a feature called 'The Idler's Club' (Fig. 0.1). The backs of five easy chairs frame the bottom of the image, facing a fireplace that occupies the middle ground. In each chair sits a young man (all of them have dark hair, although one is balding). Some turn towards each other. One has his feet up on the mantelpiece and another leans his head back as smoke escapes his mouth. Tendrils of smoke wend their way from the visible or invisible cigars of each, meeting above the fireplace to form the words 'The Idler's Club'. Beneath this image, the letterpress begins with the sentence 'Then there was another thing.'

Through this headpiece, the *Idler* declared its intention to serve as a club for contributors and readers alike. Of course, as befits a periodical edited by humorists, this claim served as a bit of a joke. The exclusivity and personal connections of a club could never be replicated in a mass-circulated magazine, especially, as the column quickly makes clear, one aimed at the recently literate classes. But, also in a manner typical of Victorian humorists, the joke carries a kernel of truth. In his 1924 memoir, Arthur Conan Doyle describes the importance of the *Idler* circle to his early career in London:

> Of the literary men whom I met at that time my most vivid recollections are of the group who centred round the new magazine, 'The Idler', which had been started by Jerome K. Jerome, who had deservedly shot into fame with his splendidly humorous 'Three Men in a Boat'. It has all the exuberance and joy of life which youth brings with it, and even now if I have ever time to be at all sad, which is seldom enough, I can laugh away the shadows when I open that book. Jerome

I

Figure 0.1 Dudley Hardy, headpiece for 'The Idler's Club', *Idler* 1, no. 1. Personal collection.

is a man who, like most humorists, has a very serious side to his character, as all who have seen 'The Third Floor Back' will acknowledge, but he was inclined to be hotheaded and intolerant in political matters, from pure earnestness of purpose, which alienated some of his friends. He was associated in the editorship of 'The Idler' with Robert Barr, a volcanic Anglo- or rather Scot-American, with a violent manner, a wealth of strong adjectives, and one of the kindest of natures underneath it all. He was one of the best raconteurs I have ever known, and as a writer I have always felt that he did not quite come into his own. George Burgin, like some quaint gentle character from Dickens, was the sub-editor, and Barrie, Zangwill, and many other rising men were among the contributors who met periodically at dinner. I was not unfaithful to 'The Strand', but there were some contributions which they did not need, and with these I established my connection with 'The Idler'. It was at this time and in this way that I met James Barrie, of whom I shall have more to say when I come to that chapter which treats of some eminent and interesting men whom I have known.[1]

Doyle sketches the portraits of key figures in this study: Jerome K. Jerome, Robert Barr, J. M. Barrie and Israel Zangwill. A few essential portraits remain to flesh out the group I call the Idlers: Barry Pain, the first to be called a 'New Humorist', who wrote for both *Punch* and the *Idler*, and P. G. Wodehouse, twenty-two years younger than Doyle, who played with him on Barrie's cricket team. Several other figures play supporting roles in the study's cast, including Robert Louis Stevenson, G. K. Chesterton and Dorothy Sayers, as well as George Burgin through his contributions to the *Idler*. These figures used humour about the club to highlight the vagaries of social belonging, often with an eye to advancing their own social and professional standing.

Despite the heavy nostalgia in Doyle's description, he places his companions in a literary hierarchy. Not only does he include Barrie alone in the category of 'eminent and interesting men', but he also stresses that he sent the *Idler* the submissions that the *Strand* 'did not need'. The Idlers' efforts to advance their professional and social standing met with various degrees of success. As the Victorian canon has adjusted over the years, Idlers have risen and fallen. Robert Louis Stevenson has never really lost his place, although today he holds it for his adventure stories rather than his essays. Doyle holds a firm place in new scholarship and on syllabi. Barrie's star is rising, although still largely for his plays rather than the early novels and periodical pieces that connect him most closely to the Idlers.[2] Zangwill, too, draws increasing attention, mainly for his explicitly Jewish work, including *The Melting Pot* and *Children of the Ghetto*. Jerome rarely features in books not explicitly focused on him, and Pain even less. However, both have attracted monograph-length studies, unlike Barr, who does not currently rate an entry in the *Oxford Dictionary of National Biography*.[3] Meanwhile, the term 'Victorian' rarely applies to Wodehouse, due to his age, although he overlapped with the Idlers' social and professional circles. Despite the prevalence of humour in the Victorian canon from Dickens to Wilde, canonicity often seems synonymous with seriousness. Even those figures who were recognised as humorists during their lifetimes often have the serious elements of their writings overemphasised.

By focusing on Jerome, this study highlights the role of humour, stylistically and socially. The attempt to mimic club talk provided stylistic continuity among these different authors and cemented the idea that the works were 'speaking' to each other. Casual talk among men appears not only in official club settings but also in more informal groups, including the 'Idler's Club' column itself, and also in mixed-sex groups, particularly in fictional portrayals of newspaper offices. In a sense, this continued the tradition begun by *Blackwood's Edinburgh Magazine* in 'Noctes Ambrosianae', a series of fictionalised conversations featuring *Blackwood's* staff and other literary figures. Yet many of the Idlers were deemed 'New Humorists' at the time – not a compliment – and seen as a break from past humour tradition in terms of style and professionalism, with an emphasis on class.

Jerome frames idling as a class-based contrast to work: 'I like work: it fascinates me. I can sit and look at it for hours.'[4] Implicitly of the clerk classes, his idlers should be working but shirk their duties. Anne Humphreys contrasts them with Walter Benjamin's flâneurs, but they also differ from Wodehouse's idle clubmen, who do not need to work by virtue of their class standing.[5] Both Wodehouse and Jerome spent time as clerks: Jerome for the railway and Wodehouse in a bank. John Carey argues that Wodehouse's upper-class characters speak in clerk's slang, continuing the stylistic precedent of New Humour.[6] The club and the magazine contrast as spaces of class-based leisure. Although magazines crossed class readership, Matthew Arnold famously decried 'the New Journalism' as making papers too accessible to the newly literate public.[7] As part of the larger Reform trajectory, the 1870 Education Act expanded literacy by beginning the creation of the state school system.[8] Jerome himself owed the later years of his education to this act. The reading public never truly resembled a club in size and configuration, but between Samuel Johnson's *Idler* and Jerome and Barr's *Idler*, readership had greatly expanded and diversified.[9]

In the field of New Journalism, the *Idler* explicitly competed with the *Strand*, similarly founded in the early 1890s. When Jerome bought the *Idler* from Barr in 1895, he changed the size and price to match the *Strand* more precisely and described his aspirations in a note 'To the Readers of "The Idler"':

Having obtained the sole control of *THE IDLER*, it is my hope not only to maintain, but to increase, its present great popularity and prestige. In circulation *THE IDLER* is second to only one other English magazine, while its literary standing is in the very foremost rank. This position *THE IDLER* at once stepped into at its birth, more than three and a-half years ago, and has maintained without trouble, in spite of the efforts of its rivals, new or old. With its circulation I am satisfied; at all events, for the present. It will never be my aim to make it a magazine for what is generally termed 'the masses', but to appeal to that growing public which possesses literary tastes and artistic sympathies.

I wish to make it a magazine that will be almost a need to thinking men and women.[10]

As other critics of Jerome have noted, his experience with class-based prejudice by no means inoculated him against class snobbery.[11] Conceding that the *Idler*'s circulation cannot match the *Strand*'s, he argues for its superior literary merit. This very number of the *Idler* carried a chapter of Doyle's serial *The Stark Munro Letters*, as well as a serial instalment of Barr's *A Woman Intervenes*. Works by other Idlers appeared in the *Strand*, including a serial of Jerome's memoir.[12] Although the *Idler* did not compete with *Punch* directly in format, price or frequency, it clearly had to contend with its influence in the print field, especially when it came to humour. The *Idler* did not frame itself as a humorous periodical, and it carried serious poetry, prose and non-fiction. Yet the character of the magazine was undoubtedly shaped by the humour of its editors, highlighted by their decision to open the first issue with a new serial by Mark Twain, *The American Claimant*. Jerome frequently complained about poor reviews of his work in *Punch*, but Pain published in both, as did John Bernard Partridge.[13] Like clubs, magazines allowed for multiple affiliations, but not without some rivalries.

The Idlers' jokes about clubs focused attention on exclusivity, particularly as it pertained to the reading public. The critique of exclusivity implies a desire to open the club, but the Idlers repeatedly stress the cosy feelings of belonging that clubs foster. Humour fuels the ambiguity of this position: through 'most ingenious paradox', contradictory viewpoints often coexist without a clear point of advocacy.[14] In fact, discomfort with humour's political ramifications may have contributed to a lacuna in explicit studies of Victorian humour between a flourishing in the 1970s and a slow revival in the early 2000s.[15] At a time when popular journalism still questioned whether women could be funny, Eileen Gillooly and Margaret Stetz drew attention to 'feminine humour'.[16] As Carolyn Williams has shown in reference to Gilbert and Sullivan, many works of humour whose gender stereotypes have appalled previous critics can be viewed as enacting more complex gender critique and gender parody.[17]

The most defining feature of the gentleman's social club is its exclusivity by sex. Perhaps for that reason, the writers who used the club as a cosy, if conflicted, metaphor for the reading public tended to be male. The major example in this study of a woman writing about the club is the trouser-wearing, androgyny-advocating Dorothy Sayers, who largely appears as a coda and whose work and biography bear no direct links to the *Idler* circle. Women certainly contributed to the *Idler* and the 'Idler's Club' column, including very funny women such as Ella Hepworth Dixon and Evelyn Sharp. But they did not engage in the same type of humour about clubs, although fictional female journalists play crucial roles in Jerome and Barr's novels. As Eve Kosofsky Sedgwick and Jack Halberstam foundationally show, women participate in masculinity: women are deeply implicated in relationships between men, in this case even through their exclusion, and women can participate in experiences of masculinity, in this case largely as readers.[18] Jerome goes out of his way to mention women as readers in the address above: he could have chosen gender-neutral language or used the masculine as generic. Men may have practised this particular style of joke about clubs, but these men advocated for gender inclusivity in social and professional spaces. At times swimming up the critical stream, I argue that many of these authors represent exclusion by sex as one of the chiefly laughable aspects of the club as an institution. In that sense, gender becomes shorthand for exclusion more broadly.

If the case of gender shows the possibilities of the Idlers' approach to exclusivity, the case of race shows its limits.[19] Although the *Idler* aspired to a global reach, non-white common readers are not depicted and explicitly welcomed in the way that women are. Zangwill's Jewish identity was understood at the time in terms of race, and he is particularly alive to the distinctions between the Ashkenazi and Sephardic ethnic and cultural groups.[20] However, despite his deep integration into the *Idler* circle, Zangwill's friends and colleagues do not explicitly integrate Jews into their fiction. Although Jerome wrote against American lynchings in *To-Day* and in his memoir, he took pains to emphasise that he did not advocate racial equality.[21] Casually racist language appears in works by nearly all of these authors, and Wodehouse employs blackface as a comic device, including having Bertie Wooster impersonate a blackface minstrel performer.[22] The 2004 Overlook edition of Wodehouse's *Uncle Fred in the Springtime* (1939) depicts Pongo dressed in blackface as a Zulu warrior on its cover.[23] Blackness operates as a sign of otherness and exclusion. The possibility that a club might admit a Black member is only raised briefly in a long list of untold anecdotes at the end of Barry Pain's *Problem Club* (1919): 'how a negro failed to get into the club, and how a girl of seventeen was actually elected – these things with many others must remain hidden in the club archives'.[24] The contrast between the treatment of race and gender could not be clearer than in this juxtaposition. Narratorial surprise hails the admission of the girl but not the rejection of the Black applicant: the surprise may instead lie in the fact of their attempt.

If the Idlers in this study were working to make print culture carry only the positive feelings of exclusivity and not the negative ones, they did not completely succeed. Indeed, they may have been trying not to throw the doors of the club completely open but only to crack them enough so that they themselves – and perhaps some others like them – could sneak through. As Benedict Anderson famously argued, newspapers and other works of print culture reinforce 'imagined communities'; his example was nations, but gender and racial affiliations certainly fall into this category. Part of what made his argument so influential was its emphasis that although there are certain real dimensions to the nation (geographic features, etc.), the community around it is collectively imagined.[25] Yet the purely fictional clubs introduce another possibility, an imaginary community.[26] Imaginary communities are not bound by physical location and can thus transcend time and space. The Failure Club does not exist, so if readers want to imagine themselves as members, who can stop them? Exclusionary language might bar the door, constantly reminding some readers that they are unwelcome. Yet readers can also decide to suspend their disbelief about demographic exclusion and make themselves members of the club. The context of light humour enables this type of negotiation, presenting the often serious business of social mobility as a comfortable laughing matter.

Clubs and print culture

The club loomed large in the Victorian imagination. Imposing as the physical edifices of club premises remain to this day in the St James's area of London, known as Clubland, print culture magnified the club's presence. Readers of newspapers, periodicals and fiction in a variety of formats vicariously experienced club life – and continue to do so as long as these texts are read. Rendering literal the notions of explicit criteria for belonging and expulsion,

along with rules for behaviour and procedures for their enforce-
ment, the club remains a powerful symbol of the institutionalisa-
tion of Victorian social power and its attendant exclusivity.

The social clubs that grew out of the London coffeehouses and
clustered in the West End in the area of St James that became
known as 'Clubland' served several pragmatic ends. Originally
an exclusive group within a public coffeehouse, the club initially
served as a manner of guaranteeing gambling wagers.[27] These
were emphatically clubs for gentlemen, with the full gender, class
and economic connotations of the word. White's claims the title
of the first club, in 1697, and it remains one of the most exclusive, including by sex. By the Victorian period, most clubs had
their own premises, or clubhouses.[28] Before hotels and restaurants
became common in the capital, clubs provided a place for members
to have a meal, entertain friends, stay overnight, send and receive
mail, among other needs. Some clubs, most notably the Bath, had
swimming pools and other bathing apparatus. As clubs for women
became more common in the 1880s, they addressed the need for
women shopping in the city to have a quiet place to rest, have a
cup of tea, and use the toilet.[29] Some clubs had separate 'town'
and 'country' membership rates, allowing for those who lived far
from London to occasionally enjoy the club's sociability – and to
have a place to stay in the metropolis.[30] Clubs served a variety
of pragmatic and personal needs, including the professional and
political.[31]

The club sometimes functioned like a group of friends, institutionalised for specific logistical purposes. But the process of exclusivity and rules for initial and continuing membership proved key
in facilitating the function of certain elements of the club, from the
initial concerns about the ability to pay gambling debts to the continuing ways in which clubs circumvent licensing laws for the sale
and consumption of alcohol. The self-policing function of clubs
served pragmatic legal as well as social purposes. New members
had to be proposed to a club, sponsored by at least one existing
member, and all members could vote with white or black balls.
Formal structures from clubs influence the ways we still talk about
social exclusivity: blackballing has become a general term, and
'old boys' club' literally means a social club for alumni of a public
school, such as the Public Schools Club.[32]

Over the course of the Victorian period, some elements of the
club changed. Smoking became more part of club life, including

dedicated smoking rooms, whereas once it had been prohibited.[33] Non-members began to be allowed as guests in clubs, some-times confined to 'Strangers' Rooms'.[34] At some clubs, members could host dinners for friends even if not all were members of that club. As restaurants became more common, some clubs met there, instead of or before acquiring their own premises. Club life retained a strong connection to the practice of men giving dinners for each other, often a formal process with a chair and familiar rituals including songs and speeches.

Clubs and print culture have an intertwined history that dates back to the coffeehouses. The West End club as such began as a way of seeking greater exclusivity within the eighteenth-century coffeehouse.[35] In addition to caffeine, these coffeehouses served up newspapers and periodicals for communal reading, particularly as the stamp duty raised the price.[36] Despite Jürgen Habermas's famous use of the coffeehouse as exemplar of the 'public sphere', he acknowledges the limits they placed on class and gender. The ability to 'disregard[] status', crucial to the operation of the coffeehouse, depends on other barriers to entry, a dynamic that only intensified in the club.[37] At the same time, the reading public in the eighteenth century was much smaller than that of the nineteenth century. Many of the debates around the club and the periodical centred around the distinction between public and private; in other words, the extent to which each served as a haven from the outside world.

Newspapers and periodicals in the Victorian period sought to associate themselves with clubs and Clubland, in part through their titles. Quite a few Victorian periodicals took their names from London streets – the *Strand*, the *Cornhill*, the *Pall Mall Gazette*, the *St James's Gazette* – many of those streets in and around Clubland. This practice may have originated with W. M. Thackeray's fictional *Pall Mall Gazette*, which parallels the gossip Major Pendennis trades in his club overlooking Pall Mall.[38] Club subscriptions could be very important for a journal's circulation. To indicate the popularity of *Home Chimes*, a review cited its presence on the table of the Athenaeum Club.[39] Club libraries provided an attraction to members: for example, Matthew Arnold praised both the books and periodicals that the Athenaeum provided.[40] Readers 'subscribed' to both a club and a magazine; each was essentially a profit-making business that provided a structure for leisure and sociability.

When it came to his personal affairs, however, Thackeray preferred a brighter line between the clubroom and the pressroom. As Patrick Leary argues, the Garrick Club Affair, which led to the rift between Thackeray and Charles Dickens, centred around the question of privacy, not only Dickens's (in the question of his affair with Ellen Ternan) but also Thackeray's: Thackeray objected to Edmund Yates publishing his 'private conversation' from the Garrick Club.[41] Indeed, many literary figures – novelists, dramatists and journalists (and in this period many wore all these hats and more) – belonged to West End clubs, some of which were founded specifically for these types of clientele, as in the Garrick Club and the Authors' Club (founded in 1891 by 'Idler's Club' contributor Water Besant).

Between Thackeray's generation and that of the *Idler* circle, the ties between Clubland and print culture grew even stronger. New Journalism, not merely a pejorative but a distinct shift in style and practice, saw the advent of the interview, the proliferation of the byline, and the increased use of the journalistic 'I' rather than 'we'.[42] In keeping with this increasing trend of inviting the public into the private life of literary figures and celebrities (at least in the imaginative form of the periodical), when Douglas Sladen revamped the biographical dictionary *Who's Who* in 1897, he included a field for 'clubs' by each entry. In part because of Sladen's own literary connections (he was a member of the Authors' Club and founded the New Vagabonds, among others), many literary figures featured in *Who's Who*.[43]

In a sense, Victorian humour began with fiction about clubs: Charles Dickens's *The Posthumous Papers of the Pickwick Club* (1836–7). In fact, the central Pickwickian characters are officially 'the Corresponding Society of the Pickwick Club', tasked with travelling and sending back their papers 'to the Pickwick Club, stationed in London'.[44] The physical space of the Pickwick Club principally features in the opening chapter. As Louisa May Alcott vividly renders in *Little Women* (1868–9), readers of the popular novel could imagine themselves members of the club, even across gender lines.

The club has served Victorians and Victorianists alike as a model of masculinity. The 'clubman' was an established type in the period. Scholars of Victorian masculinity identify the club as being crucially related to domesticity, although how is a matter of debate. In his influential study, James Eli Adams claims that clubs, like other all-male spaces such as boys' schools, 'undermined the sway of domesticity by challenging the family as the boy's primary source of identity'.[45] More recently, Amy Milne-Smith counters that the club instead comprises a 'form of domesticity': 'clubland was a rival domestic space, in many ways surpassing what the family could hope to provide'.[46] Adams's argument that Victorian brotherhoods were mistrusted as the century progressed as 'the sign of the closet'[47] has led some critics to stress the homoerotic element of representations of clubs, including in fiction also studied here.[48] This is an important perspective, and certainly one the texts support, but I am less interested in the erotics of these texts than in their larger social significances – which may indeed encompass the erotic, among other things. After all, Eve Kosofsky Sedgwick's famous exploration of the homosocial emphasises the fluidity or 'continuum' of relationships between men in this period, in which the Wilde trials were cementing the heterosexual–homosexual binary.[49] Particularly in the context of mass readership, these texts made themselves available to a variety of readings.

The *Idler* did not invent the practice of representing the staff of the periodical as a club. 'Noctes Ambrosianae' ran in *Blackwood's Edinburgh Magazine* from 1822 to 1835, purporting to depict conversation among its contributors at Ambrose's Tavern in Edinburgh. *Fraser's* and other periodicals imitated the feature, and 'The Idler's Club' can be seen as continuing the tradition.[50] Yet the *Idler*'s innovations, which largely follow conventions of New Journalism, change the nature of the club and make it more open to readers, particularly of the clerk classes. Furthermore, the 'Idler's Club' column clearly identifies itself as collaboratively written, unlike 'Noctes Ambrosianae', which is assumed to be singly authored, although it was published anonymously in the convention of the time. 'The Idler's Club' appears differently on the page: as a series of essays that imitate speech, with 'speakers' identified in headnotes, unlike the 'Noctes' script form, a format that Jerome would use in *Tea-Table Talk* (1903) and various single-authored columns.[51] Indeed, the 'Idler's Club' column used a tavern headpiece a few years into its run that recalled the *Blackwood's* setting.[52] But in earlier periodicals, table talk served to identify a coterie audience or in-group, as in the *Punch* table, which only came to public circulation through Leary's publication of the British Library manuscript of Henry Silver's diary. The public nature of the club distinguished the Idlers, including the extent to which the illusion of the club remained incomplete and the club merged with the periodical. Inviting readers, especially from the clerk classes, into the club blurred the lines between upper-class idling at the club and lower/middle-class idling through reading light literature.

The Idler's Club forms

The figures who created clubs for the unclubbable have strikingly similar biographies which intertwine. Many of the core *Idler* group were born within five years. Jerome and Doyle were born within a month of each other on 2 and 22 May, 1859; Barrie a year later; and Zangwill and Pain both in 1864. Two men born in Scotland in 1850 helped lay their path: Robert Louis Stevenson and Robert Barr.

Unlike his more famous countryman, Barr did not grow up in Scotland. When he was four years old, his family moved to Canada. In 1876 he joined the staff of the *Detroit Free Press*, and in 1881 he crossed the Atlantic to become the editor of its London edition, the first of an American newspaper.[53] Like many of the Idlers, Barr combined journalism and fiction writing (the line between the two was never totally clear, and New Journalism blurred it further), often writing under the pseudonym Luke Sharp. Barr's journalistic success laid the groundwork for the *Idler*, as Jerome writes in his memoir, *My Life and Times*, part of which appeared in the *Strand* in 1925:

> Barr had made the English edition of the Detroit Free Press quite a good property; and was keen to start something of his own. He wanted a popular name and, at first, was undecided between Kipling and myself. He chose me – as, speaking somewhat bitterly, he later confessed to me – thinking I should be the easier to 'manage'. He had not liked the look of Kipling's jaw.[54]

Although this comparison may seem unlikely, Kipling and Barr did in fact have a significant correspondence, and it bears repeating that Kipling, too, made an early splash as a humorist.[55] Jerome continues, 'the title was mine': it clearly plays on Jerome's 1886 collection of essays, *Idle Thoughts of an Idle Fellow*.[56] The *Idler* first appeared in February 1892, with Barr and Jerome at the helm.

In Jerome's youth, his family clung to the underside of the middle class.[57] His father, born Jerome Clapp, changed his name to Jerome Clapp Jerome and gave his son the same name (Clapp became Klapka by 1880).[58] Before Jerome's birth, Clapp engaged in a series of ill-fated ventures that lost the family money, property and status. Jerome was born in Walsall, and the family moved to London in time for Jerome to attend grammar school at age ten, quite soon after the passage of the 1870 Act. When Jerome was twelve, his father died, so after leaving school at age fourteen he became a railroad clerk at Euston Station.[59] He inched his way onto the literary scene by publishing in newspapers and periodicals; he credits writing letters to *The Times* as an early start.[60] A brief stint as an actor supplied the material for Jerome's first book, *On the Stage – and Off*, serialised in the *Play* and published as a book in 1885.

Jerome principally credits his literary start to F. W. Robinson (1830–1901), editor of *Home Chimes*. He emphasises the connections that Robinson and *Home Chimes* facilitated: 'Swinburne, Watts-Dunton, Doctor Westland Marston and his blind son Philip, the poet, Coulson Kernahan, William Sharp, Coventry Patmore, Bret Harte, and J. M. Barrie, were among my fellow contributors to *Home Chimes*.'[61] Barrie's own account of his start in literary London instead places Frederick Greenwood and the *St James's Gazette* at the centre of his success story, which forms a key portion of his chapter in this study. Zangwill also contributed to *Home Chimes*, although he does not appear in this passage. Some biographers have questioned how and when Jerome became aware of Zangwill, but I suspect it was through Robinson and *Home Chimes*.[62] A paragraph in the 1891 Dundee *Evening Telegraph*, which will be discussed in greater detail in Chapter 5, names Zangwill and Barrie as guests at a dinner for Robinson.[63] It seems likely that Jerome was among the other guests.

By the time the *Idler*'s first issue appeared in 1892, it featured an 'Idler's Club' with a clear cast of characters, including Barr, Jerome, Zangwill, Barry Pain and Eden Phillpotts. Zangwill had just published *The Bachelors' Club* (1891), his first breakaway success. He would become more famous for his writing featuring Jewish characters and settings, particularly *Children of the Ghetto* (1892), described as the 'first Anglo-Jewish best-seller',[64] and *The Melting Pot* (1908), first performed in America.[65] But throughout his career, and especially in this early period, Zangwill straddled the Jewish and mainstream audience. Born in Whitechapel to an Ashkenazi Jewish family, he wrote not only about the tribulations of the religious and ethnic minority a generation after emancipation, but also about some of the internal distinctions and prejudices between Sephardic and Ashkenazi Jews. Like many of the Idlers, he began as a journalist, on the staff of the weekly *Jewish Standard* in 1888. In this early period, in addition to publishing in other mainstream periodicals such as *Home Chimes*, Zangwill edited his own weekly, *Puck*, which he renamed *Ariel* and framed as a competitor to *Punch*.[66] The *Jewish Standard* folded in 1891 and *Puck* in February 1892,[67] just in time for Zangwill to devote his attention to the new *Idler*. Among the Idlers, Zangwill's Jewish identity was neither secret nor strongly emphasised. Like many periodical authors in the wane of anonymous publication, Zangwill occasionally went by his first initial (obviously J. M. Barrie and P. G. Wodehouse are still known in that way), which in his case downplayed his ethnic identity. The extent of Zangwill's personal and professional network can in part be seen during his participation in the Zionism/territorialism debate in the early twentieth century. In the *Fortnightly Review*, he published letters on the subject from his contacts, including Barrie, Jerome, Arthur Pinero, Thomas Hardy, H. G. Wells, Mary Ward, Doyle, Arthur Quiller-Couch, W. S. Gilbert, and H. Rider Haggard.[68] Not all letters agreed with his Zionist stance, and a few sound antisemitic.

Many in this core *Idler* group are still known as 'New Humorists', which initially carried all the negative force of 'new' as *fin-de-siècle* epithet. One of Jerome's biographers identifies him as the 'father' of New Humour,[69] but Jerome in his autobiography points out, 'It was to Barry Pain that the reproach "new humorist" was first applied. It began with a sketch of his in the "Granta" – a simple little thing entitled "The Love Story of a Sardine."'[70] Scholars attempting to codify New Humour emphasise the class dimension of the critique, for both authors and audiences. Critics tend to agree that New Humour was characterised by slang, but whether it be clerk's slang, American slang or college slang is a matter of debate.[71] Recently Jonathan Wild has argued that the term came from Andrew Lang's generational frustration at being classed with Pain in the 'Whitefriars Library' series.[72] The core group of New Humorists is fairly small and does not completely overlap with the main figures in this study, although all contributed to the 'Idler's

Club' column: Jerome, Pain, Zangwill, W. W. Jacobs, W. Pett Ridge, Barr, W. L. Alden and G. B. Burgin.[73] Although the stylistic influence on humorists such as Wodehouse is quite clear (perhaps especially through Jacobs),[74] New Humour did not apply even to all of the historically and stylistically linked figures in this study, such as Barrie. In a way, New Humour functioned as a type of anti-club: a group to which members did not especially want to belong. The Idler's Club, as we shall see, was much more capacious and positive in affect.

Although initially emblematic of 'New Humour', Barry Pain had access to two exclusive institutions not shared by other key figures in this study: *Punch* and Oxbridge. (Sayers attended Oxford before women could receive degrees, but she does not form part of the *Idler* circle.) Born in Cambridge, Pain attended its university and published in the student periodical *Granta*, whose founding editor, R. C. Lehmann, was a member of the *Punch* table from 1890 to 1920.[75] Pain never penetrated into the inner *Punch* circle, but he published in the weekly and it carried a favourable review of his first book.[76] Jerome had a sort of feud with *Punch*, who referred to him in their reviews as 'Arry K'Arry, combining the classist epithet 'Arry with an unpleasant Orientalist joke.[77] Like many Idlers, Pain was extremely prolific, producing over sixty books. He is best known today for his *Eliza* series, some of which appeared in *To-Day*.[78] These stories largely mock the pretensions of suburban clerks towards upward mobility, although, as Jonathan Wild points out, they convey more sympathy with the clerks' anxieties than the Grossmiths' *Diary of a Nobody*, which first appeared in *Punch*.[79]

In 1895, Jerome bought the *Idler* from Barr, as we have seen.[80] This made him editor and proprietor of two periodicals: he had founded *To-Day*, a literary, two-penny weekly, in 1893. In 1897, Samson Fox brought a libel suit against *To-Day* for an item in its business column that accused him of misleading investors. Although Jerome had not written the piece, he was liable as the paper's editor and proprietor. Jerome lost the case, and although the damages were only one farthing, the legal costs amounted to nine thousand pounds.[81] Jerome declared bankruptcy and was forced to sell both papers. Barr eventually bought the *Idler*, and Pain became the editor of *To-Day*. Jerome continued to write plays, books and periodical pieces, including for *To-Day* until the paper folded in 1905.

Jerome dedicated *Novel Notes* (1893), which depicts a group of four writers who set out to write a novel jointly but find conversation more compelling than writing, 'To / big-hearted, big-souled, big-bodied / friend / Conan Doyle.'[82] 1893 was the first peak of Doyle's Sherlock Holmes fame, the year that closed with Holmes's (temporary) death in 'The Final Problem'. Although Doyle was not known as a humorist, his Diogenes Club, as we shall see, falls squarely in the phenomenon of humorous fictional club. His contributions to the *Idler* included *The Stark Munro Letters* (1894–5) and several short pieces including an instalment in the series *My First Book* (later published in book form). As his memoir shows, Doyle had the *Strand* for fame but the *Idler* for community.

Doyle met Barrie at one of the '*Idler* At-Homes', weekly 'tea-parties' that Barr and Jerome held at the *Idler*'s offices, encompassing a larger social circle than those who published in the periodical.[83] In January 1892, Doyle wrote to his mother, 'I went in to the "Idlers'" dinner and met J. M. Barrie, Jerome K. Jerome [. . .] I dine again with some of them on Friday, and I hope that Jerome & Barrie may dine with me next week.'[84] Jerome makes more of his friendship with Barrie in his public writing than the reverse, perhaps due to Barrie's generally cultivated air of unclubbability, and perhaps due to the growing gap in their relative financial, literary and social standings. Yet Doyle's grouping of them as a unit in this letter indicates their closeness, as does, in a less direct way, a letter Barrie wrote to a Jerome biographer.[85] Of course, Barrie and Doyle had a shared bond, not only as Scots but also as alumni of Edinburgh University. Doyle's description of Barr, above, also highlights his Scottish origins, and both emphasised their connections to Robert Louis Stevenson, a fellow alumnus who contributed to *My First Book* in the *Idler* and the serial that launched Jerome's weekly, *To-Day*.[86] Barrie corresponded with Stevenson, who wrote to Henry James of his admiration for Barrie's Thrums novels.[87]

Doyle joined Barrie in another clublike pursuit: cricket. The sport was closely linked to Clubland: the Marylebone Cricket Club (MCC), better known as Lord's, appears in *Who's Who* alongside other clubs, including those associated with cards, golf and yachting.[88] Less formally, cricket provided clublike structures, silly names and all, including an Idlers' team. Barrie's team, the subject of a recent monograph, brought together many of the figures in this study, most notably Doyle, Jerome and Wodehouse (not all at the same time). Barrie irreverently titled his cricket team the Allahakbarries, a misappropriation of the Arabic phrase which Barrie (mis)translated 'Heaven help us' in a self-deprecating joke of cultural appropriation.[89] Doyle captained the Idlers' cricket team and the Undershaw XI, named for his house (and the number of players on a team).[90] Members of this group played opposite each other as Artists v. Writers and Married v. Single.[91] While Doyle was serving as a doctor in the Boer War, his friends honoured him by playing under the name 'Arthur Conan Doyle's XI'.[92] Doyle was the best cricketer of the group. As Barrie put it, writing about himself in the third person, 'the more distinguished as authors his men were the worse they played. Conan Doyle was the chief exception to this depressing rule. . . . Jerome once made two fours.'[93] Two fours is a low score in cricket; therefore, this contains a backhanded compliment to Jerome's writing. At one point, the Allahakbarries played the *Punch* cricket team, although several *Punch* men played on Barrie's team, including A. A. Milne, with Bernard Partridge as a key link.[94]

A photograph taken at an Authors v. Artists game on Doyle's forty-fourth birthday in 1903 shows a twenty-two-year-old P. G. Wodehouse standing in the back row, pipe in mouth, a few men over from Doyle and Barrie.[95] Wodehouse's first novel, *The Pothunters*, had been published the previous year, and he was working to establish himself in mainstream periodicals. Although Wodehouse came from an ancient family that encompassed landed gentry, he, too, qualified as something of an outsider. During his childhood, his parents had lived and worked in Hong Kong while he and his brothers went to school in England, including Dulwich College. The family's finances, however, prevented Wodehouse from following his brother to Oxford as the family had expected. Already involved in school periodicals, Wodehouse served two years in the London branch of the Hong Kong and Shanghai Bank (now HSBC) before he could support himself on his literary earnings in 1902. Wodehouse played on Barrie's cricket team, where he met Doyle, with whom he corresponded.[96] There is no evidence that Wodehouse and Jerome ever met, but Wodehouse clearly admired Jerome, referring to him in fiction and quoting him, through their mutual acquaintance W. W. Jacobs, in his letters.[97] Few critical works connect Wodehouse to his Victorian colleagues,[98] although, like Jerome, Wodehouse and his characters are often described as relics of a previous era.

Most of the Idlers were members of London social clubs at various points in their lives. None belonged to the most exclusive echelon of White's, Boodle's and Brooks's. But as a group they belonged to literary and dramatic clubs, as well as the more explicitly social and some political clubs. Doyle and Barrie belonged to the Athenaeum Club, which prided itself on requiring excellence in a field as a prerequisite for membership, one of their few biographical links to G. K. Chesterton.[99] Jerome, Pain, Doyle and Barrie belonged to the Authors' Club.[100] (This may not be an exhaustive list; lifetime club membership is actually a tricky thing to research.) Doyle belonged to several sporting clubs, including the MCC and the Royal Automotive.[101] In terms of political clubs, Doyle and Barrie belonged to the Reform (not heavily political, but liberal) and Wodehouse to the Constitutional, a Conservative club.[102] Zangwill belonged to the Maccabeans, a Jewish club, but also to the Vagabonds and Dramatists' as well as the Playgoers'.[103] The Playgoers' Club stands out as a key club for a sub-group of the Idlers: Jerome and Zangwill each served as its president.[104] Barrie served as 'principal guest' at the Playgoers' twentieth annual dinner, a reminder that membership alone does not tell the whole story of clubs' social function.[105] Even within the ranks of theatrical clubs, the Garrick may have been out of reach for some of these Idlers, although Barrie and Wodehouse did belong.[106]

Part of the reason theatrical clubs feature so heavily in the Idlers' memberships is that most of them wrote for the theatre, and in fact many were most successful as dramatists during their lifetimes. Jerome received consistent success as a playwright, despite his claim that 'Max Beerbohm was always very angry with me.'[107] His plays appeared on stage – mainly in London, but also in New York – and in print consistently throughout his novel-writing career, from *Barbara* in 1886 to *The Soul of Nicholas Snyders* in 1927.[108] *The Passing of the Third Floor Back* (premiered 1908, published 1910) formed an important part of his contemporaneous reputation, highlighting, as Doyle says above, his serious side. Barrie's current reputation, of course, hinges on *Peter Pan*, which had its breakout success on the stage. Today, his plays are much more studied than his novels. Through their mutual theatre connections, Jerome introduced Barrie to his future wife, then the actress Mary Ansell,[109] although their well-publicised divorce case made this a dubious distinction. Zangwill's posthumous reputation relies heavily on his play *The Melting Pot*. Wodehouse too had great success on the stage, mainly in musical comedy in partnership with Guy Bolton and Jerome Kern.[110] He holds the record for the most simultaneously running shows on Broadway, five.[111] Doyle and Barrie collaborated on a comic opera libretto, chiefly notable in that its failure resulted in Barrie's story 'The Adventure of the Two Collaborators', a Sherlock Holmes parody published in Doyle's memoirs, originally 'written on the fly leaves of one of his [Barrie's] books'.[112] This small gem of a story, in which Barrie and Doyle visit Holmes and Watson, resulting in Holmes's downfall, indicates the creative play within their circle, even in a work not originally written for mass publication.

Although most reached their peak of fame in the Victorian period, many of the Idlers lived on surprisingly far into the twentieth century. Barr died in 1912 (still relatively young at sixty-two, but older than Stevenson, who had died in 1894). Zangwill also died at sixty-two, in 1926, and Jerome the following year at sixty-eight. Barry Pain lived till 1928 and Doyle 1930. Barrie died in 1937 at age seventy-seven, but he was not the last survivor of his generation. Eden Phillpotts, a core contributor to the 'Idler's Club', died in 1960, a couple of years short of a century, and wrote essays about guided missiles and cybernetics.[113] Wodehouse was almost as long-lived, dying in 1975, the year after he was knighted. Doyle had also been knighted, principally for his services in wartime. In the early twentieth century, honours on the basis of literary achievement became more common; in 1907 W. S. Gilbert was the first to be knighted on the strength of his contributions as a dramatist, and Barrie was made a baronet less than a decade later on the same basis.

Today, these figures who were so closely associated around the turn of the century have extremely different reputations. Sherlock Holmes, Peter Pan and Jeeves seem a motley crew, although all are active in the popular imagination. Israel Zangwill has garnered more attention recently for his serious Jewish writing. Barry Pain is less well known, but is 'best remembered' for his *Eliza* books;[114] his *Dictionary of National Biography* entry concludes, 'Although Pain is best-known today for his humorous working-class sketches, it was his serious writing that earned critical acclaim during his lifetime.'[115] Despite his absence from the *DNB*, Barr appears in the *Dictionary of Literary Biography* in the 'Mystery Writers' volume, highlighting his Eugène Valmont stories and his status as one of the early parodists of Sherlock Holmes (in a story published in the *Idler*).[116]

Jerome's *Times* obituary highlights *Three Men in a Boat (To Say Nothing of the Dog)* and *The Passing of the Third Floor Back*, but generally resigns Jerome to the dustbin of history: 'Jerome was an industrious writer, but he never equalled these two successes, and in his later work the sentiment which had always marked his writing tended to degenerate into sentimentality. He had not, in fact, kept pace with the changes of public taste, and remained to the end in the naivete both of his laughter and his tears a typical humorist of the 'eighties.'[117] Jerome's sentimentality came under fire more than his humour during his career as a whole. But if most of the figures in this study, with the exception of Jerome, Wodehouse and Pain, are not primarily known as humorists, this may be by dint of significant effort. Jerome frequently and publicly complained about being pigeonholed as a humorist, often through humorous stories about not being taken seriously.

Humour and sociability

The context of the club highlights the social and relational function of humour. Sigmund Freud famously described the 'social process' of the joke in terms of relationships between three parties: the person who tells the joke, the object of the joke, and the audience.[118] In mass-circulated media, particularly print fiction, this diagram becomes more complex, as the 'person who tells the joke' might be seen as the author, the narrator, a character, or even someone reading the text aloud. Humour can generate a variety of social feelings, positive and negative, from disdain or even hatred to pleasure and fellow-feeling. In other words, humour can bring individuals or groups closer together or drive them apart. Jokes can trigger negative emotions either as part of their operation (laughing 'at' vs laughing 'with') or because they misfire. Many taxonomies of humour or comedy (the two terms have distinct histories but often describe the same body of texts and theories) differentiate along the lines of affect, either explicitly or implicitly.[119] Yet taxonomies struggle to capture the complex ways in which a work of humour mobilises layers of affect in a diverse readership. Therefore, this study rarely adopts or invents taxonomies for humour, instead focusing on rich description of individual case studies.

Works explicitly focused on Victorian humour have been undergoing a revival in the twenty-first century. In the 1970s and early 1980s, several works charted a grand narrative of Victorian humour – sometimes under the term 'comedy' or 'wit'.[120] This work often focused on cultural attitudes towards humour, tackling the complex roots of the stereotype of Victorians as humourless. Robert Bernard Martin's *Triumph of Wit* presents as its thesis the movement over the Victorian period 'from a belief in amiable, sentimental humour to an acceptance of intellect as the basis of comedy'.[121] Although Wilde does not figure in Martin's study, his ascendance in views of the *fin de siècle* fits this narrative nicely. The New Humorists did not figure in Martin's argument, nor in other treatments of 'amiable' or 'benign' humour, which Stuart Tave identifies as the dominant mode of the late eighteenth and early nineteenth centuries and Richard Carlson in the early twentieth centuries, including Wodehouse and Doyle.[122] Even recent works, such as the excellent collection *Victorian Laughter and Comedy*, subscribe to the idea that the century moved away from 'conviviality' towards 'dissent' or 'a resistance *to* laughter'.[123] In that sense, although the Idlers were often described as New, they may be seen as a throwback to a more Dickensian – and specifically Pickwickian – mode, a mantle that Jerome tried to claim through a story of a childhood meeting with a man he believed to be Dickens.[124] More recent studies of Victorian humour tend to focus on a particular medium, as in Brian Maidment's study of caricature and visual culture, or otherwise narrow the scope to focus on the specifics of a set of material, as I do here.[125] In terms of the place of the Idlers in the overarching narrative of Victorian humour, I think that the binary between 'amiability' and 'intellect' or 'wit' is overstated. As we shall see, these figures are often amiable, but not always so, and the same jokes that strike some readers as friendly feel to others like a slap in the face.

In all the excellent work on the 'feelings of [Victorian] reading', humour figures less than sorrow, sentimentality or 'ugly feelings'.[126] Little work has been done on the insights humour can bring to the questions raised about the feelings of Victorian reading. For instance, Thackeray has been a major figure in works about reading, in particular the early interjection in *Vanity Fair* about 'Jones, who reads this book at his club', yet the major scholars of reading who employ this quotation do not explicitly address its obvious humour.[127] Methodologically, humour exacerbates the question of how to access readers' feelings. Scholars of reading feelings often rely on theories of sympathy, as readers are invited or inspired to share the feelings of characters depicted in literature, sparking a complex critical conversation around the mechanisms and limits of sympathy.[128] But while humour can work in this way – laughing with characters – humour can also run directly counter to characters' feelings: laughing at characters. Especially if one considers Freud's social model of the joke as always involving a joke-teller, a reader also laughs 'with' someone. That someone may be a character, but also an imagined narrator, author or larger community of readership.

While humour itself is a feeling, or set of feelings, I also trace the ways in which these works mobilise other feelings and play on the 'structure of feeling' established in both the club and the mass-circulated printed text.[129] Like other feelings, too, humour can fail – and humour can result from the failure to elicit other feelings, as in the famous remark attributed to Oscar Wilde, 'One would have to have a heart of stone to read the death of Little Nell without laughing.'[130] This also speaks to the distinction between humour that seems intentional and that which seems unintentional. One important feeling related to humour is that of belonging. Thus, disruptions to the immersive reading experience, which have only recently been discussed in terms other than condemnatory, may form a fundamental part of the construction of feelings in a humorous text.[131] Laughter can form an interruption to a reading, whether a silent reader startles themselves with an unexpected vocalisation or an oral reader pauses to ride the laugh.

Part of this study's mission is recovery: of the works of some under-studied writers, such as Jerome and Pain; of lesser-known works by some more canonical writers such as Stevenson and Barrie; and of the connections (personal, professional and formal) between members of this circle. Although most of these figures ended up being members of at least one West End club, joking about clubs helped them do social work on multiple fronts with different possible readings for different audiences. As they advanced their own social ambitions, they maintained a connection to the growing clerk classes by representing the difficulty of social negotiation and the complexities of social belonging. At the same time that they acknowledged the attraction of the club as a mark of social achievement, they called attention to the arbitrariness of the social system. Humour allowed them to represent the club simultaneously as deeply important and ridiculous.

Chapter descriptions

This book starts with the 'Idler's Club' column and works outwards from Jerome K. Jerome to P. G. Wodehouse. Chapter 1 begins an argument that the Idlers redefined the club as an inclusive space; it focuses on the 'Idler's Club' column in its collaborative form from 1892 to 1901. The 'Idler's Club' column explicitly compares the periodical and the club – in the context of a joke. This chapter thus affords a sustained discussion of the club as a metaphor for print culture, and the related case of smoking as a metaphor for reading (a particularly masculine metaphor closely associated with the club in these texts). Part of the essential joke comparing the club to a magazine, within the pages of the *Idler*, is that the magazine is preferable, particularly because of its inclusion of women.

The contrast between the club and the newsroom continues in Chapter 2, mainly through a reading of Jerome's novel *Tommy and Co.* (1904), which depicts the staff of a periodical and a club, with some overlapping personnel. The eponymous Tommy is a newspaperwoman whose unique personality and unconventional relationship to gender enlivens the 'company' and makes the club seem stifling by comparison.

Israel Zangwill's *The Bachelors' Club*, with which Chapter 3 begins, bridges the discussion of the exclusion of women with the in-depth study of male friendship which will occupy the rest of the study. In the works of prolific club-creators Zangwill and Barry Pain, Chapter 3 considers the function of club rules in fictional, humorous clubs. Their stories frequently begin by stating the club rules, and these rules go on to provide a source of humour and often to drive the plot – which almost always involves the threat of a character being expelled from the club because of a rule violation. These rules thus represent social fears – the fear of transgressing a line and being socially shunned – but also social desires. Clear and directly stated rules of social behaviour can seem appealing to those aspiring to social mobility (or to the socially awkward).

Chapter 4 treats mysteries that pit the male friendship dyad against the more sinister club. The structure of rules cast as comforting, if silly, in Chapter 3 appears decidedly more sinister in mysteries by Robert Louis Stevenson, Arthur Conan Doyle, G. K. Chesterton and Dorothy Sayers. Nevertheless, clubs often provide the solution to a mystery, giving meaning to initially illegible actions.

Chapter 5 focuses on the solitary clubman, in a study of unclubbability focused on the works of J. M. Barrie. Generally, the term 'unclubbable', which tellingly arose before its positive opposite, refers to disposition. Yet it defines sociability by reference to 'such qualities as fit one to be a member of a club', which in most cases included gender and class.[132] This chapter puts pressure on the distinction the word 'unclubbable' seeks to elide between disposition and demographics. Many of Barrie's works feature unclubbability, complementing his own self-representation. As a figure who experienced a stratospheric rise in social standing and wealth over the course of his lifetime, Barrie used unclubbability to frame his social awkwardness as a matter of disposition rather than of breeding.

Chapter 6 examines P. G. Wodehouse's clubs, from the Drones to the Ganymede and beyond. Wodehouse provides the most sustained, and possibly the most successful, example of a club presented as simultaneously emotionally accessible to the common reader and also fundamentally silly. Wodehouse highlights the role of class impersonation, latent in the works of many of his predecessors in this study. The genial affect of the Drones Club also helps counterbalance some surprisingly macabre jokes about violent socialist revolution.

Humour is built on contradiction: formally, it often presents two contradictory or conflicting meanings simultaneously.[133] Thus humour uniquely accommodates both paradox and the diverse reactions of a mass reading public. Even after the laughter fades, both meanings are left hanging. The club is attractive. The club is rebarbative. The club provides an ideal model for democratic sociability. The club ignores the reality of life outside its doors and represents the worst elements of Victorian hegemony. We want to belong to clubs. We think clubs are pernicious. All these conflicting attitudes towards clubs may exist within a single person; they certainly exist within the mass reading public. Moreover, the very act of joking about clubs and the social order they represent claims power for author and reader alike. The genial style that characterised the *Idler* and its circle only furthers this transgressive work: adopting a position of ease asserts the privilege not to become too vehement. Rather than break the windows of the club from outside, as rioters did in 1886,[134] the Idlers imaginatively invited all readers in to put their feet up on the mantelpiece.

Notes

1   Doyle, *Memories and Adventures*, 118.
2   Bold and Nash's collection includes one essay on Thrums, by Margery Palmer McCulloch.
3   Cloy, *Barry Pain and the New Humour*. Works on Jerome include those by Moss, Connolly, Faurot and Oulton.
4   Jerome, *Three Men in a Boat*, 244.
5   Humpherys, 'Putting Women in the Boat', 6.
6   Carey, *The Intellectuals and the Masses*, 59.
7   Mussell, 'New Journalism', 443; Weiner· *Papers for the Millions·*
8   Boos, 'The Education Act of 1870'.
9   Altick, *The English Common Reader*.
10 Jerome, 'To the Readers of "*The Idler*"', 97–8.
11 Wild, *The Rise of the Office Clerk in Literary Culture, 1880–1939*, 69.
12 Jerome K. Jerome Society, 'Periodical contributions by Jerome'.
13 Partridge illustrated Jerome's *Stage-Land* (1889), and Jerome wanted him for *Three Men in a Boat*. Illustrations in the *Idler* include G. B. Burgin's 'The Lyceum Rehearsals' in March 1893. The *Idler* carried an interview with Partridge in 1897. Jerome K. Jerome to J. W. Arrowsmith, 11 March 1889. Typed copy in Jerome K. Jerome collection. Daniels, 'An Afternoon with Mr Bernard Partridge', 358–74.
14 Gilbert, *The Pirates of Penzance*, in *The Complete Annotated*, 237.
15 Earlier works: Gray, 'The Uses of Victorian Laughter' and 'Victorian Verse Humor, 1830–70'; Henkle, *Comedy and Culture*; Kincaid, *Dickens and the Rhetoric of Laughter*; Martin, *The Triumph of Wit*; Pearsall, *Collapse of Stout Party*; Polhemus, *Comic Faith*. More recent works include Lee, *Victorian Comedy and Laughter*; Maidment, *Comedy, Caricature and the Social Order*; Nicholson, '"You Kick the Bucket; We Do the Rest!"'; Gillooly, *Smile of Discontent*; Howes, 'Comic/Satiric Periodicals'; Wagner-Lawlor, *The Victorian Comic Spirit*. Further discussion follows below.
16 Gillooly, *Smile of Discontent*; Stetz, 'The Laugh of the New Woman'; Stetz, *British Women's Comic Fiction, 1890–1990*.
17 Williams, *Gilbert and Sullivan*.

18 Halberstam, *Female Masculinity*. Sedgwick, *Between Men*.

19 The fact that most of these authors are white is no reason to 'demarcat[e] the "racial" as opposed to the '*non*racial'". Chatterjee, Christoff and Wong, 'Introduction: Undisciplining Victorian Studies', 371.

20 Rochelson, *A Jew in the Public Arena*, 54.

21 See Oulton, *Below the Fairy City*, 120. She cites 'TO-DAY', *TO-DAY*, 30 June 1894, p. 242.

22 Betensky, 'Casual Racism in Victorian Literature'. Wodehouse, *Thank You, Jeeves*.

23 Wodehouse, *Uncle Fred in the Springtime*.

24 Pain, *Problem Club*, 235.

25 Anderson, *Imagined Communities*.

26 I approach this idea elsewhere but stop short of using the term 'imaginary community'. Fiss, '*The Idler*'s Club', 417; Fiss, 'Pushing at the Boundaries of the Book'.

27 'White's Club originally formed as an association of gentlemen who could be trusted to pay their gambling losses.' Milne-Smith, *London Clubland*, 21.

28 Milne-Smith uses the term 'clubhouses', though most period texts use the term 'premises'. Milne-Smith, *London Clubland*, 29, eg.

29 Doughan and Gordon, *Women, Clubs and Associations in Britain*.

30 *Who's Who 1897*.

31 Thévoz, *Club Government*.

32 Forrest, *Foursome in St James's*.

33 Milne-Smith, *London Clubland*, 33–4.

34 Milne-Smith, *London Clubland*, 31.

35 Milne-Smith, *London Clubland*, 19.

36 Altick, *The English Common Reader*, 48.

37 Milne-Smith likewise stresses the coffeehouses' exclusivity. Habermas, *The Structural Transformation of the Public Sphere*, 36; Milne-Smith, *London Clubland*, 20.

38 I discuss this point at greater length in '*The Idler*'s Club'. Barbara Black also discusses the connection between the *Pall Mall Gazette* (both fictional and non-fictional) and the club. Black, *A Room of His Own*, 129; Fiss, '*The Idler*'s Club', 416; Thackeray, *Pendennis*, 439.

39 'Magazines for January', 8.

40 Lubenow, '*Only Connect*', 126.

41 Thackeray, qtd in Leary, *The Punch Brotherhood*, 94.

42 Mussell, 'New Journalism', 443.

43 Sladen, *Who's Who*. From ongoing work in collaboration with Troy Basssett.

44 Dickens, *The Pickwick Papers*, 2. Elsewhere, I discuss the role of newspaper excerption in the reception of the novel and the creation of the Wellerism. Fiss, 'Out With It, as the Subeditor Said to the Novel'.

45 Adams, *Dandies and Desert Saints*, 64.

46 Milne-Smith, *London Clubland*, 111.

47 Adams, *Dandies and Desert Saints*, 17.

48 Black, *A Room of His Own*, 192.

49 Sedgwick's category of the 'homosocial' is explicitly a response to Adrienne Rich's 'lesbian continuum' and she calls both 'homosocial continuums'. Sedgwick, *Between Men*, 25; Rich, 'Compulsory Heterosexuality', 648.

50 Leary, *The* Punch *Brotherhood*, 6, 14; Leary, '"Fraser's Magazine" and the Literary Life, 1830–1847', 105–26; Black, *A Room of His Own*, 129.

51 Christie, '"Where Personation Ends and Imposture Begins"', 175–94.

52 Anne Humpherys extensively discusses the shifts in headpieces over the course of *The Idler*'s Club column. Humpherys, 'Putting Women in the Boat'.

53 Cox, 'Robert Barr', 14–22.

54 Jerome, *My Life and Times*, 166. Serialised as *Confessions of a Humorist* in 1925. Jerome K. Jerome Society, 'Periodical contributions by Jerome'.

55 Benfey, *If*, 84, 147, 174.

56 Jerome, *My Life and Times*, 166.

57 Biographer Joseph Connolly compares Jerome's childhood to that of Dickens. Faurot speaks of his parents' 'eager[ness] to preserve their gentility'. Connolly, *Jerome K. Jerome*, 12; Faurot, *Jerome K. Jerome*, 21.

58 Oulton, *Below the Fairy City*, 40.

59 Faurot, *Jerome K. Jerome*, 21.

60 Jerome, *My Life and Times*, 79–80.

61 Jerome, *My Life and Times*, 76.

62 All three contributed to *Home Chimes*; the question is whether Zangwill met either Jerome or Barrie at this stage. In his memoirs, Jerome describes meeting Barrie through Robinson and alludes to other famous writers in *Home Chimes*. Zangwill biographer Meri-Jane Rochelson repeats the suggestion that Jerome may have

noticed Zangwill's work in the *Jewish Standard*, but she seems dubious. Carolyn Oulton notes that Jerome and Zangwill both contributed to *Home Chimes*. Jerome, *My Life and Times*, 2–3; Oulton, *Below the Fairy City*, 54; Rochelson, *A Jew in the Public Arena*, 37.

63 'Notes mainly Personal', *Evening Telegraph* (Dundee), 10 June 1891.

64 Winehouse, 'Israel Zangwill's *Children of the Ghetto*: A Literary History of the First Anglo-Jewish Best-Seller'. Referenced in Rochelson, *Jew in the Public Arena*, 51.

65 Biographer Meri-Jane Rochelson points out that 'Zangwill's obituary appeared on the front page of the *New York Times*.' Rochelson, *Jew in the Public Arena*, 17.

66 Rochelson treats this in detail and also frames an argument about Zangwill's 'forming [of] an Anglo-Jewish literary identity'. Rochelson, *Jew in the Public Arena*, 37–8.

67 Baker, 'Zangwill, Israel (1864–1926)'; Taunton, '*Puck*'.

68 Rochelson, *Jew in the Public Arena*, 159–60.

69 Connolly, *Jerome K. Jerome*.

70 Jerome, *My Life and Times*, 189–90.

71 John Batts calls New Humour synonymous with American humor, which elides some of the distinctively British class dynamics. Jonathan Wild and John Carey identify clerk's slang in Wodehouse's upper-class characters. Cloy, *Muscular Mirth*, 7; Batts, 'American Humor', 91–113. Wild, *The Rise of the Office Clerk in Literary Culture*; Carey, *The Intellectuals and the Masses*, 58–9.

72 Wild, 'What was *New*', 294.

73 Cloy, *Muscular Mirth*, 7; Wild, 'What was *New*', 291.

74 Cloy, *Muscular Mirth*, 7.

75 The *Punch* table itself functioned as a type of club; see Leary, *The Punch Brotherhood*.

76 Cloy, *Muscular Mirth*, 21.

77 Jerome, *My Life and Times*, 74; Jerome, *Novel Notes*, xiv.

78 Ten Eliza stories are listed in the table of contents of *To-Day* vol. 9 (1896).

79 Wild, *The Rise of the Office Clerk in Literary Culture*, 59.

80 The *Dictionary of National Biography* states that this transition happened '[a]fter a disagreement with Barr', but no other source substantiates this, including Oulton, who reports the transition as commonplace (87). Atkinson, 'Jerome, Jerome Klapka (1859–1927)'.

81 Connolly, *JKJ*, 103; Jerome, *My Life and Times*, 194.

82 Jerome, *Novel Notes*. Originally serialized in the *Idler*, 1892–3.

83 Jerome, *My Life and Times*, 167; Bassett, 'Robert Barr's Life at *The Idler*', 510–24.

84 Arthur Conan Doyle to Mary Doyle, 6 January 1892, in Lellenberg et al., *Arthur Conan Doyle*, 305.

85 J. M. Barrie to Alfred Moss, 19 January 1928, in Jerome K. Jerome Collection. Barrie mainly refers Moss to Jerome's own memoirs.

86 *The Ebb Tide* appeared in *To-Day* attributed to Robert Louis Stevenson alone, but Lloyd Osbourne was later credited as a co-author.

87 Birkin, *J.M. Barrie and the Lost Boys*, 18.

88 Sladen, *Who's Who* (1897), 30. Graves says that the Portland is 'to cards what St Andrews is to golf or the MCC is to cricket'. Graves, *Leather Armchairs*, 32.

89 Barrie, *Greenwood Hat*, 98.

90 Telfer, *Peter Pan's First XI*, 84, 133–4.

91 Telfer, *Peter Pan's First XI*, 108, 134.

92 Telfer, *Peter Pan's First XI*, 149.

93 Barrie, *Greenwood Hat*, 100–1.

94 Telfer, *Peter Pan's First XI*, 162–3, 45.

95 Telfer, *Peter Pan's First XI*, facing 121.

96 P. G. Wodehouse to Arthur Conan Doyle, 9 August 1912, in Ratcliffe, *P.G. Wodehouse*, 83.

97 Oulton, *Below the Fairy City*, 12. P. G. Wodehouse to Leonora Wodehouse, February 14, 1939, in Donaldson, *Yours, Plum*, 75.

98 Nicola Humble's article is an exception, though her rationale is stylistic rather than biographical. Humble, 'From Holmes to the Drones', 90–103.

99 *Who's Who* (1904), 431; *Who Was Who* 1929–40, 71. *Who Was Who* 1929–40, 246.

100 *Who's Who* (1904), 811, 1173, 431. Authors' Club current website, http://www.authorsclub.co.uk/ (accessed 8 April 2016).

101 *Who Was Who* (1929–40), 383.

102 *Who's Who* (1904), 811, 431. *Who's Who* (1908), 2002.

103 Rochelson, *Jew in the Public Arena*, 2.

104 Findon, *The Playgoers' Club 1884 to 1905*.

105 Findon, *The Playgoers' Club 1884 to 1905*, 71.

106 Thwaite, *A. A. Milne*, 310.

107 Jerome, *My Life and Times*, 75.

108 Dates are for published plays. See 'Jerome the Dramatist' and the excellent bibliography in Nicholas, ed., *Idle Thoughts on Jerome K. Jerome*, 87–96, 198–201.

109 Jerome, *My Life and Times*, 140.

110 Wodehouse and Bolton, *Bring on the Girls!*

111 Wodehouse, *The Complete Lyrics of P.G. Wodehouse*, xvii. As of 2017, the record holds; see Ring, 'P. G. Wodehouse'.

112 Doyle, *Memories and Adventures*, 102.

113 Phillpotts, *One Thing and Another*, 34, 51.

114 Murphy, 'Pain'.

115 Murphy, 'Pain'.

116 Barr [Luke Sharp], 'Detective Stories Gone Wrong: The Adventures of Sherlaw Komes', 413–24.

117 'Mr J. K. Jerome', *The Times*, 15 June 1927.

118 Freud, *The Joke and Its Relation to the Unconscious*, 135, 139, 140.

119 Meredith, 'An Essay on Comedy', 43; Hunt, 'On the Combination of Grave and Gay', 91–3; Martin, *The Triumph of Wit*, ix.

120 Gray, 'The Uses of Victorian Laughter' and 'Victorian Verse Humor, 1830–70'; Henkle, *Comedy and Culture*; Kincaid, *Dickens and the Rhetoric of Laughter*; Martin, *The Triumph of Wit*; Pearsall, *Collapse of Stout Party*; Polhemus, *Comic Faith*.

121 Martin, *Triumph of Wit*, vii.

122 Carlson, *The Benign Humorists*; Tave, *The Amiable Humorist*.

123 Lee, 'Introduction', 22.

124 Jerome, *My Life and Times*, 37. He refers to an incident fictionalised in *Paul Kelver* (161–6), which featured Dickens saying 'Damn Mr Pickwick!'

125 Maidment, *Comedy, Caricature and the Social Order*; Nicholson, '"You Kick the Bucket; We Do the Rest!"'; Gillooly, *Smile of Discontent*; Howes, 'Comic/Satiric Periodicals'.

126 Ablow, *The Feeling of Reading*; Bown, 'Rethinking Victorian Sentimentality'; Ngai, *Ugly Feelings*.

127 Dames, *The Physiology of the Novel*, 76; Flint, 'Women, Men, and the Reading of *Vanity Fair*', 259; Stewart, *Dear Reader*, 50.

128 Adela Pinch contends that the long eighteenth century has a 'tendency to characterize feelings as transpersonal, as autonomous entities that do not always belong to individuals but rather wander extravagantly from one person to another'. Siann Ngai argues that 'ugly feelings can be described as conducive to producing ironic distance in a way that the grander and more prestigious passions,

or even the moral emotions associated with sentimental literature, do not'. Ngai, *Ugly Feelings*, 10; Pinch, *Strange Fits of Passion*, 3.

129 Williams, *The Long Revolution*, 64.

130 This remark has proved difficult to trace, but it is widely cited, as in Nicola Bown, 'Introduction: Crying Over Little Nell', in Bown.

131 Nicholas Dames's chapter on Thackeray presents Victorian readerly attention as wave-like. Elsewhere I discuss the role of partial readerly immersion in forming community in Victorian children's literature. Dames, *The Physiology of the Novel*, 121; Fiss, 'Pushing at the Boundaries of the Book'.

132 *OED Online*, s.v. 'clubbable', last modified Dec. 2020.

133 This is often known as the 'incongruity theory' of humour, one of the most pervasive and also most formal accounts of the causes of humour. Freud alludes to its pervasiveness. Jim Holt's accessible overview of humour describes the major theories of humour. Holt, *Stop Me if You've Heard This*, 81–7; Freud, *The Joke and Its Relation to the Unconscious*, 3.

134 Milne-Smith, *London Clubland*, 24.

Club Chatter, Gossip and Smoking: The 'Idler's Club' Column as a Reader's Space

The 'Idler's Club' column positioned the club as an imagined space of reading for the magazine as a whole. In this way, it resembles the metaphor of the 'imagined fireside' in Victorian children's literature, which aimed to bring together diverse readers, particularly children and adults.[1] Like the fireside, the club smoking room is a place where reading could literally take place, but also a space in which informal oral interaction cements community.[2] While children's literature imagines intergenerational reading to be the ultimate oral expression of community formation, the *Idler* and its ilk choose club talk, or gossip. Gossip carries strong gender and ethical connotations – as much today as when Patricia Meyer Spacks defended its pleasures and purposes. Although Spacks often uses the term 'serious gossip', which would contrast with humour, she also defines it fundamentally as 'idle talk', and the *Idler* certainly seeks to inhabit a similar 'space of intimacy'.[3] Despite gossip's frequent and most pejorative associations with women, Amy Milne-Smith claims club talk as an essential form of male gossip, crucial to the formation of community within clubs.[4] The Garrick Club Affair indicates club gossip's destructive force, which took an even more virulent form in the Wilde trials.[5] Framing club talk as a positive force, then, required some effort on the part of the 'Idler's Club' contributors, even though they made it look easy.

The 'Idler's Club' column saw considerable change over the course of its lifetime, in part through changes in the editorship of the *Idler*. From the first issue in February 1892, the column was co-authored, beginning in the voice of proprietor and co-editor Robert Barr (side notes identified contributors). At the close of the first volume, more formal topics appeared at the opening of the column, which eventually became the 'Subject for Discussion' in the beginning of the third volume.[6] In 1895, Jerome K. Jerome bought the paper from Barr and became sole editor. As part of his ambitions to expand the *Idler*'s reach to rival the *Strand*, Jerome extended the 'Idler's Club' network and brought the 'subjects for discussion' on to slightly more serious topics. In 1898, however, Jerome's libel trial and bankruptcy forced him to sell the paper (see Introduction). As the paper cycled through several editors before Barr bought it back in 1902,[7] the column languished, dropped out entirely in some issues, and became an explicitly reader write-in column, openly soliciting contributions and listing compensation:

> NOTE.—The subject to be discussed by *The Idler*'s Club in next month's number is:—Which is the most painful, Wit or Humour? Idlers are invited to join in the discussion, but are warned that space is limited. Expositions are limited to 250 words; the remuneration for published items will be half-a-guinea. Matter must be sent in before the 10th.[8]

When Barr bought back the paper, he put an end to this practice and made it a single-authored column whose authorship rotated. The semi-fictional club invited readers in, but the explicit invitation of readers to be Idlers also introduced a business element that disrupted the club's illusion.[9]

The 'Idler's Club' creates a truly imagined space, a fictional club, the type that readers could already imagine through the real or vicarious experience of London's Clubland. Readers could use this imagined space as a gateway to such imagined communities as literary London. Victorian travel writing, according to Alison Byerly, served as a metaphor for larger trends in Victorian reading, representing a 'way of belonging to two places at once'.[10] The 'Idler's Club' likewise provides an intermediary space between readers' actual locations and the world of the stories in the main part of the magazine. Its imagined smoking room enables readers to imagine the snug intimacy of a private club from which to engage in periodical reading.[11] However, the exclusive nature of the club cannot be denied, and gender serves as its most prominent marker of exclusivity. In an article on Jerome's editorship of the *Idler* and *To-Day*, Anne Humphreys argues that both periodicals practised a separate-sphere approach to gender and repeatedly calls the magazine 'masculinist'.[12] I place the emphasis differently: although Jerome was not the most outspoken advocate for women of his time, the presence of women in the *Idler*'s pages fell off decidedly after he sold the paper. The *Idler*'s masculine metaphors of clubs and smoking are rendered more accessible for all readers through the twin removes of fictionality and humour. Readers can partake of this imagined sociability even if they never pass through a club's portals or pick up a cigar.

Smoking as a metaphor for reading

The most common 'Idler's Club' headpiece depicts five men sitting in armchairs with their backs to the viewer, facing a large fireplace (Fig. 0.1). One man has his feet on the mantel; two others sit back, one with his head lolling onto the back of the chair. The man on the far right turns towards his fellows, revealing his profile, in a listening posture. His eyebrows are lifted and his mouth turns up in amusement or intrigue. All five men hold lighted cigars or cigarettes, two in their hands and three in their mouths, and the smoke travels upwards, mingling to form the words 'The Idler's Club'. This illustration served as a headpiece for the column in the first volume of the *Idler* and returned periodically, including for a column on smoking.[13] It concretely creates the image of the club as a space, and it establishes an analogy between the words in the magazine and smoke: pleasurable, light, ephemeral and non-utilitarian.

Famously, anxieties around reading in the nineteenth century and elsewhere played out through the metaphor of eating. Women in particular encountered chastisements to cease gorging on the sweetmeats of novels and instead consume the nutritious food of history.[14] So dominant has the eating metaphor become that Janice Radway warned of its 'theoretical, methodological, and political consequences'.[15] This chapter investigates metaphors for reading that provided a counterpoint to the eating metaphor: the club and smoking. These metaphors derive from masculine culture but, just as the eating metaphor was applied to both sexes despite its gendered connotations, so these modes of reading can apply to female readers as well. The 'Idler's Club' column and the *Idler* magazine as a whole employed the metaphors of smoking and a club, linked together in the image of the club smoking room in the column's frequent headpiece.

As a metaphor for reading, smoking differs significantly from eating. Although the metaphor became associated with women as it was frequently used to police their reading, eating is, of course, necessary for life and everyone does it. Generally speaking, the comparison between women's reading habits and eating is often an attempt at a method of control, often by (male) figures of authority: women are cautioned to curb their dangerous appetites, particularly for novels, which are often compared to sweets on which women might easily gorge themselves if not held back by more judicious regulations.[16] Smoking, on the other hand, is optional and coded masculine in this period – even when women smoked. Not yet understood as an addiction, smoking here is often framed as a habit rather than a compulsion – although, as we shall see in Chapter 5, J. M. Barrie uses it in an extended study of deep longing. In her study of Holmes's smoking and tobacco papers, Susan Zieger argues that Holmes's approach forms a watershed that began to conceptualise both smoking and media addiction, but she actively resists the term 'reading' for the phenomenon she describes.[17]

The *Idler* participated in a larger practice of representing smoking in periodicals, which Mathew Hilton traces in a study of smoking in nineteenth- and twentieth-century British popular culture. A number of periodical articles featuring tobacco draw a parallel between the act of smoking and the act of reading: the articles call themselves 'whiffs' or 'pipefuls' of information and seem to usher or secure the reader's place in 'the fraternity of smokers'.[18] Hilton takes this literally, imagining a smoking reader, yet the reading metaphor can be figurative, applied to non-smoking readers. Not only did smoking and tobacco sales benefit from these types of periodical puff pieces, but so, too, did periodical literature benefit from the association with smoking: Joseph Hatton and *Idler* publisher Andrew William Chatto engaged in these pieces.[19] Smoking serves as a metaphor for a particular type of reading. Just as eating provided a gendered metaphor for reading, complete with a mass of connotations, so too did smoking.

While eating is often a condemnatory metaphor for reading, with an emphasis on setting limits, smoking is a more ambiguous metaphor. It is often applied to one's own reading, or even the reading of the particular article at hand. Most examples of the eating metaphor occur in commentary about texts rather than the pieces themselves, and generally contain finger-wagging.[20] Readers are not invited to 'savour this sweetmeat'. Smoking carries contradictory implications when used as a metaphor for reading. Most of these articles represent smoking as a minor vice, and frequently emphasise its positive qualities: relieving stress, promoting meditation and, above all, being a form of sociability that paradoxically, as Hilton elegantly demonstrates, represents itself as fundamentally individualistic. When smoking is applied as a metaphor for reading, it is often with a humorous, self-deprecating tone – again, in contrast to the metaphor of eating, which typically reprimands the (usually female) reader, occasionally using humour to do so.

Just as readers could contribute to a sense of clubbability through the fellowship of the periodical press without actually belonging to a club, or even having seen the West End in person, so too could they enjoy some of the ethos of smoking without actually indulging themselves. And indeed, as the first 'Idler's Club' headpiece shows, clubs and smoking carried a strong imagined connection (even though some actual West End clubs had debates about where and whether to allow smoking).[21] The culture of smoking as cultivated in print culture stressed collectivity, in part through knowledge of tobacco that could be gained in reading periodical pieces.[22] Smoking and reading shared a common image problem: that of passivity, particularly in a culture that gendered consumption as passive and thus characteristic of women and the masses.[23]

The connection between reading and smoking in the 'Idler's Club' headpiece plays out elsewhere in the *Idler* and the work of its contributors. Barry Pain had a regular column entitled 'In the Smoking Room' for *Black and White*, starting in early 1892.[24] Jerome's *Novel Notes*, his first serialised novel to appear in the *Idler* (1892–3), chronicles a 'pipe party', a group of four friends who aspire to write a novel together.[25] The novel remains, as the title suggests, in note form, but the loosely connected stories serve as a testament to their fellowship – which the preface added to the 1893 book casts nostalgically into the past. The book also adds a dedication to Doyle, implying a link between the *Idler* circle and the men depicted in the novel.[26] The final illustration of *Novel Notes*, in both periodical and book form, depicts a solitary smoker; the words 'The End' are formed from smoke emanating from his pipe (Fig. 1.1). The melancholy of the single smoker suits the novel's close, even before the whole piece is cast in retrospective nostalgia. Yet in its original serialisation, the issue closed with the 'Idler's Club' and its headpiece of communal smoking.

Smoking appears in this context as both a solitary pleasure and a communal pursuit – like reading. Indeed, although eating can

Figure 1.1 J. Gülich, final illustration from *Novel Notes* (both book and serial). Personal collection (book).

also be communal, nineteenth-century depictions of reading as a metaphor, particularly in respect to women, stress solitary, illicit eating, especially of sweets, just as visual depictions stress solitary reading.[27] Jerome's dedication to *Idle Thoughts of an Idle Fellow* (1886) praises 'the companion of my idle hours', delaying through hyperbole that this is not a human companion, but 'my . . . Pipe'.[28] Smoke may be ephemeral, but the vessel – the pipe – becomes a treasured companion. In the analogy with reading, the pleasure of the reading experience may be fleeting, but repetition builds relationships. A photograph of Jerome in his study with his pipe appears in the *Idler* to illustrate his entry in the series 'My First Book' (Fig. 1.2). Throughout their work, those in the *Idler* circle invoke different specific technologies of smoking, often unpacking their meaning (for the uninitiated or non-smokers). Barry Pain's Failure Club eschews the church-warden pipe in favour of 'the more convenient briar'.[29] Conversely, a member of his Problem Club indicates his superior class standing – and personality – by lighting 'a cigar that can only be obtained by the favour of the planter'.[30] Class and personality manifest through smoking paraphernalia.

In *The Bachelors' Club*, Zangwill describes lighting a fellow's cigar from one's own as 'the masculine substitute for a kiss'[31] (Fig. 1.3). Obviously, to current critics, this line suggests a homo-erotic reading, but it takes us back to Eve Sedgwick's original sense of 'homosocial', a response to Adrienne Rich's 'lesbian continuum'.[32] At the time, the notion that any interaction between

Figure 1.2 Jerome K. Jerome. Photo by Fradelle and
Young, from *My First Book*. Personal collection.

men fell on the spectrum with sex sparked much critical excitement about sexual implications, but Sedgwick's insistence on the
nuances involved in the movement along the whole continuum
is, in a way, more radical. Giving this encounter a 'just reading',
in Sharon Marcus's formulation (responding to Sedgwick),
reflects the difficulty of acknowledging male friendship – or men
caring about men more broadly – in a social landscape that does
not afford many models or much vocabulary for such interactions.[33] The kiss in Zangwill's analogy is not necessarily a heterosexual one but could be a homosocial one: between female
friends, sisters, even mothers and daughters. These women have
the kiss in their vocabulary, whereas their male equivalents do
not.[34] Clearly, the passage conveys deep intimacy. Furthermore,
the intimate moment Zangwill describes occurs not between
clubmen but between a member of the Bachelors' Club and a
cabman whom he has just discovered to be his successful novelist father's ghost-writer; out of guilt, the clubman will marry
the cabman's daughter. The cigar-lighting is thus a gesture of

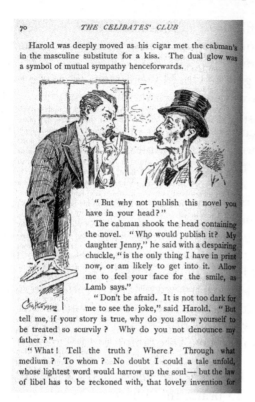

70   *THE CELIBATES' CLUB*

Harold was deeply moved as his cigar met the cabman's in the masculine substitute for a kiss. The dual glow was a symbol of mutual sympathy henceforwards.

" But why not publish this novel you have in your head?"

The cabman shook the head containing the novel. "Who would publish it? My daughter Jenny," he said with a despairing chuckle, " is the only thing I have in print now, or am likely to get into it. Allow me to feel your face for the smile, as Lamb says."

" Don't be afraid. It is not too dark for me to see the joke," said Harold. " But tell me, if your story is true, why do you allow yourself to be treated so scurvily ? Why do you not denounce my father ? "

" What ! Tell the truth ? Where? Through what medium ? To whom ? No doubt I could a tale unfold, whose lightest word would harrow up the soul — but the law of libel has to be reckoned with, that lovely invention for

Figure 1.3 George Hutchinson, illustration in *The Bachelor's Club*. Personal collection.

cross-class intimacy – a masculine pleasure shared across demographic boundaries, as these novels themselves were, including with their female readers.

Jerome and other members of the Idler's Club seem very aware of the gender implications of smoking. The first 'Idler's Club' column to include women focuses on the pros and cons of smoking. The first female contribution bears the caption, 'A lady defends lady smokers.'[35] This contributor points out the acceptance of female smoking in continental Europe and calls for similar tolerance in England. Later in the discussion, Grant Allen, a regular contributor and future author of notorious New Woman novel *The Woman Who Did* (1895), supports the practice of women smoking, albeit in facetious terms that reinforce some misogynistic stereotypes: 'If women smoked, they would spend hours in quiet meditation, instead of spending them in costly shopping or devastating conversation.'[36] Yet the wider context of humorous idle talk makes it difficult to tell how serious Allen's comments are; this statement could also be read ironically to indicate that men waste time in smoking. His next sentence is more clearly disingenuous: 'The cigarette would wean them from the excessive tea in which they now indulge.'[37] Another contributor labelled simply 'Angelina' argues against smoking in men: 'Well may we women loathe tobacco, for she is our most insidious and dangerous rival.'[38] Women join in the sociable debate of the Idler's Club, whether or not all of them literally take up a cigarette. The issue of women smoking was clearly a New Woman issue, emblematic of women's participation in a variety of traditionally male activities, such as breadwinning.

Jerome later used women's smoking as an opening gambit in his early twentieth-century essay 'Woman and Her Behaviour' (from the To-Day 'Idle Thoughts' series). He begins by posing the question, 'Should women smoke?' Yet he ultimately refuses to answer the question, saying 'I like women who smoke,' and 'I also like the woman who does not smoke.'[39] In fact, he objects to the notion that he should have an opinion on the subject: 'It may be a sign of degeneracy, but I am prepared to abdicate my position of a woman's god, leaving her free to choose her own life.'[40] He goes on explicitly to praise the 'pluck' of female pioneers in securing a place for 'the working woman of today': 'There were ladies in those days too "unwomanly" to remain helpless burdens on overworked fathers and mothers, too "unsexed" to marry the first man that came along for the sake of their bread and butter. They fought their way into journalism, into the office, into the shop.'[41] Jerome is by no means anxious to bar women from the sociable cigarette or women readers from his own literary 'pipe club'. Certainly some readers might have felt excluded. But the Idler and its clubs also present the opportunity to peer into a lifestyle the reader might not otherwise share. Where else but in fiction could a woman gain at least the illusion of being in a room of all men?

In fact, an illustration in the August 1896 issue of the Idler labels a woman reader as 'An Idler' (Fig. 1.4).[42] This woman seems absorbed in the book she holds, a slight volume in paper wrappers. Perhaps she is reading the Idler itself, which would make her not only an idler, but an Idler: a member of the circle of readers implied in the magazine's circulation. Reading is another kind of idling, a more acceptably feminine version of pipe smoking, although not

Figure 1.4 Hounsom Byles, 'An Idler', *Idler* 10 (1896): 127. University Libraries, University of North Carolina at Chapel Hill.

completely unobjectionable.[43] The experience of reading Jerome and his fellow New Humorists is especially idle, following a desultory train of thoughts. As Nicholas Dames demonstrates through Thackeray's work, absorptive reading could be seen as a type of laziness in the Victorian conception of attention.[44] Even a reader who appears still and absorbed is lazily floating from anecdote to anecdote along Jerome's gently winding stream of consciousness. Jerome's Idler's Club, after all, included women before the gender integration of actual London clubs.[45] Unlike the exclusive *Punch* table, whose literary talk only gradually filtered into print culture, often creating an extra layer of meaning obscure to the general reading public, the 'Idler's Club' appears to invite all who can spend a shilling – or borrow from one who can – to join in their idle conversation.[46]

The establishment of the 'Idler's Club': A close environment

In its first volume, and even its first issue of February 1892, the 'Idler's Club' column clearly established the club as a metaphor for reading and made the class implications of that metaphor clear. In the beginning, the column represented its contributors as convivial clubmen and simultaneously as literary figures with clear ties to the magazine's production. The opening of the first column introduces the central joke and leans on the inherent tension between a club and a magazine. In explicitly referring to the 1870 Education Act and expansion of literacy, the first column makes the magazine's central joke the juxtaposition of two forms of class-based leisure: the West End club and magazine reading.

The first column begins conversationally, in the voice of Robert Barr (identified in a side note):

> Then there was another thing. It was felt that the time had come when a new monthly magazine ought really to be published. Whether the founders of our present system of education realised the possibility or not, the working of the scheme has resulted in a large increase to the number of people who can read. You would imagine that the demand would have created a supply. But look at our bookstalls to-day! Almost nothing on them. Here is a great reading population crying out for printed matter, and yet nobody seems to pay any attention to the appeal. Think what an opportunity the recent festive holiday season might have supplied to an enterprising publisher, yet no one seems to have thought of bringing out a Christmas number![47]

Barr clearly positions the *Idler* as meeting the need created by the Education Act 1870. Barr makes his joke at the obvious-ness of the desire to satisfy the new market, rather than at the expense of the new readers. Here as elsewhere, Barr plays his own straight man, letting the joke turn on his feigned obliviousness. Yet in making the situation seem absurdly simple – more education results in more readers, who then require more reading material – he makes a case against the stigmatisation of New Journalism.

Barr's editorial declaration adopted a markedly different tone towards readers than its competitors. Only a year earlier, the editor of the *Strand Magazine*, establishing his own formal editorial voice in the third person, 'respectfully place[d] his first number in the hands of the public'.[48] This editorial statement appears more conventionally, at the beginning of the first issue, under the heading 'Introduction', decorated with a floral motif and a large drop cap. Although the *Strand* alludes to the same market referenced in the *Idler*, it does not propose to lower itself to the level of common readers: 'It may be said that with the immense number of existing Monthlies there is no necessity for another. It is believed, however, that THE STRAND MAGAZINE will soon occupy a position which will justify its existence.'[49] It thus makes an argument for the magazine's excellence and even its exceptionalism, implying that it will rise above the throng in a way that accepts an elitist hierarchy. The *Idler* mocks such an argument, content to simply mingle among the masses (though in time its rhetoric would change). Crucially, Barr does not shy away from identifying the reason for the 'immense number of existing Monthlies'. Readers who benefited from the Education Act were not those whose fathers put them down in the club books at birth. The 'Idler's Club' was a club for them, one that required no connections to join but which afforded imaginative connections to a cosy group of journalists making idle conversation.

When it came to class, Jerome was quite distinct about the demographic of his audience, avoiding the lowest echelon. Corresponding with J. W. Arrowsmith about the terms for the book publication of *Three Men in a Boat*, Jerome insists that the book be priced at 3s 6d rather than one shilling: 'I am better known to the say, 3/6 public than I am to the 1/-. The 1/- public only take a book that is a rage, a 3/6 public know an author and look for him. I'm sure we could get a good sale at 3/6, and then come down to a 1/- issue after. The 2 classes of buyers are so distinct.'[50] Jerome's own experiences of his family's struggle to maintain a vestige of middle-class standing – not to mention his own attempts at class mobility – attuned him to fine distinctions of class. Yet even as he complained of *Punch* mocking his own debt to the Education Act with the moniker 'Arry K 'Arry, he used the stock lower-class figure 'Arry in his fiction.[51] When Jerome took over the *Idler*, he made a similar distinction in his address to readers: 'It will never be my aim to make it a magazine for what is generally termed "the masses", but to appeal to that growing public which possesses literary tastes and artistic sympathies.'[52] The *Idler*'s inclusivity had its limits.

The first 'Idler's Club' column directly imitated club talk, accentuating the collaborative nature of the column. Side notes in Gothic type and archaic diction identify changes in speaker. Each section is several paragraphs long, and sometimes one speaker continues for several sections in a row, creating the impression of garrulous speech rather than snappy dialogue – those who admire the sound of their own voices. These sections often begin with conversational gestures rather than the diction of the formal essay. Most strikingly, Barr begins the column, 'Then there was another thing.'[53] Other contributions begin with tags such as 'Oh, by-the-bye.'[54] These loose conversational links themselves become a kind of joke, as when Jerome follows Zangwill's remarks on the absurdity of the timing of Christmas numbers with 'By-the-bye, talking of Christmas, have you noticed how, of late years, the custom of sending valentines to those we love, and to those we are supposed to love, has steadily declined?'[55] The artificiality of this connection suggests the type of club conversation in which members are not really listening to each other, but it doesn't really matter because the conversation is so trivial.

This type of self-reflexive, self-deprecatory humour characterises the entirety of the first column, with many of the jokes turning on the speaker, his colleagues, and/or the journalistic profession. In this vein, Zangwill begins one set of remarks, 'Has anybody read Mrs Grimwood's book? Several of you have reviewed it, I know.'[56] This comment would be quite at home in his fictional Mutual Depreciation Society, which was introduced in the same issue: it impugns not only those present but journalistic reviewing practices more generally. Nevertheless, the tone remains light, a glancing blow on the way to other matters. Jerome employs more overtly self-deprecatory humour in his valentine anecdote. In the manner that made *Three Men in a Boat* so popular, he genially makes his own ineptitude the subject of his humour.

The imitation of club talk invokes the intimacy of gossip, in Spacks's recuperative sense.[57] Indeed, a precursor to the column was Jerome's single-authored column for *Home Chimes*, 'Gossips' Corner'. One column begins by commenting on its own headpiece (Fig. 1.5):

What I am anxious to find out just now is the name and address of the gentleman who designed the picture that stands at the top of these pages. I also wish to know what time he is most likely to be found

GOSSIPS' CORNER.

Figure 1.5 Headpiece for 'Gossips' Corner' in *Home Chimes*. Beinecke Rare Book and Manuscript Library, Yale University.

at home. This corner, dear reader, is a spot where you and I meet together to have a quiet gossip, and a creature that, I suppose, calls itself a man, goes and heads it with a sketch of a couple of donkeys. I want to know whom those donkeys are intended for? Don't tell me it's only a seascape with figures. Seascape with figures be—I know what he means. Now my idea was for the picture of a Grecian temple with myself, in a white sheet, as Socrates, or Plato, and an eager throng of wondering listeners (representative of the British public) grouped picturesquely around me. Two donkeys, indeed! When I get hold of that artist I'll tell him what I think of him with a brickbat.[58]

Jerome treats his reader as a confidential companion, who in turn catches some of the flak from his self-deprecating humour. The comparison to the donkeys is, of course, Jerome's creation more than the artist's. Indeed, the notion that the art is commissioned with a knowledge of the column's content is as much a self-aggrandisement as the comparison between Jerome and Plato. The content of his gossip is much less important than the relationships it forges. The triviality is part of the charm, the ephemerality an essential mechanism of community formation in a club or a periodical readership.

The 'Idler's Club' continues in this tradition, at one point referring to itself as a 'page of gossip'. Unlike columns such as Yates's

'Lounger at the Clubs', its gossip was not malicious.[59] Instead it used gossip in the spirit of the general New Journalistic trend of celebrity interviews: a backstage pass to the literary world. George R. Sims, in the May 1892 'Idler's Club' column, remarks on J. M. Barrie's not having taken a curtain call as author of *Walker London* and proceeds to tell self-deprecating anecdotes about how he himself is uncomfortable taking curtain calls. Of course, these anecdotes reinforce and puff his own celebrity status as well as Barrie as a member of the *Idler* circle. The relaxed atmosphere of the 'Idler's Club' fosters a sense of intimacy with literary celebrities, as one might gossip at the club about one's mutual acquaintances.

A potential danger in presenting the *Idler* as a club was that its smoking room might seem too close and self-contained, creating a claustrophobic atmosphere for readers. A review of the *Idler*'s first issue in the *Spectator* identified it as the 'organ of the so-called "New Humorists"', saying, 'Who these are, and how they joke, may be gathered from the final article, entitled "The Idlers' Club", and perhaps also from a rather too painfully funny story, "The English Shakespeare", by Mr I. Zangwill.'[60] This story, which would later be incorporated into *The Old Maids' Club* (discussed further in Chapter 3) describes a club of journalists who band together to form a sort of cartel, puffing each other's work in print yet meeting in private as the Mutual Depreciation Society, a club whose rules stipulate that members must insult each other. *The Spectator* continues, 'There is obviously a danger that the New Humorists may form themselves into a close coterie, and may commit the mistake of thinking that the public are much more interested than they actually are, in the jokes they make at each other's expense.'[61] The downsides of the magazine as club emerge here as a potential threat. 'The public' remains an unknown quantity and may not feel the sense of affiliation with the Idlers (let alone the New Humorists) that they encourage through this feature. *The Spectator* also indicates that some of the critical disdain for New Humorists derived from their style.

The light style of the Idlers' humour reveals itself through contrast. In the May 1892 'Idler's Club' column, Zangwill parodies Oscar Wilde's characteristic epigrams as he addresses him directly: 'I say these things to make it quite clear that I speak to you more in anger than in sorrow. You are much too important to be discussed seriously, and if I take the trouble to give you advice it is only because I am so much younger than you.'[62] The parody points to differences in their style and their satiric targets. Wilde also practises self-conscious triviality, but his triviality elevates itself into a highly wrought art form, laughing from a distance at those who are unselfconsciously, prosaically and irredeemably trivial. The Idlers, however, practice a more realistic triviality, embracing its ephemerality and seeking to close the distance between themselves and their readers. The New Humorists' self-referential, self-deprecatory humour invites readers to laugh at the writers' expense, rather than the other way around. Yet as generous as the 'Idler's Club' members could be to their readers, their geniality slipped away when addressing the aesthete. The conclusion to Zangwill's section on Wilde has an uncharacteristic bite: 'He takes such broad views that he has grown narrow. What he wants is a little knowledge of life, and twelve months' hard labour.'[63] The unwitting prophecy in the last clause makes the comment more chilling in hindsight. Zangwill was more of an 'insult comic' than his fellows, but his Society for Mutual Depreciation and other representations of groups, such as *The Bachelors' Club*, unfold within a context of good humour. The 'Idler's Club' column did not approach the 'malicious joy' of John Wilson's contributions to *Blackwood's*, for instance.[64] Wilde styled himself as an individual, but the Idlers emphasised their group identity. Epigrams occur less often and usually within the context of rambling conversation.

Although it resembles the record of a clublike conversation, the 'Idler's Club' series subtly references general readers as participants, which distinguishes it from previous periodical table talk. In fact, an inconsistency in the punctuation of the club name is surprisingly telling: it is sometimes rendered the 'Idler's Club' and other times the 'Idlers' Club'. Is it a club based around the *Idler* magazine (the *Idler*'s Club) or a club for those who enjoy idling (the Idlers' Club)? 'Idlers', after all, could describe those who enjoy the perusal of light periodical literature. The Hounsom Byles 'Idler' plate appeared in 1896 on its own page in the *Idler*, facing the end of a J. F. Nisbet story, 'The World, the Flesh and the Devil', and before Jerome's column 'Letters to Clorinda', purportedly addressed to a specific female reader (Fig. 1.5). Labelled 'An Idler', a woman sits on a rocky promontory, attention fixed on a small volume in her hand, presumably a number of the *Idler*. This embrace of Idlers as readers rather than speakers in the club increases in that period of the periodical's development, as we shall soon see.

Zangwill might imagine an interpolation by the general reader rather than his fellow journalists when he says in the first column, 'What's that you say? All this has been said before? Naturally.'[65] Readers do not merely eavesdrop on this conversation; they are part of it. Later 'Idler's Club' columns make reference to the larger fraternity of Idlers, as in September 1892, when Zangwill says, on the subject of places to spend one's holiday, 'Naturally, one does not go to the trouble of accidentally lighting upon an unsuspected haven, to give away the secret to ten million other Idlers.'[66] Still, references to common readers are relatively rare, possibly because they threaten the illusion: it is hard to feel cosy in a group of ten million. In this respect the 'Idler's Club' echoes the experience of actual London clubs. Large West End clubs such as the Carleton had membership lists that numbered in the thousands, making it impossible for all of the members of the club to actually know each other. Clubs did not always offer literal friendship, but rather the promise that members could become friends given the opportunity to chat in the smoking room. Through the club metaphor, the *Idler* suggested the same thing about magazine readership.

In fact, in the first 'Idler's Club' column, Barr intentionally blurs the distinction between contributor and reader: 'Oh, by-the-bye, if anybody gets his MSS. sent back from this magazine, he must understand that it is the Sub-editor's doing. So far as Jerome and myself are concerned, we are always ready to take anything we can lay our hands on. Indeed, that has been the principle that has guided us from childhood. But our Sub is a cold, calculating villain, without a spark of kindly feeling in him.'[67] In the guise of a genial good cop incapable of spurning anyone, Barr invites the common reader to consider themselves a potential contributor, an imaginary member not only of the immediate 'Idler's Club' but also of the select company of its chummy coterie. The here-unnamed subeditor becomes the fall guy, although the actual sub, G. B. Burgin, became a frequent 'Idler's Club' contributor. Given the clear context of New Journalism that Barr established at the beginning of the column, this appeal seems to democratise the audience. Rather than dismissing his readers' intelligence, Barr welcomes them into the club of fellow journalists. Yet the paragraph goes on to speak slightingly of the reading public's taste through its characterisation of the sub: 'As for his taste in literature, it is simply beneath contempt. He invariably rejects the most brilliant stories and articles that are sent into the office; and passes on to us only that rubbish that his experience tells him the British public will care for.'[68] This insults the reader, but it makes up for this by insulting everyone else as well, including the contributors to the 'Idler's Club' whose 'rubbish' appears in the journal. Barr thus treats the reader as a member of the Mutual Depreciation Society. After all, good-natured teasing often cements bonds of fellowship.

Yet Barr's private correspondence shows that he took the task of manuscript selection very seriously. Writing to Maud Russell Loraine Sharp, later Emarel Freshel, whom he had met on a trans-atlantic ocean voyage, Barr vigorously defends the *Idler*'s editorial process:

> Your notion about 'inner circles' in literature is entirely wrong. Take this magazine for instance. Every article, story, & poem is read by three persons who are not only unbiased but whose living depends on their work being carefully & intelligently done. If all three condemn a ms it goes back. If two praise it the sub-editor reads it & if it is good in his opinion & is in handwriting, it is sent away to be type-written & then I read it.
>
> We have 3 years' stuff on hand, most of it by utterly unknown men & women. If you can suggest a fairer or more impartial system than that I'll adopt it. Editors are as anxious to find budding geniuses as the B. G.'s are to be found. The success of their publications depends on it.[69]

Despite a flourish of humorous abbreviation of the type that would come to characterise Bertie Wooster, Barr seems very anxious to present the *Idler* as an open field, a business and a meritocracy, not an old boys' club.

A tension lurks in the 'Idler's Club' between leisure and commerce. While readers of the magazine are idling, in the sense of avoiding work, for the contributors, this *is* work.[70] They are, as it were, professional idlers. Occasionally, especially given the meta-textual bent of the column, this paradox comes explicitly to the fore, including in the first issue. As part of a humorous discussion of the *Idler*'s plans, Barry Pain refers to his employment status: 'I have decided to make these proposals in *The Idler*, because previous to the publication of this number, I have found absolutely nothing in *The Idler* to which I have been able to take objection. It can look back upon its past without a blush. I am speaking in a perfectly disinterested spirit, and with a full determination to be paid for this conversation.'[71] The tail end of this amusingly meaningless compliment alludes to the jarring fact that these men are indeed being paid. Although they speak in the guise of idle clubmen for the benefit of readers seeking to be idle as well, they are in fact working journalists. The conflation between the 'Idler's Club' as an editorial feature and a band of cosy club members was thus occasionally revealed to be unstable. As the topics solidified and the contributors became farther flung, less care was taken to format the column as a conversation. Yet the early columns set the tone and context for the later discussions; if they began to take themselves more seriously, they still maintained the idea of the 'Idler's Club' as an imagined community.

Widening the club

Over the years of the 'Idler's Club' column's collaborative status, it widened its scope significantly. From 1892 to 1901, a total of 280 contributors had their work appear in sections of the column. This collection begins to resemble an actual club in scope: not as many as the 3,700 members of the Constitutional, but not as few as the fictional clubs created by the core Idlers, which tend to have around twelve members or trace a smaller group of five or six friends.[72] Of course, not all of these contributors wrote at the same time: for the most part, the columns contained about six or eight contributors, mimicking the size of a conversation in a smoking room. Inevitably the column took on a slightly different character: less close in both senses, more open to air that dissipated the cigar smoke. Perhaps Jerome and Barr were actively trying to respond to *The Spectator*'s caution against the disadvantages of a close coterie. As the club expands, the metatextual humour remains but the link to talk weakens.

Contributors included George Bernard Shaw, Clement Scott, Florence Marryat, F. W. Robinson, Dr Arabella Kenealy, Walter Jerrold (son of Douglas), Arthur Waugh (father of Evelyn) and Rutland Barrington, best known as a staple of the D'Oyly Carte Opera Company. Even Andrew Lang, who originally coined the term 'New Humour' derisively, joined the club in June 1899, after Jerome had left the editor's position.[73] As Linda Hughes and the Curran Index have recently highlighted, Lang also contributed anonymous comic verse to *Punch*.[74] Lang's 'Idler's Club' contribution begins a column on 'Spirit Manifestations', an all-male discussion that does *not* include Doyle. He never contributed directly to the 'Idler's Club' column, although the July 1892 column responds to his article about the North Pole in the same number.

The introduction of an explicit topic, in vols 3–5 labelled 'Subject for Discussion', provided formal cohesion without the need for contributors to actively collaborate in the writing. The first column resembles conversation so closely that it is easy to imagine it having been written in the *Idler* offices, perhaps even around the same table or desk – in the manner of the famous *Punch* table. But the topics for discussion facilitated the composition of the pieces in a more distributed way. As time goes on, the conversations are less interleaved, which reduces the illusion of response. The side notes, however, continue not only to identify the speakers but also to stitch the conversation together in a way that suggests response. For instance, 'A Substitute for Swearing' (July 1894) begins with the side note 'Barr introduces bad language'.[75] His contribution is broken into several sections, each with its own side note, such as 'The English language at fault'.[76] The segue into the next speaker appears in a side note: 'Dr Percival does not approve of swearing.'[77] Even though correspondents do not return, as they did in the early days, the side notes make the change of speaker an artefact of the change in sub-topic. The familiar cast of characters frequently appear towards the beginnings and ends of the column, heightening a sense of continuity.

This particular column also raises a question about the reliability of the side notes in identifying contributors. 'Dr Percival' and the contributor that follows, 'The Captain of HMS training ship "St Vincent"' may be fictitious pseudonyms by other *Idler* writers: Thomas Percival, author of *Medical Ethics*, died in 1894, and the allusion to 'the big, big "B"' in the Captain's portion suggests that he may be a spoof of Gilbert's Captain from *HMS Pinafore* – or he might in fact have been Cecil Thursby, who occupied that position at that time.[78] Subsequent sections claim to be written by the headmasters of various schools and colleges, which seems more likely. The 'Colonial College' segment immediately follows the *St Vincent* and begins, 'As we never use a big, big "D" at the Colonial College [. . .]', suggesting conversation – or that it was written by the same *Idler* staff. On the other hand, the allusion to *Pinafore* may simply have occurred to many of the contributors.

Throughout the collaborative run, some contributor identifications are clearly pseudonyms. The clearest example is a whole column, 'How I Bring Up My Parents', whose authors are identified as children of literati, including 'Miss Vera Beringer', whose mother, Aimée Beringer, contributed to several other 'Idler's Club' columns under 'Mrs Oscar Beringer'; 'Master W. Alden'; 'Miss Elsie Jerome' and 'Miss Beerbohm Tree'.[79] The first 'Idler's Club' column to include women carries several pseudonyms, including for the women (inviting the question as to whether they were, in fact, included). In addition to 'a lady' and 'Angelina', a stock name for a woman used by *Punch* and in Jerome's writings, 'James I' chimes in. The monarch refers to 'my booklet, *A Counterblaſt to Tobacco*, imprinted *Anno* 1604', and generally uses archaic diction, complete with ampersands and long s's.[80] Zangwill replies directly, using a similar style, and even the sidenotes gloss this as 'Zangwill reaſoneth with ye monarch.'[81] The paratext clearly has a playful dimension and contributes significantly to the metatextual slant of the column as a whole.

Side notes featured from the first issue, in Gothic font and diction, perhaps inspired by the notion that a side note resembles a manuscript gloss. The blackletter font disappeared after the first issue, but the diction remained, and here resurfaced. At times the column manifested different layouts, as in 'The Same Story' (June 1894), which presents an outline of a story's plot, followed by iterations by different authors. Each iteration has a title and byline that cut across the page. Another column uses bylines across the page on a more conventional column, 'Is a Corrupt Government Better than an Honest One?' (March 1895). This format may have derived from the small number of contributors: only Spencer Jerome, Israel Zangwill and Frank Smith.

The column with the most contributors directly followed in April 1895 on the subject 'Who Shall be Laureate?', drawing twenty-two contributors, including Oscar Wilde, George Bernard Shaw, George Gissing, E. Nesbit and John Strange Winter (Henrietta Stannard), as well as 'Idler's Club' regulars Zangwill, Pain and G. B. Burgin. The first response in the column, by Sir Edwin Arnold, humorously reveals the mechanisms by which the editors now solicit contributions:

You have honoured me, Mr Editor, by asking, 'Will you contribute about two hundred words on the man you think should be the next

Poet Laureate, and the reasons for your choice?' And you offer profit as well as honour by adding, 'I shall be happy to pay your customary rates for this contribution.' I am sensible of the honour, but not desirous of the honorarium; so I will reply – too briefly for reward – 'The man whom Her Majesty chooses.'[82]

Jerome chose to run the entirety of the letter rather than its final phrase and also chose to put it first in the column, in a bout of metatextual humour. Unlike earlier columns, there is no attempt to stitch these into a conversation. For instance, multiple contributors suggest the same candidates (mainly Swinburne, William Morris and Kipling) without acknowledging that the same figures have been suggested earlier in the column. Other contributors refer to the editor's request more obliquely, including John Strange Winter, who rejoins, 'That person is not a man, but a woman – that person is myself.'[83] She continues to state that 'every poet, major or minor' thinks 'himself' the finest of the poets, but her point about gender continues to linger.

The question of women's representation in the 'Idler's Club' is a complex one: the column is not exclusively male, but neither do women hold an equal share in it. A conservative count of contributors shows 48 women out of the total 280, with 27 not coded for gender (see Appendix). At 17 per cent of the contributors, they make up only 14 per cent of the total entries during the time of the collaborative column. This may seem a dismally small fraction, but other factors contextualise it. As the Appendix shows, women's contributions to the 'Idler's Club' grew progressively to a high-water mark of 35 per cent in 1897 – but Jerome sold the paper in 1898.

In 1892, Barr sought to present the *Idler* as inclusive of women in his private correspondence with Maud Sharp. He highlights the *Idler* At-Homes, weekly 'tea-parties' at the *Idler*'s offices, which came as near to a meeting of the Idler's Club as possible although they comprised such figures as Barrie, who never contributed to the *Idler*.[84] Joanne Shattock has likened literary parties to clubs in their networking function for women writers in the 1840s and 1850s.[85] Barr assures Sharp: 'The "Idler" at-homes are not men's affairs. Mrs Jerome who is a lovely woman & Mrs Barr who is also . . . Well I need only say she is an American woman & that ought to be enough . . . are always there to receive the ladies. Jerome & I are there of course but we are only useless impediments. The rooms overflow with ladies of talent.'[86] Barr's letter shows that he wanted to present the *Idler* as an open, mixed-sex community that blended the personal and the professional.

The most important factor in 'Idler's Club' contributors was the clublike inner circle. And that circle was male. The five most frequent contributors (see Appendix) – who comprised both founding editors, the subeditor, W. L. Alden, and Barry Pain – contributed 17 per cent of the entries, which is more than all the women combined. Alden was the most frequent contributor, appearing in the column at least once every year until 1901, never equalling his initial eight contributions per year, but frequently contributing five times in a year. Jerome himself contributed progressively less as the years went on. Eliza Lynn Linton, the most frequent female contributor with ten contributions, died in 1898 yet made her presence felt in the column. All of the contributors to the first volume were male. Zangwill contributed to every 'Idler's Club' column in the first volume. As the column grew, that central cast of characters often appeared as the first or last entry in a column. Side notes frequently identify those contributors by last name only, although this practice varies.[87]

Although the early 'Idler's Club' columns mimicked the ebb and flow of conversation, often to comic effect, later columns called attention to the textual materiality of the column and its production. 'Some Literary Typewriters' (April 1894) opens with what purports to be Barr's record of successful mastery of the typewriter in six days.[88] The first entry, in monotype that mimics the typewriter, contains mis-capitalisations, misspellings and stray marks; by the sixth day, the writing appears smooth and even. Joseph Hatton's entry begins with what looks like the facsimile of a typescript annotated by hand, and Justin McCarthy's lapses into a similar passage in the middle, with more minor annotations.[89] Hubert Herkomer's entry contains a passage in his handwriting, and Dr Parker's concludes the column, entirely in handwriting – and entirely in the third person, with no side note.[90] His entry follows Burgin's, which has no overt reference to his own role as subeditor. The typographical play in the 'Idler's Club' column indicates that its metatextual humour extends past the club-talk framework. The illusion of the club does not have to stand up to the wide expansion of contributors, because the audience has been in on the joke from the beginning.

The reader in the *Idler*'s club

The 'Idler's Club' column draws out some of the ramifications of the club smoking room as a metaphor for reading, including the difficulties of using a metaphor from embodied face-to-face contact for the unique sociability of reading. In Jerome's address to readers when he assumed full ownership and editorship of the magazine, he wrote of the *Idler*, 'I hope to make it a friend wherever the English tongue is spoken.'[91] He figures the magazine simultaneously as personally intimate in its relationship and global in its scope – a difficult balance to maintain. Humour could help, in part by pulling back the curtain on the mechanics of the construction of community – ironically an intimate gesture. For instance, the *Idler* ran a series of caricatures by Scott Rankin called 'People I Have Never Met', featuring well-known literary figures, many of whose work appeared in the magazine, such as Andrew Lang and Mark Twain. The work's title accentuates the mechanism of literary celebrity and literary sociability that enables one to envision an author whom one has never met. Indeed, it goes a step further in implying that the artist himself is relying on second-hand sources to construct the portraits and attendant relationships. Jerome himself features in one such caricature, threatening the illusion of a physical Idler's Club: if Rankin has never met Jerome, not all *Idler* contributors gathered even at the *Idler* At-Homes.[92]

The most direct account of readers embodying the Idler's Club carries complex ramifications for gender. In the July 1892 column, Eden Phillpotts writes,

> There has come to my ears a very gratifying circumstance from the North of England, and the significance of the Idlers' Club is thereby proved to demonstration. Sundry young ladies, the admired of sundry young and old gentlemen, recently designed an entertainment with a view to giving pleasure, securing moneys for a charitable object, and, perhaps, themselves gaining some well-deserved attention. *Tableaux vivants* were the order of the day, and amongst them, sandwiched between the 'Execution of King Charles I' and 'The Finding of Moses in the Bulrushes', was presented a living reproduction of the Idlers' Club, as it appears above this page of gossip. The difficulties were not small, but these entertainers met and mastered each in turn. Young men with cigarettes and pipes gladly volunteered their services.[93]

Notably, the idea of staging a tableau is said to originate with female readers. Their inclusion of the 'Idler's Club' in the programme indicates not only their own familiarity with the piece but their expectations that their audience will recognise it. However, the women themselves did not embody the Idlers: they recruited men to enact the scene. Phillpotts humorously recounts the difficulty of finding a bald man with legs long enough to reach the mantelpiece, but this detail itself suggests the arbitrary nature of the identity of the lounging figures. Of course a club wouldn't limit itself to bald men with long legs (unless it was a comic club of the kind described in the Idlers' novels), and thus it might not be limited to male readers. Certainly, female readers could imagine themselves into the space of the club, if not into the particular bodies depicted in the illustration.

Through the 'Idler's Club' column, the *Idler* answered the implicit question Barr posed in the first issue: how could the *Idler* distinguish itself among the glut of magazines, not to mention other print material, competing for the attention of a rapidly expanding mass reading public? The answer was by offering readers an image to counterbalance the anonymity of mass print culture – a club in which to imaginatively situate their leisure-time reading. As a periodical organised by light humorists but not explicitly or exclusively identified with humour, the *Idler* was uniquely situated to supply this need. The 'Idler's Club', particularly in its early days, maintained a humorous tone that enabled it to strike a delicate balance between exclusivity and inclusivity. The quality of the contributors' deadpan and self-deprecatory humour allowed readers to interpret many remarks as either sober or facetious – or, more frequently, a combination of both. Because the club refused to take itself too seriously, readers were free to do the same. Instead of being schooled by belletristic writers who addressed them and one another in tones of cultivated propriety, readers were encouraged to join the club on an equal basis and to listen to the editors' chummy chit-chat. They were also encouraged to minimise the distinction between reader and writer and between the vocation of literary journalism and the casual perusal of its labours. In the global market of print that swelled year by year, they could find in the 'Idler's Club' a welcoming refuge that was snug in the centre of busy, jostling London, friendly as a shared cigar.

Notes

Material from this chapter first appeared as 'The Idler's Club: Humor and Sociability in the Age of New Journalism'. *Victorian Periodicals Review* 49, no. 3 (2016): 415–30. Published by The Johns Hopkins University Press.

1 Fiss, 'Pushing at the Boundaries of the Book', 265–6, 273.

2 Obviously, this resembles Benedict Anderson's concept of 'imagined communities' – the major distinction being that he referred to nations; here, fictional spaces create imaginary communities. Anderson, *Imagined Communities*; Fiss, 'The Idler's Club', 417.

3 Spacks, *Gossip*, 15, 26.

4 Milne-Smith, *London Clubland*, 89.

5 Milne-Smith, *London Clubland*, 99, 102–3.

6 Parker et al., 'Idler's Club' (March 1893).

7 In the *Dictionary of Nineteenth-Century Journalism*, Anne Humpherys names some of these editors as Arthur Lawrence and Sidney Sime, but also erroneously states that the magazine 'disappeared' in 1898. Humpherys, 'Idler (1892–1898)'.

8 'Note', 201.

9 Anne Humpherys notes that the going rate for the 'Idler's Club' contributions had been a guinea, so there were some savings in having readers contribute. Humpherys, 'Putting Women in the Boat', 22.

10 Byerly, *Are We There Yet?*, 28.

11 This notion echoes that of the 'imagined fireside', which I identify as a trope in Victorian children's literature. Fiss, 'Pushing at the Boundaries of the Book', 264.

12 Humpherys, 'Putting Women in the Boat', 16, 12.

13 Parker et al., 'Idler's Club' (November 1892). Anne Humpherys extensively discusses the shifts in headpieces over the course of the 'Idler's Club' column.

14 Flint, *The Woman Reader*, 50–1.

15 Radway, 'Reading Is Not Eating', 7–29.

16 Flint, *The Woman Reader*, 50. Flint cites many examples of food metaphors; it's not all an equation of novels to sweets.

17 Zieger, 'Holmes's Pipe', 25, 40.

18 Hilton, *Smoking in British Popular Culture 1800–2000*, 22, 34.

19 Zieger, 'Holmes's Pipe', 39.

20 Flint cites Francis Bacon's injunction that 'Some *Bookes* are to be Tasted, Others to be Swallowed, and Some Few to be Chewed and

Digested' as influential: often when books are described as healthful food it is with the emphasis that only some books (or genres, etc.) fall into this category. Flint, *The Woman Reader*, 50.

21 Milne-Smith, *London Clubland*, 33–4.

22 Hilton, *Smoking in British Popular Culture 1800–2000*, 23.

23 Hilton, *Smoking in British Popular Culture 1800–2000*, 20. Patrick Brantlinger has perhaps the clearest focus on this issue as it pertains to both women and the lower classes. Brantlinger, *The Reading Lesson*.

24 Cloy, *Muscular Mirth*, 21.

25 Jerome, *Novel Notes*, 1.

26 Jerome, *Novel Notes*.

27 Flint, *The Woman Reader*, 50–2, 18. One of Flint's examples invokes communal eating as a contra-example, depicting eating alone what should be shared.

28 Jerome, *Idle Thoughts*. Susan Zieger ties smoking reveries with ephemeral print culture, focusing especially on material explicitly meant to be read while smoking. I was especially influenced by the 2013 MLA paper that became this article. Zieger, 'Holmes's Pipe'.

29 Pain, *One Kind and Another*, 272.

30 Pain, *Problem Club*, 67.

31 Zangwill, *Bachelors' Club*, in *Celibates' Club*, 70.

32 Sedgwick, *Between Men*, 2. Rich, 'Compulsory Heterosexuality', 648.

33 Marcus, *Between Women*, 3; Sedgwick, 'Paranoid Reading and Reparative Reading', 123–51.

34 'Women regularly kissed each other on the lips, a gesture that could be a routine social greeting or provide intense enjoyment.' Marcus, *Between Women*, 57.

35 Parker et al., 'Idler's Club' (November 1892), 460.

36 Parker et al., 'Idler's Club' (November 1892), 465.

37 Parker et al., 'Idler's Club' (November 1892), 465.

38 Parker et al., 'Idler's Club' (November 1892), 468.

39 Jerome, *The Angel and the Author*, 215, 216.

40 Jerome, *The Angel and the Author*, 216.

41 Jerome, *The Angel and the Author*, 219.

42 Humpherys uses this image as part of her argument for separate spheres for men and women in the pages of the *Idler*. Humpherys, 'Putting Women in the Boat', 15.

43 Flint, *The Woman Reader 1837–1914*.

44 Dames, *The Physiology of the Novel*, 73.

45 'While by the end of the [nineteenth] century women's clubs became more common, and women were admitted as guests to many clubs, women's clubs never achieved the permanence of their male counterparts, and it would take almost a century for women to become full-fledged members of any of the principal London clubs. Clubland remained a distinctly masculine space throughout the nineteenth and early twentieth centuries.' Milne-Smith, *London Clubland*, 31.

46 Leary, Punch *Brotherhood*, 87.

47 Barr et al., 'Idler's Club' (February 1892), 106.

48 'Introduction', 1. The *Strand* had a feature entitled 'The Strand Club', but contra the *Dictionary of Literary Biography* entry on Robert Barr, it began in 1905. 'The Chronicles of the Strand Club – No. 1', 66–71.

49 'Introduction', 1.

50 Jerome K. Jerome to J. W. Arrowsmith, 11 March 1889. Typed copy in Jerome K. Jerome Collection. Quoted in Connolly, *JKJ* 72.

51 Jonathan Wild notes Jerome's use of the stock lower-class figure 'Arry in his fiction; Jerome bristled at having the term itself applied to him in *Punch*. Wild, *The Rise of the Office Clerk in Literary Culture*, 69. Jerome, *My Life and Times*, 74; Jerome, *Novel Notes*, xiv.

52 Jerome, 'To the Readers of "The Idler"', 98.

53 Barr et al., 'Idler's Club' (February 1892), 106.

54 Barr et al., 'Idler's Club' (February 1892), 110.

55 Barr et al., 'Idler's Club' (February 1892), 113.

56 Barr et al., 'Idler's Club' (February 1892), 110.

57 Spacks, *Gossip*, 46.

58 Jerome, 'Gossips' Corner', 155.

59 Barr et al., 'Idler's Club' (July 1892), 719.

60 'Current Literature', 209.

61 'Current Literature', 209.

62 Alden et al., 'Idler's Club' (May 1892), 481–2.

63 Alden et al., 'Idler's Club' (May 1892), 483.

64 Christie, 'Where Personation Ends and Imposture Begins', 179.

65 Barr et al., 'Idler's Club' (February 1892), 112.

66 Scott et al., 'Idler's Club' (September 1892), 110.

67 Barr et al., 'Idler's Club' (February 1892), 110.

68 Barr et al., 'Idler's Club' (February 1892),110–11.

69 Robert Barr to Maud Russell Lorraine Sharpe, later Freshel, 15 August 1894, in Bassett, 'Robert Barr's Life at *The Idler*: Four Unpublished Letters', 521.

70 Anne Humpherys contrasts the idler with the *flâneur*, emphasis-
    ing that the former is constructed in opposition to work. In a dif-
    ferent context, Deidre Lynch describes the ways in which literary
    professions – in her case, the study, not the production, of literature –
    demand affective work. Humphreys, 'Putting Women in the Boat', 6.
    Lynch, *Loving Literature*, 5.
71 Barr et al., 'Idler's Club' (February 1892), 109.
72 Joseph Hatton, who contributed to the 'Idler's Club' column, lists
    this figure as the limit of the members. Hatton, *Club-Land*, 35.
73 Hatton et al., 'The Idler's Club' (June 1899). Wild, 'What was *New*',
    294.
74 Hughes, 'Anti-Elitist Elitist Verse Forms' [forthcoming]. *The Curran
    Index*.
75 Barr et al., 'Idler's Club' (July 1894), 658.
76 Barr et al., 'Idler's Club' (July 1894), 659.
77 Barr et al., 'Idler's Club' (July 1894), 661.
78 *Wikipedia*, s.v. 'Cecil Thursby', accessed 6 June 2020.
79 Beringer et al., 'Idler's Club' (October 1895), 292–9.
80 Parker et al., 'The Idler's Club' (November 1892), 466.
81 Parker et al., 'The Idler's Club' (November 1892), 467.
82 Arnold et al., 'The Idler's Club' (April 1895), 401.
83 Arnold et al., 'The Idler's Club' (April 1895), 412.
84 Jerome, *My Life and Times*, 167.
85 Shattock, 'Professional Networking, Masculine and Feminine', 134.
86 Robert Barr to Maud Russell Lorraine Sharpe, later Freshel, 8
    November 1892, in Bassett, 'Robert Barr's Life at *The Idler*: Four
    Unpublished Letters', 518.
87 An early contributor is identified only by the last name 'Kennedy',
    and I have been unable to place them. I have assumed, when I say all
    the contributors to the first volume were male, that this writer was
    as well.
88 Barr et al., 'The Idler's Club' (April 1894), 321–3.
89 Barr et al., 'The Idler's Club' (April 1894), 328.
90 Barr et al., 'The Idler's Club' (April 1894), 332, 336.
91 Jerome, 'To the Readers of "*The Idler*"', 100.
92 Ramkin, 'People I Have Never Met – Jerome K. Jerome', 100.
93 Barr et al., 'Idler's Club' (July 1894), 719.

2

The Pressroom and the Clubroom: Working Women and Idling Men in Jerome K. Jerome's *Tommy and Co.*

After the end of the collaborative 'Idler's Club' column, Jerome K. Jerome revisited the relationship between the club and the periodical through a different medium: fiction. *Tommy and Co.* appeared as a book in 1904, although, fittingly, its chapters had previously appeared in a slightly different order in the US *Saturday Evening Post* and the UK *Cassell's Magazine* and *Windsor Magazine*.[1] By this time, Jerome had lost his libel case and with it the editorship and ownership of both *To-Day* and the *Idler*. The central role of the periodical *Good Humour* and its social network revisits his editorial days in an affectionate haze. Yet the central figure in this social network is not a clear Jerome stand-in (unlike the J of *Three Men in a Boat* and other works), but the eponymous Tommy, who first appears as an androgynous street urchin and whose fluid approach to gender continues after her sex is revealed.

The organisation of *Tommy and Co.* as a book emphasises Tommy's role in bringing the community together. The first story to be published eventually became the fourth chapter, and it features a more conventional newspaperwoman with an unhappy ending to her story. 'The Temptation of Miss Ramsbotham', sub-titled in the US 'The Love Story of an Unmanageable Woman', was published in November 1902 in the US *Saturday Evening Post* and *Cassell's* Christmas number.[2] Over a year later, the rest of the book proceeded like a more usual serial, with the rest of the chapters in order appearing in the weekly *Saturday Evening Post* towards the end of the month, then in the *Windsor Magazine* for the following month. Each appeared under a stand-alone title highlighting the individual stories told within. A few contain the fictional periodical's title, as in 'Good Humor Obtains the Marble Soap Advertisement' and 'Dick Danvers Comes to Life: A Good Humor Story'. However, all of the titles were rewritten for the book to show the role played by the main character of the story or chapter in the periodical's development, without using *Good Humour*'s title: 'Peter Hope Plans His Prospectus', 'William Clodd Appoints Himself Managing Editor', 'Gridley Junior Drops into the Position of Publisher', 'Miss Ramsbotham Gives Her Services', 'Joey Loveredge Agrees – on Certain Terms – to Join the Company', 'The "Babe" Applies for Shares', and 'Dick Danvers Presents His Petition'. Tommy is not named in any of the book's chapter titles, unlike the stories: chapter 1 was titled 'The Stolen Interview: "Tommy" Shows Aptitude for Journalism' in the *Saturday Evening Post*, and *Windsor Magazine* merely used that subtitle, which puts Tommy's name in quotation marks, unlike the book title. Tommy's central role in the title (which could easily have been *Good Humour*) indicates her central role not only in the narrative – which forms a loose bildungsroman, with the first and last stories featuring her unconventional birth and unconventional marrige – but also in the periodical and its community.

The double meaning of 'company' here (in the book's title and the title of chapter 5) plays on the periodical as both business and communal experience, not unlike the 'Idler's Club'. Indeed, the '*Idler* At-Homes' and *Idler* cricket team – and the seemingly genuine pleasure Arthur Conan Doyle reported in the company of this group – indicate that the *Idler* had a similar mixture of professional and personal camaraderie to the one depicted in *Tommy and Co*. But instead of representing the magazine as a club, the novel creates a male club, the Autolycus Club, to serve as a foil. The Autolycus Club is not an active evil, but it encourages callow immaturity in its members. Meanwhile, Tommy holds both the periodical (as the subeditor) and the community around it together. Tommy's gender fluidity supports the strengths of *Good Humour* not only as a periodical, but as a community. The 'Idler's Club' compares the periodical to a club, but *Tommy and Co*. insists on the periodical's superiority, precisely because of its greater inclusivity.

A man's view of newspaperwomen

Ironically, given the number of female contributors to the *Idler* detailed in Chapter 1, it was the *Idler*'s male editors who wrote the most humorous, appealing accounts of women in journalism.

In addition to Jerome's *Tommy and Co.*, Robert Barr wrote *Jenny Baxter, Journalist*, which appeared in book form in 1888, four years before he founded the *Idler*. His eponymous heroine's femininity may be more conventional than either major female journalist in Jerome's *Tommy and Co.*, but her enjoyment in both her femininity and her work makes hers seem like an enjoyable profession.

Conversely, the funny female 'Idler's Club' contributors could not quite muster humour when it came to describing female journalists. Ella Hepworth Dixon, a humorist and journalist who contributed four times to the 'Idler's Club', might have been expected to write a humorous account of women in journalism. Her 1930 memoir *As I Knew Them* comes close, although as the title suggests, its focus is more clearly on the celebrities that she met, not exclusively through her work.[3] Her novel *The Story of a Modern Woman* (published in 1894, the same year she was writing for the 'Idler's Club') tells the story of a female journalist, but its dominant tone is sombre. If there is humour, it is largely ironic, dark social satire, not the light tone of her novel *My Flirtations* (1892) or the work of Jerome. The protagonist's work in journalism is largely portrayed as gruelling and deleterious to her health: 'We've got to be dosed with poison to make us fit to sit at a desk and write – twaddle.'[4] This perspective was important in the project of advancing early feminism; an exemplar of the 'New Woman Novel', this type of social commentary attempted consciousness-raising about the plight of the working woman. But I would be surprised if any female reader of the 1890s closed *The Story of a Modern Woman* and thought, 'That settles it: I'll take up a career in journalism!' Which may have been Dixon's point. Likewise, humorist and 'Idler's Club' contributor Evelyn Sharp's New Woman novel *The Making of a Prig* (1897) depicts a young woman earning her living in London (though as a teacher, not a journalist). Like Dixon, Sharp emphasises the trials and hardships of her protagonist. And while Sharp frequently stresses Katherine's 'sense of humour', which 'carrie[s] her though' to a comparatively happy ending, the novel itself is not particularly funny, nor particularly designed to inspire young women to enter the workforce.[5]

Barr's 1888 novel, *Jennie Baxter, Journalist*, however, might elicit that reaction in a female reader. The eponymous heroine approaches her profession as an adventure, although it is clear from the inception that she needs the money. Still, she begins in a stronger financial state than Dixon's Mary: she seeks a salaried position on a paper because 'the income she made was reasonably good, but hazardously fitful'.[6] Barr understood the ramifications of a salaried staff position on a paper, and that women rarely held them.[7] Yet Barr also takes care to stress the physical aspects of Jennie's femininity. He introduces the reader to Jennie as she 'makes her toilette', and tells us by the end of the novel's first sentence that 'she was an exceedingly pretty girl'.[8] Delicately and carefully, Barr indicates the lengths to which Jennie is willing to use her feminine charms as she 'set[s] out . . . to capture an editor': 'Quite sensibly, she depended upon her skill and her industry as her ultimate recommendation to a large salary, but she was woman enough to know that an attractive appearance might be of some assistance to her in getting a hearing from the editor, even though he should prove on acquaintance to be a man of iron, which was tolerably unlikely.'[9] In fact, the editor is unaffected by her appearance, but it does influence the doorman. Because he shows her up to an antechamber, she overhears a crucial conversation that enables her first success. While her femininity gives her some opportunities (just as it forestalls some), her journalistic skills as well as her quick wit and iron nerve see her through.

The same holds true throughout Jennie's adventures as a member of the *Bugle* staff: her gender occasionally opens doors, but she passes through them on her own. In the process, she outwits powerful men. Her first adventure, a case of diamonds stolen from an Austrian princess, pits her against one of Barr's several parodies of Sherlock Holmes, in this instance known as Cadbury Taylor. Taylor underestimates Jennie, and fails to read her correctly (in an imitation of one of Holmes's parlour trick deductions). However, unlike Barr's earlier Holmesian parody, 'Detective Stories Gone Wrong: The Adventures of Sherlaw Kombes' (1892), this is not due to Taylor's incompetence, but Jennie's cleverness in planting false clues. When it comes to the mystery both are trying to solve, Jennie is far ahead of Taylor. In her undercover position as secretary to the Princess, she discovers that the diamonds have merely been mislaid. Furthermore, she repairs the marital rift between the Prince and Princess by giving them a talking-to, interrupting Taylor's incorrect denouement, ushering him and his client, the Princess's American father, out of the room. Her plain-spokenness as well as her cleverness earns her a story, an entrée into her next adventure and – perhaps most surprising – the friendship of the Princess.

In the course of this friendship, Jennie and the Princess discuss the benefits and enjoyment of work. The Princess writes to Jennie asking her to involve her in a case, saying, 'You don't know how much I envy you in your newspaper office.'[10] Jennie writes back, 'It is perfectly absurd for you to envy one who has to work as hard as I. You are the person to be envied. It is not all beer and skittles in a newspaper office, which is a good thing, for I don't like beer, and I don't know what skittles is or are.'[11] This helps contextualise the book's ending, wherein Jennie decides to marry and leave the newspaper business. These events are related in time, but not explicitly connected causally. The obstacles to her union are typical of a comic plot: mistaken identity and her own reluctance to admit her feelings. She finally agrees to marry Lord Donal Stirling after outwitting him for the third time, agreeing in the process to relinquish the documents she has stolen from him, which she calls 'the fruits of her greatest achievement'.[12] Even with this concession, she still manages to accomplish the core task set by her editor, and from the beginning of the caper, the duplicity with which she gains these fruits makes her uncomfortable. She decides to leave the newspaper business but attributes this decision to her financial reward from the Austrian government rather than her marriage: 'I am rich, therefore I am going to give up my newspaper career. I suppose that is why women very rarely make great successes of their lives. A woman's career so often is merely of incidental interest to her; a man's career is his whole life.'[13] Despite this statement, by many standards Jennie has made a 'great success' of her life: she rapidly rises to prominence in her profession and proves her worth to powerful people. Light-hearted to the end of the novel, she does not take herself too seriously and appears happy with all her decisions.

'A new species'

The question of Tommy's gender dominates the first chapter of *Tommy & Co.*, in which she first appears. For the first half of the chapter, Tommy effectively has no gender. With considerable dexterity, Jerome avoids using gendered pronouns for her. A major tactic he uses is to examine Tommy piecemeal and use the pronoun 'it' in reference to a part of her body. This device leads to portions of Tommy's body being imbued with agency: 'The door opened, and a small, white face, out of which gleamed a pair of bright, black eyes, was thrust sideways into the room.'[14] Tommy is made strange by virtue of her gender ambiguity, but it is also clear that her primary affiliation is to the world of print culture.

If Tommy is 'a new species', the 'genus' is Printer's Devil:

> To Peter Hope, hack journalist, long familiar with the genus Printer's Devil, small white faces, tangled hair, dirty hands, and greasy caps were common objects in the neighborhood of that buried rivulet, the Fleet. But this was a new species. Peter Hope sought his spectacles, found them after some trouble under a heap of newspapers, adjusted them upon his high, arched nose, leant forward, and looked long and up and down.
>
> 'God bless my soul!' said Mr Peter Hope. 'What is it?'[15]

Peter's surprise is not necessarily occasioned by the piecemeal features that have previously been described, but by Tommy's choice of clothes:

> Over a tight-fitting garibaldi of blue silk, excessively décolleté, it [the figure] wore what once had been a boy's pepper-and-salt jacket. A worsted comforter wound round the neck still left a wide expanse of throat showing above the garibaldi. Below the jacket fell a long, black skirt, the train of which had been looped up about the waist and fastened with a cricket-belt.[16]

The combination of the boy's cap and jacket with the skirt seem to occasion Peter's discomfort. Tommy's clothes fail to signal gender, which may explain the emphasis on the body underneath. 'Décolleté', a word more associated with ladies' evening gowns than printer's devils, may be employed ironically here, but it is hard to tell.

The threat of sexuality, ambiguous in this description, soon becomes clearer as Peter further questions his visitor: 'For answer, the figure ... stooped down and, seizing the front of the long skirt, began to haul it up.'[17] Peter exclaims 'Don't do that!',[18] clearly assuming the worst – that the Printer's Devil is actually the different genus Streetwalker, and that he will be forced into an undesired sexual confrontation with a minor. Reassuringly, Tommy seeks only to fish a job reference out of the pocket of a pair of trousers worn under the skirt, having heard that Peter sought a housekeeper. However, Peter does want to know what's under Tommy's skirt, although he doesn't want to see it for himself. He ends up asking her to submit to a medical examination, convincing her that it's normal procedure for new employees. Of course, it's more in keeping with the inspection of prostitutes mandated by the Contagious Diseases Act – although Jerome takes pains to make the doctor friendly, comic and sympathetic.

Clearly, Peter seeks to pin Tommy to one gender or another, primarily for his own social comfort. In his first conversation, he struggles with how to address her, and thus asks her 'bluntly',

'Are you a boy or a girl?'
'I dunno.'
'You don't know!'
'What's the difference?'[19]

Peter does not answer the question, presumably out of embarrassment. Yet Jerome also leaves it hanging, a question that Tommy will continue to pose, implicitly and explicitly, throughout the novel – and one which her 'company' will also take up.

Tommy's ignorance underscores the ways in which gender is indeed a social category. Clearly, Tommy must have an awareness of her own anatomy, but she lacks the context in which to interpret it. A gender catechism from Mrs Postwhistle reveals the confusion on that front:

'Nobody ever told you whether you was a boy or a girl?'
'Nobody as I'd care to believe. Some of them called me the one, some of them the other. It depended upon what was wanted.'[20]

For Tommy, biology does still not quite make a difference: she can act as a boy or a girl, according to 'what was wanted'. Roles are fixed to a gender, but Tommy can float between genders. By first appearing to Peter in the garments of both genders, she signals her readiness for a range of gendered activities.

Decades later, Dorothy Sayers would ground a theory of gender – and of feminism – in the practice of women wearing trousers:

Let me give one simple illustration of the difference between the right and the wrong kind of feminism. Let us take this terrible business – so distressing to the minds of bishops – of the women who go about in trousers. We are asked: 'Why do you want to go about in trousers? They are extremely unbecoming to most of you. You only do it to copy the men.' To this we may very properly reply: 'It is true that they are unbecoming. Even on men they are remarkably unattractive. But, as you men have discovered yourselves, they are comfortable, they do not get in the way of one's activities like skirts, and they protect the wearer from draughts about the ankles.'[21]

Here and in a later essay, she uses trousers as a metaphor for the human, or *Homo*, a territory that she says men have claimed for themselves, but is in fact a middle ground between male (*Vir*) and female (*Femina*).[22] To indicate the territory of *Vir*, which she says no woman needs to or wants to invade, she uses the metaphor of braces (as in suspenders), which she calls 'unnecessary and unsuited to the female form'.[23] Tommy's utilitarian approach to gender similarly manifests in sartorial metaphors, but at this stage she seems genuinely not to consider essential distinctions between genders. For her, all gender differences are performed.

When Peter finds out Tommy's gender, he does not describe her gender as biological but uses Tommy's own utilitarian language, describing her gender as contingent on her activities:

'If you are to be a housekeeper, you must be a girl.'
'Don't like girls.'
'Can't say I think much of them myself, Tommy. We must make the best of it. To begin with, we must get you proper clothes.'
'Hate skirts. They hamper you.'[24]

Peter and Tommy's shared casual misogyny forms part of the joke, and part of the reason for Tommy to dislike the idea of living as a girl. Peter takes up Tommy's method of framing gender and clothes as related to occupation, rather than insisting on gender as essential or biological. Thus Tommy's view of gender continues, as she insists, 'They do hamper you. You try 'em.'[25] Although Peter does not take her up on her offer, another member of the *Good Humour* 'company' later does and concurs with Tommy's assessment.

Tommy's medical examination to determine her gender is explicitly likened to a birth:

> Peter, alone, paced to and fro the room, his hands behind his back, his ear on the alert to catch the slightest sound from above.
> 'I do hope it is a boy,' said Peter, glancing up.
> Peter's eyes rested on the photo of the fragile little woman gazing down at him from its stiff frame upon the chimney-piece. Thirty years ago, in this same room, Peter had paced to and fro, his hands behind his back, his ear alert to catch the slightest sound from above, had said to himself the same words.
> 'It's odd,' mused Peter – 'very odd indeed.'[26]

Tommy's name has already reminded Peter of his late son, in a manner that begins to trigger his Scrooge-like transformation from the anti-sentimental journalist who resembles Jerome's critics to a 'Pickwickian' espouser of good humour:[27]

> For no reason whatever, as he told himself, his memory would persist in wandering to Ilford Cemetery, in a certain desolate corner of which lay a fragile little woman whose lungs had been but ill adapted to breathing London fogs; with, on the top of her, a still smaller and still more fragile mite of humanity that, in compliment to its only relative worth a penny-piece, had been christened Thomas – a name common enough in all conscience, as Peter had reminded himself more than once. In the name of common sense, what had dead and buried Tommy Hope to do with this affair? The whole thing was the veriest sentiment, and sentiment was Mr Peter Hope's abomination.[28]

The slippage between the two Tommy Hopes exemplifies Marjorie Garber's figure of 'the changeling boy, the fantasy child who personates change, and exchange'.[29] As in Garber, the exchange occurs across gender lines in a manner that destabilises gender categorisation. J. M. Barrie in particular often emphasises 'Boy or girl?' as a question immediately following birth; by rolling the clock back to that birth's anticipation, Jerome cements the link between the Tommies.

Despite Peter's fears about her gender and its dangers – poignantly compared to the dangers of childbirth – Tommy's gender does not in fact prevent her from fulfilling the Tommy Hope destiny:

> Out of the shadows crept to Peter Hope an old forgotten dream – the dream of a wonderful new Journal, price one penny weekly, of which the Editor should come to be one Thomas Hope, son of Peter Hope, its honoured Founder and Originator: a powerful Journal that should supply a long-felt want, popular, but at the same time elevating – a pleasure to the public, a profit to its owners. 'Do you not remember me?' whispered the Dream. 'We had long talks together. The morning and the noonday pass. The evening still is ours. The twilight also brings its promise.'[30]

Jerome describes this journal in much the same language he used as an editor to describe the *Idler*, particularly stressing its place at the upper end of the lower bracket, 'elevating' its readers' class prospects as well as their spirits. Tommy is at the heart of the Dream: a child enables Peter to have this dream, in part as the gradual successor to the editorship. Over the course of the novel, Tommy does not explicitly realise the editorship. Peter starts her out as a printer's devil, and she quickly rises to the position of journalist, then subeditor. Further success is hinted at but not spelled out, so it is not clear whether Peter's dreams of her editorship are specifically realised. Almost as soon as her sex is revealed, as Peter tries to change her name to 'Jane', we flash forward to her future success: 'A sweet-faced, laughing lady, known to fame by a title respectable and orthodox, appears as an honoured guest to-day at many a literary gathering. But the old fellows, pressing round, still call her "Tommy".'[31] Her male name gives her access to (or is an index of) male sociability: she is one among the 'old fellows'. But we are simultaneously assured of Tommy's literary fame, gained through a 'title respectable and orthodox' – presumably gender-appropriate. She gains fame as a woman, and retains male friendship. Above all, she retains both a 'sweet face' and a sense of humour.

Before the end of the first chapter, however, Tommy must prove herself capable of stepping into this role. Her first real adventure in journalism involves jumping onto a moving train to secure an interview with an elusive prince. To accomplish this task, she returns to her androgynous clothes and her utilitarian approach to gender. Her interview is secured by her combination of gendered traits: the trousers and daring of a boy (which the Prince assumes she is) and the intriguing reality that she is in fact a girl. Jerome moreover implies that some of her most tenacious qualities are the result of her true gender – although in misogynistic terms. When Tommy persists in justifying herself and arguing with the Prince, he comments, 'There is not the least doubt as to which sex you belong to.'[32] Like Jennie Baxter, Tommy's journalistic persistence aligns with expectations of women.

What is perhaps more surprising than Tommy's initial gender ambiguity is its retention. Although Tommy seems to be relatively settled in her new family, job and gender identity, when she is reintroduced (as all characters are) in subsequent stories, her gender ambiguity returns. In the second chapter, which centres around the making of William Clodd's fortune (which enables him to found a paper with Peter Hope), Clodd's first encounter with Tommy makes him question her gender. The narrative itself offers him no aid, describing Tommy first as 'a decided voice'. Again, Tommy is referred to as 'it', though, as with the earlier narrative reference, this has a clear gender-neutral referent:

> The owner of the decided voice went on writing. Clodd, having done as he was bid, sat himself in the easy-chair before the fire and smoked. Of the person behind the desk Mr Clodd could see but the head and shoulders. It had black, curly hair, cut short. Its only garment visible below the white collar and red tie might have been a boy's jacket designed more like a girl's, or a girl's designed more like a boy's; partaking of the genius of English statesmanship, it appeared to be a compromise. Mr Clodd remarked the long, drooping lashes over the bright, black eyes.
>
> 'It's a girl,' said Mr Clodd to himself; 'rather a pretty girl.'
>
> Mr Clodd, continuing downward, arrived at the nose.
>
> 'No,' said Mr Clodd to himself, 'it's a boy – a cheeky young beggar, I should say.'[33]

Like Peter, Clodd finds Tommy's gender difficult to determine. But while Peter's principle confusion lies in her clothes, not her features, here the reverse is the case. Clodd tries to tie Tommy's features to personality traits and thus to gender traits, but he is flummoxed. Although her eyes (again 'bright') seem 'pretty', her nose suggests an attitude that Clodd cannot reconcile immediately with femininity – or at least, he could reconcile pretty eyes more easily with masculinity.

Clodd also seeks guidance in Tommy's clothes, but while they are ambiguous, they are certainly more conventional than the motley outfit compiled in the previous chapter. In fact, as Clodd notes, gender ambiguity itself is somewhat conventional, even fashionable in the age of the New Woman and New Man. Yet while this fact provokes a joke, it is by no means the type of now-critically-recognisable dig at the unappealing masculinity of the New Woman. Instead, the joke is on 'the genius of English statesmanship'. In other words, Jerome uses this joke to associate this type of gender ambiguity in fashion with quintessential Englishness and with conventionality and respectability. Even the fact that the joke seems to be a somewhat old one reinforces the notion that there is fundamentally nothing 'new' or unsettling about this fashion trend.

Tommy resists easy legibility. But her illegibility does not appear threatening. When Clodd, still puzzled by Tommy's gender, asks her name and she replies 'Tommy [. . .] I mean Jane', he makes only a mild joke at the evident contradiction, saying 'Make up your mind, [. . .] don't let me influence you.'[34] At face value, this accepts Tommy's right to determine her own destiny, her own gender expression. As a joke, it comments on the absurdity of a person not knowing her own name, let alone gender. But it remains good-natured: the easy-going surface meaning dominates. Gender and identity are confusing to Tommy, and by extension to everybody around her. Again, the question 'What's the difference?' seems to hang in the air. In subsequent stories, she is often introduced as the 'subeditor' of *Good Humour*, which seems to be the best description of her.

Androgyny and *Good Humour*

The other members of Tommy's social circle do not merely condone Tommy's androgyny; some of them practice their own unconventional inhabitation of gender roles. Johnny Bulstrode, nicknamed 'the Babe', has his own trousers-and-skirt episode, in which he dresses as a woman to help Tommy overturn Clodd and Peter's belief that 'Cadging for advertisements isn't a woman's work.'[35] However, Johnny has a problem: his disguise works too well. Although this episode contains a good deal of cross-dressing comedy, ultimately it fosters mutual understanding and sympathy across gender lines.

Tommy inspires Johnny's turn, but only indirectly. Her gender non-conformity does not preclude male interest: 'Most of the members of the Autolycus Club looked in about once a day to see if they could do anything for Tommy.'[36] Johnny is among them, and Tommy turns him away rather crossly because Clodd and Peter have forbidden her from seeking a crucial advertisement for the paper from a man said to be 'susceptible to female influence'.[37] Johnny has the idea for his impersonation after a messenger boy cheekily calls him 'miss':

> The Babe, by reason of his childlike face, was accustomed to insults of this character, but to-day it especially irritated him. Why at twenty-two could he not grow even a moustache? Why was he only five feet seven and a half? Why had Fate cursed him with a pink-and-white complexion, so that the members of his own club had nicknamed him 'the Babe', while street-boys as they passed pleaded with him for a kiss? Why was his very voice, a flute-like alto, more suitable – Suddenly an idea sprang to life within his brain.[38]

Unlike Tommy, Johnny does not choose his gender ambiguity, but has it thrust upon him by virtue of his appearance. His catalogue of features shows the fluidity of biological traits that often mark gender, and they 'irritate' him perhaps because he associates them with his failure to woo Tommy more effectively. The club here appears as an enforcing agent of masculinity: they are the ones who nickname him 'the Babe'.

The Autolycus Club, true to its namesake Roman god of trickery, creates the problem with Johnny's impersonation. The actual seeking of the advertisement goes completely smoothly. After visiting the businessman, who tells him to return a few days later to confirm the deal, Johnny returns home in a cab only to discover that he has neglected to bring any money with him. Hitching up his skirt, he outruns the cabman home, but his regular landlady is out and her substitute won't let a young lady in to respectable lodgings for single gentlemen. Seeking out his friends at the Autolycus Club, he claims to be Miss Bulstrode, Johnny's sister, who has been robbed on the way to visit her brother. One of his friends, however, recognises his clothes, having happened to visit the shop as the parcel was being done up. The club gets in on the joke. Pretending to believe his charade, they secure him lodging with Mrs Postwhistle (another recurring character) under the stipulation that she not lend 'Miss Bulstrode' any money. They then proceed to take 'Miss Bulstrode' out on the town, and one of them cultivates a serious flirtation. Increasingly alarmed, Johnny has no doubt that they buy his act. But they begin truly to believe when a fellow club member reports having travelled up to town with Miss Bulstrode herself on the day in question. Panicked, they release Mrs Postwhistle – the only character to figure Johnny's disguise out for herself – from her promise not to lend him money. Johnny meets up with his sister and resolves to play his own trick on the boys by allowing them to continue in their belief, though in time the whole story comes out.

For Johnny, the life of a woman is confining, and not just because his friends keep him a prisoner. Like Tommy, he puts on gender identities as easily as a garment, but he also finds that skirts 'hamper' him. On his first venture out, he encounters the difficulties of women's dress. First Johnny experiences the effects, then he discerns the cause. Only after he has knocked down two people, the second of whom (a woman; most of the men are quite polite to Johnny) advises him to 'take something for that squint', does he realise that the veil is his problem, and he nearly faints before he realises 'it's these damned stays! No wonder girls are short-tempered, at times.'[39] Rather than Johnny's cross-dressing emphasising the essential difference between men and women, it allows him literally to see from their perspective – and to identify the cause as social expectations on women (clothes) as opposed to inherent or essential differences. Although Johnny does not always behave in a ladylike manner, his actions can still be interpreted within a female framework. When he swears at an errand boy for overhearing his distress (the boy was going 'to offer sympathy'), 'a passing flower-girl' exclaims, 'Well, I never . . . Calls 'erself a lidy I suppose.'[40] Johnny's friends pretend to interpret his request for cigarettes as a New Womanish move – which they puritanically refuse. Johnny finds these new gender expectations as confining as his stays.

This episode portrays the distinction between men and women as both arbitrary and punitive. Johnny can slip out of his stays at the end of the chapter, but what of his sister? The difference between them is so minimal that it almost disappears. During the end of their joke, they appear together, each in gender-appropriate dress, and the Club easily takes Miss Bulstrode for the same figure they've been entertaining, who was Johnny in women's dress. Only after Johnny's slip of the tongue indicates their deception do the club members put the two side by side and see a difference. At the end of the chapter, 'Miss Bulstrode ke[eps] the appointment made for Monday afternoon' and secures the key advertisement.[41] Presumably Mr Jowett cannot discern the distinction either. In making the visit herself, the respectable Miss Bulstrode proves Tommy's original point: that women can solicit advertisements and maintain their respectability. Despite her similarity to Johnny, and her slight involvement in his antics, Miss Bulstrode's propriety is never questioned. The following chapter sees Tommy returning triumphant after securing an advertisement. Johnny's experiment in gender-bending has improved Tommy's lot.

Miss Ramsbotham

Like Miss Bulstrode, the female journalist Miss Ramsbotham demonstrates women's involvement in the public sphere without going to the extremes of Tommy's androgyny. Although her story appears in the middle of the novel, it was the first story to be published, and the only one to appear in *Cassell's Magazine* (in the 1902 Christmas number). Miss Ramsbotham may have been a sort of first draft of Tommy, in the sense that Jerome (like Barr) was thinking through the position of a female journalist. Her story is much more conventional than Tommy's; thus its ultimate position in the middle of the novel ends up highlighting Tommy's greater success in navigating gender expectations. Miss Ramsbotham is a much more conventional New Woman, yet her story emphasises her masculinity and its obstacles to romance.

Miss Ramsbotham is a quintessential member of the journalistic 'club', but she is hampered in romantic endeavours by her very companionableness: 'An ideal wife, she was an impossible sweetheart. Every man was her friend.'[42] She is not able to cultivate the feminine mystique that attracts men. As she puts it, men can have 'Two kinds of love': admiring beauty and protecting 'the weak and helpless'.[43] The self-sufficiency that makes her a good journalist is coded as too masculine. The central plot of her chapter begins when she suddenly becomes engaged to a young playboy, to the disbelief of her friends. Love changes her, however. She loses her 'sense and humour', at least in the presence of her fiancé.[44] Furthermore, she seems destined to play the man in her relationship as well: 'All the little offices of courtship he left to her.'[45] Eventually he becomes attracted to a beautiful young girl who works in a bun shop.

Miss Ramsbotham appears to absorb the blow, arranging things quietly so that the young man will go away for a time while Miss Ramsbotham takes the young girl under her wing to facilitate her transition into a higher class of society. As the *Good Humour* circle observes, Miss Ramsbotham becomes more convention- ally beautiful and fashionable, while the young girl gains weight and spoils her looks. Miss Ramsbotham later confesses that she enabled and even nudged along the transformation. Notably, Miss Ramsbotham's transition to conventional femininity is described as a fall. When the man returns, he rejects his altered younger love and tries to rekindle his romance with Miss Ramsbotham. She is less interested in marriage than in proving her attraction, and she remains an old maid. To Peter Hope, she reveals that she rejected her beau partly because she realises she had been judging him on his looks, just as he had judged the women.

Unlike Tommy, Miss Ramsbotham's blending of gender roles gives her the worst of both worlds romantically. Yet Jerome places the blame on men's lack of discernment as well. Miss Ramsbotham decides to wait for a man who likes her 'thin and in these clothes, just because I am nice, and good company, and helpful'.[46] But she is destined to remain an old maid:

> A charming, bright-eyed, white-haired lady occupies alone a little flat in the Marylebone Road, looks in occasionally at the Writers' Club. She is still Miss Ramsbotham. Bald-headed gentlemen feel young again, talking to her: she is so sympathetic, so big-minded, so under- standing. Then, hearing the clock strike, tear themselves from her with a sigh, and return home – some of them – to stupid shrewish wives.[47]

These men have chosen not to embrace the kind of companionate marriage they could have had with Miss Ramsbotham. Still, she continues to engage in the sociability of a literary club – in this case, literally. The women-only Writers' Club partially constituted a response to the all-male founding of the Authors' Club in 1891. Walter Besant's fellow 'Idler's Club' contributor John Strange Winter (Henrietta Stannard) served as its first president, beginning in 1892.[48] The gentlemen in the extract above seek out the society of female journalists in their own club – while many men's clubs remained completely closed to women as visitors.

As published in the *Saturday Evening Post*, Miss Ramsbotham's story had some variations. It carried no references to *Good*

Humour or any of its circle. Her friend who in the book carries tales to the circle is identified merely as 'a fellow-journalist'.[49] The material about the Ladies' Page, discussed below, is entirely absent. Also, the last paragraph, which skips to Miss Ramsbotham's spinster old age, is missing; the story ends merely 'That is the man I am waiting for.'[50] This ending leaves a greater possibility open, and emphasises that Miss Ramsbotham deserves a man who will accept her as she is.

The novel's interpolated section of the 'company' of *Good Humour* shows the general support for Miss Ramsbotham, particularly admiration of the men. Upon hearing of her engagement, William Clodd declares, 'Lucky man, whoever he is. Half wish I'd thought of it myself.'[51] Another exchange points out that Grindley junior also married an intellectual woman, although she's also pretty. Miss Ramsbotham's story, then, becomes embedded in a community in which marriage is only one fate for a competent, intelligent, working woman. The title of the story, 'The Temptation of Miss Ramsbotham', both implicitly compares her to Christ and represents her makeover into conventional femininity as a 'temptation' which she is right to reject, despite the personal cost. Although the novel's version of Miss Ramsbotham more definitively forecloses her ending, it puts her in the context of a variety of types of intellectual and working women. Spinsterhood is not the worst outcome, and Miss Ramsbotham retains her sociability, particularly through her club.

The subeditor's happy endings

Miss Ramsbotham's more foreclosed ending in the novel also puts more pressure on the ending of Tommy's story. Despite the fact that Jerome, like Barr, knew many women writers, married and single, he struggles on the one hand with the narrative pressure to define a happy ending for a woman as a marriage and on the other, with the narrative and actual unconventionality of a married woman continuing to work. Tommy's story ends up with multiple endings, perhaps as a result.

Unlike Miss Ramsbotham's, Tommy's attractiveness to men is unquestioned; however, the final chapter that treats her romance plot begins with Peter and Clodd worrying about her future. They argue over Clodd's decision to buy her a piano as a means of bolstering her femininity and marriage prospects. Peter says of his hopes for Tommy, 'I want her ... to be a sensible, clever woman, capable of earning her own living and of being independent; not a mere helpless doll, crying for some man to come and take care of her.'[52] Miss Ramsbotham's single status then serves as an encouraging precedent. Tommy expresses ambivalence towards the theoretical prospect. But she does in fact meet a love interest, Dick Danvers, and, unlike others who encounter her at the *Good Humour* office, he does not question her gender affiliation, perhaps because he observes her playing the piano.

From the first, Tommy meets Dick on terms of equality, even superiority, taking her professional position relative to his into account. When he interrupts her piano practice, her body language and short answers indicate her defensiveness at having been caught practising – perhaps because it is a feminine art, perhaps because she is conscious of doing it badly. She holds her 'chin at an angle that, to anyone acquainted with the chart of Tommy's temperament, might have suggested the advisability of seeking shelter'.[53] When Dick enquires for the editor and then the subeditor, Tommy replies, 'I am the sub-editor.' This announcement provokes a brief, mute confrontation: 'The stranger raised his eyebrows. Tommy, on the contrary, lowered hers.'[54] Yet Dick remains cognisant of his professional position as a supplicant author, submitting poetry to the paper: 'The stranger's manner was compounded of dignified impudence combined with pathetic humility. His eyes both challenged and pleaded.'[55] This combination is reminiscent of the young waif who arrived at the identical office in the first chapter. Like Peter in that chapter, Tommy overcomes her initial gruff common sense and takes pity on the impoverished writer, accepting the work to discuss with Peter. They decide to give him his asking price of half a crown, Peter suggesting 'We'll enter it as "telegrams".'[56] Charitably, they accept his low-market-value poetry and adopt him into the 'Company'.

Dick joins the paper's staff and the subeditor takes charge of helping him acclimate to the proper professional style:

Even Tommy liked him in her way, though at times she was severe with him.

'If you mean a big street,' grumbled Tommy, who was going over proofs, 'why not say a big street?' [*sic*] Why must you always call it a "main artery"?'

'I am sorry,' apologized Danvers. 'It is not my own idea. You told me to study the higher-class journals.'

'I didn't tell you to select and follow all their faults. Here it is again. Your crowd is always a "hydra-headed monster"; your tea "the cup that cheers but not inebriates".'[57]

This demonstrates Tommy's capability at her job, and the joke is on the circumlocutions of 'the higher-class journals'. This type of joke also relies on the reader's knowledge of degrees and styles of periodicals – funnier, perhaps, when the story itself appeared in a relatively 'high-class' weekly, the *Saturday Evening Post*.

Tommy's gruff manner not only signals her competence – and the degree to which she does not allow her burgeoning affection for Dick to stand in the way of her business sense – but also provides some humour as it contrasts with the romantic subtext, increasingly clear as the passage continues:

'I am afraid I am a deal of trouble to you,' suggested the staff.

'I am afraid you are,' agreed the sub-editor.

'Don't give me up,' pleaded the staff. 'I misunderstood you, that is all. I will write English for the future.[']

'Shall be glad if you will,' growled the sub-editor.

Dick Danvers rose. 'I am so anxious not to get what you call "the sack" from here.'

The sub-editor, mollified, thought the staff need be under no apprehension, provided it show itself teachable.[58]

Now Dick, not Tommy, takes the pronoun 'it', although throughout this passage, Tommy is occasionally referred to in gender-neutral terms. Yet is the language really that which might be applied to a male work encounter? The last paragraph in particular seems to be intentionally relying on the ways in which this both is and isn't a usual business encounter as it grapples with the question of what it means for a woman, particularly a young, attractive woman, to be the boss of a man. Some of the humour seems to come from Tommy's good-faith efforts to play the role of subeditor despite the personal attachment she is forming. This is as much about masculinity as about femininity: Tommy is providing essentially one model of masculinity in her gruff approach to the job, and Dick models another in his response.

But soon the feminine re-enters – in the next line, in fact:

'I have been rather a worthless fellow, Miss Hope,' confessed Dick
Danvers. 'I was beginning to despair of myself till I came across you
and your father. The atmosphere here – I don't mean the material
atmosphere of Crane Court – is so invigorating: its simplicity, its sincerity. I used to have ideals. I tried to stifle them. There is a set that
sneers at all that sort of thing. Now I see that they are good. You will
help me?'[59]

Dick addresses Tommy in some of the conventional angel-in-the-
house manner. Yet he talks about both Tommy and Peter as doing
the same moral work. Significantly, the workplace environment is
framed as salutary, although clearly the work and domestic spaces
blur in Crane Court – as in the *Idler* At-Homes. Again, Tommy
manages this balancing act because, not in spite, of her unconventional gender presentation. Dick's stress on sincerity also has
ramifications for arguments about humour: *Good Humour*, with
and without italics, has a moral influence.

But the terms in which Tommy responds to Dick's 'confession'
are extremely gendered and conventional:

Every woman is a mother. Tommy felt for the moment that she wanted
to take this big boy on her knee and talk to him for his own good. He
was only an overgrown lad. But so exceedingly overgrown! Tommy
had to content herself with holding out her hand. Dick Danvers
grasped it tightly.[60]

The first sentence puts Tommy resolutely into terms of gender
essentialism. Of course, literally not every woman is a mother.
However, this does give Tommy another gendered way of relating
to Dick, one that also places her in a position of authority. The
humour places Dick at a disadvantage as an overgrown child – a
man who can't fit on Tommy's appropriately feminine knee. Yet
the passage culminates in a gesture of equality – holding out her
hand. Especially if Tommy is still seated at her desk, a handshake
across a desk suggests a courtship on rather novel, equal grounds.
The work context also prevents this gesture from being entirely
in the realm of courtship. With increasing possibilities for non-
romantic sociability between men and women comes additional
confusion as to romantic intentions.

As Tommy falls for Dick, she has a brief period of increased femininity, not unlike Miss Ramsbotham. In a way, her increasing signs of femininity stick out to her friends because she has hitherto charted such a steady course through the shoals of gender. Clodd, arguing to Peter that Tommy is in love with Dick, points out her increasing self-consciousness:

> Why are there never inkstains on her fingers now? There used to be. Why does she always keep a lemon in her drawer. [sic] When did she last have her hair cut? I'll tell you if you care to know – the week before he came, five months ago. She used to have it cut once a fort-night: said it tickled her neck. Why does she jump on people when they call her Tommy and tell them that her name is Jane. [sic] It never used to be Jane.[61]

Tommy is trying to become a more conventional woman – presumably to impress Dick, because, like Peter with the piano, she worries that a man couldn't be attracted to a girl named Tommy. But these changes in Tommy's behaviour also indicate the degree to which she had achieved a stable gender presenta-tion. Her friends are dismayed rather than pleased. Clodd says of Dick, 'I distrust the man [. . .] He's not our class.'[62] From his first appearance, and an extended joke about an umbrella, Dick clearly comes from a higher class, making him seem out of place among the journalists. The 'comic umbrella', Maria Damkjær argues, is itself a marker of class and gender porousness.[63] By this point in the novel, Tommy's gender ambiguity ruffles fewer feathers than Dick's class ambiguity.

Tommy's reactions to Dick provoke a greater split between her personal and professional selves. Peter tells Tommy that Dick has gone away to America, to gauge her reaction, as she is again cor-recting proofs:

> Tommy looked up. There was trouble in her face.
> 'How do you spell "harassed"?' questioned Tommy! [sic] 'two r's or one.'
> 'One r,' Peter informed her, 'two s's.'
> 'I thought so.' The trouble passed from Tommy's face.[64]

Jerome's proofs could have used a Tommy: although the exclama-tion point punctuates the joke, Jerome is generally more subtle.

Tommy masks her 'trouble' with her feelings by concentrating on spelling – and perhaps she's making a point about being harassed by the whole situation. She conceals her feelings from Peter, entirely the subeditor. But when Tommy processes this conversation, she enacts an imaginative split between her 'Tommy' and 'Jane' sides:

> Of what use was Peter in a crisis of this kind? Peter couldn't scold. Peter couldn't bully. The only person to talk to Tommy as Tommy knew she needed to be talked to was one Jane, a young woman of dignity with a sense of the proprieties.
>
>   'I do hope that at least you are feeling ashamed of yourself,' remarked Jane to Tommy that same night, as the twain sat together in their little bedroom.
>
>   'Done nothing to be ashamed of,' growled Tommy.[65]

Tommy is self-reliant to a fault: even her proper parent in this case is herself. But it is her feminine half. Tommy is the 'growling' part of her, reminiscent of the androgynous street urchin who did not know but rather hoped she was a boy. Jane talks sense and speaks in complete sentences.

After Jane's prodding, Tommy agrees to send Dick away – so 'he could be on the staff of some big paper'.[66] However, the conversation does not go as planned:

> He rose and came to where she stood with one foot upon the fender, looking down into the fire. His doing this disconcerted her. So long as he remained seated at the other end of the room, she was the subeditor, counselling the staff for its own good. Now that she could not raise her eyes without encountering his, she felt painfully conscious of being nothing more important than a little woman who was trembling.[67]

As in her bedroom, Tommy undergoes a gendered bifurcation, here between 'the sub-editor' and 'a little woman', the latter explicitly unimportant. All the work Tommy has done to fashion a gender identity seems to melt in the face of romance. Dick dominates the conversation, telling her how he has been a 'blackguard',[68] but that Tommy has saved him – or enabled him to save himself. He also frames her moral improvement of him as 'work': 'Will you not finish your work?'[69] But it is never explicitly discussed whether this will become her only work after they are married. After describing his caddish ways, Dick asks Tommy, 'Will you not trust me?' She replies by 'put[ting] her hands in his' and saying 'I am trusting you . . . with all my life. Don't make a muddle of it, dear, if you can help it.'[70] There is a degree of passive femininity as she is metaphorically putting her life in his hands, trusting him to take care of her life. Yet her last sentence betrays both her characteristic sense of humour and a remnant of the boss or mother. Tommy recognises his power over her: that he can 'make a muddle' of her life if he's not careful. She herself labels the scene unconventional: 'It was an odd wooing, as Tommy laughingly told herself when she came to think it over in her room that night.'[71] Her ability to laugh at herself proves an essential part of her character – and ties her to Dixon and Sharp's fictional female journalists.

The periodical story ends with Tommy accepting Danvers's proposal, but the book continues on. Almost as soon as the engagement is announced, the narration states, 'The marriage did not take place till nearly fifteen years had passed away.'[72] Jerome introduces the barriers to Tommy and Dick's marriage through the trope of the fallen woman:

> The past is not easily got rid of. A tale was once written of a woman who killed her babe and buried it in a lonely wood, and later stole back in the night and saw there, white in the moonlight, a child's hand calling through the earth, and buried it again and yet again; but always that white baby hand called upwards through the earth, trample it down as she would. Tommy read the story one evening in an old miscellany, and sat long before the dead fire, the book open on her lap, and shivered; for now she knew the fear that had been haunting her.[73]

On the face of it, this story bears no direct reference to Tommy's situation. In Jerome's fiction, not uniquely among Victorians, the fallen woman often concentrates pathos and sentimentality, particularly as regards death and maternity. In this case, Tommy's fear is for Dick's past, since he has described himself as a 'blackguard'. Yet no male figure directly appears in this story. Perhaps Dick is the fallen woman, or Dick's guilt becomes Tommy's guilt, although the tale also features a persistent, androgynous child.

The encounter with the fallen woman, when she manifests in the flesh, explicitly makes a woman out of Tommy. Shortly after Tommy and Dick's engagement, Dick's former lover appears to try to win him back, confronting Tommy. Only gradually do Tommy and Dick realise that she is pregnant – and she explains that her husband has died without returning from a trip, so it would be clear that the child was conceived through adultery. Tommy convinces Dick to marry her, for the sake of the child and for the sake of rectifying the 'wrong' he has done: 'You see, dear, we all do wrong sometimes. We must not let others suffer for our fault more – more than we can help.'[74] As her rival begins to try to disclose her pregnancy, Tommy is described as a 'child' in her lack of comprehension (shared by Dick).[75] The moment of realisation comes not from words but actions: 'She [the rival] staggered towards him, and the fine cloak slipped from her shoulders; and then it was that Tommy changed from a child to a woman, and raised the other woman from the ground with crooning words of encouragement such as mothers use, and led her to the inner room.'[76] Again, Tommy's femininity is described in terms of maternity: a position of relative power and wisdom, although clearly, as the pregnant woman vividly demonstrates, not necessarily of either. Tommy becomes a woman through valuing solidarity with another woman over pursuing her own interests. This is also framed as a decisive gender shift: 'from a child to a woman', out of the gender ambiguity of childhood.

Unlike Miss Ramsbotham, who undermines her rival in love, Tommy embraces her – quite literally. What does this say about women, gender, journalism and community? Miss Ramsbotham may have been infected with masculine vices (from which the separate spheres doctrine would otherwise have shielded her), but Tommy, with her unusual upbringing and impressive workplace competence, still finds her way to womanhood when it counts. Of course, womanhood here means self-sacrifice. And she inspires similar sacrifice in Dick, although he expresses it in very traditional gendered terms: 'it came to him that it would be a finer thing to be worthy of her than even to possess her'.[77] The fact that Dick still thinks of marriage to Tommy in terms of possession shows how little Tommy's assertions have changed the balance of power.

This plot device allows Tommy to have a career as a single woman. Part of her explanation to Dick about why he should do right by his mistress has to do with her status as a working woman. When he asks what would happen to her if he 'did her bidding', she replies, 'I? Oh, I shall cry for a little while, but later on I shall laugh, as often. Life is not all love. I have my work.'[78] And once he leaves, 'Tommy was glad it was press-night. She would not be able to think for hours to come, and then, perhaps, she would be feeling too tired. Work can be very kind.'[79] So Tommy's status as a working woman enables her to be womanly in the best sense: to have compassion for her rival and uphold higher ideals, in part because love is not the only factor in her life. Yet Jerome clearly wants her to be able to have both a career and marriage, as the narrator states fairly explicitly:

> Were this an artistic story, here, of course, one would write 'Finis'. But in the workaday world one never knows the ending till it comes. Had it been otherwise, I doubt I could have found courage to tell you this story of Tommy.[80]

Sure enough, about fifteen years later the other woman conveniently dies, and Dick returns to the offices of *Good Humour* with his young daughter in tow. Though a happy ending is prefigured, it is not actually narrated. As the story ends, Peter and Clodd take the daughter out for tea to give Dick and Tommy a chance to have their reunion in private. The girl asks, however, to wait so that she can see Tommy as she approaches the building. The book closes:

> So they waited in the open doorway of a near printing-house till Tommy drove up. Both Peter and Clodd watched the child's face with some anxiety. She nodded gravely to herself three times, then slipped her hand into Peter's.
> Tommy opened the door with her latch-key and passed in.[81]

This child seems to possess some of the self-possession and serious resolve that characterised Tommy as a child. Jerome may have drawn from his own experiences as a step-parent: Elsie Jerome, credited in the 'How I Bring Up My Parents' column, was five years old when Jerome married her mother.[82]

Meanwhile, Tommy's own fate is left open, like the door. It seems unlikely that she will retreat into domesticity; instead she may become like one of the married female journalists who contribute to the 'Idler's Club', such as John Strange Winter (Henrietta Stannard), John Oliver Hobbes (Pearl Craigie), Aimée Beringer and Eliza Lynn Linton. Tommy's story thus has three endings: the ending of the periodical, in which an early marriage with Dick is implied; the half-ending above that implies her continued work as an unmarried journalist; and the delayed marriage with Dick, narrated earlier in the story, which also gains her a daughter. All these roads lead to the narrative present indicated in the first chapter, in which Tommy 'appears as an honoured guest to-day at many a literary gathering'.[83] Her literary work continues, although it also blurs the line between the social and professional.

'Why should not the paper as a whole appeal to her?'

Both Jerome and Barr explicitly denounce the idea of a women's page or column within their fiction. In *Jennie Baxter, Journalist*, Barr derides women's columns in favour of placing women in the main section of the paper and the newsroom. The novel opens as his eponymous heroine begins her campaign to be hired as a permanent staff member of the *Daily Bugle*, 'which was considered at that moment to be the most enterprising morning journal in the great metropolis of London, England'.[84] The editor attempts to give her the brush-off, saying, 'if you will write your address on this card I will wire you if I have any work – that is, any outside work – which I think a woman can do. The woman's column of the *Bugle*, as you are probably aware, is already in good hands.'[85] Jennie returns 'rather shortly', 'I do not aspire . . . to the position of editor of a woman's column. I never read a woman's column myself, and, unlike Mr Grant Allen, I never met a woman who did. . . . What I wish is a salaried position on your staff.' The editor clarifies his position, 'I may tell you frankly that I don't believe in women journalists. The articles we publish by women are sent to this office from their own homes. Anything that a woman can do for a newspaper I have men who will do quite as well, if not better, and there are many things that women can't do at all which men must do.'[86] Jennie proceeds to prove him wrong and embarrass him by scooping one of his staff members and publishing the story in a rival paper. Humbled, the editor offers her the desired position, which is not a woman-specific one. In the process, Barr nods to 'Idler's Club' contributor Grant Allen's infamous New Woman novel, *The Woman Who Did*. Unlike Herminia Barton, Jennie does not flout convention for its own sake, but rather presents her common sense as intrinsically feminine.

A crucial element in Miss Ramsbotham's fall from grace occurs when she suggests that she create a 'Ladies' Page' for *Good Humour*. Peter dislikes the idea, saying of the female reader, 'why should she want a special page to herself? . . . Why should not the paper as a whole appeal to her?'[87] Despite recognising the idea as a good business venture and the direction in which journalism is heading, only the thought of Tommy's financial future convinces him to accept her offer. Part of the problem with the plan, as far as business ethics is concerned, is that Miss Ramsbotham expects to receive favours from the fashion industry as part of her plan to become 'one of the most stylish women in London'.[88] However, she refuses to accept payment from Peter. Ann Humphreys uses *To-Day*'s women's page as part of her argument that both of Jerome's papers maintain a separate-spheres logic of gender relations. Here, however, Peter Hope seems to speak with the voice of moral authority and authorial weight, calling the separation of men's and women's pages a commercial success but a moral failing – perhaps because it emphasises the differences between the sexes rather than their common ground.

Jerome also describes Miss Ramsbotham as the author of *Good Humour*'s 'Letters to Clorinda' feature, which was in fact the title of a recurring piece he wrote under his own name for the *Idler* from 1896–7.[89] In their article on 'Idler's Club' contributor Grant Allen's complex status as male writer of New Woman fiction, Vanessa Warne and Colette Colligan suggest that he was uncomfortable identifying as a male New Woman author, citing a *Punch* cartoon represented him as an awkward, laughable female impersonator.[90] Here, Jerome seems comparatively at ease, implying his own ability to write for women as well as men in *Tommy and Co.* and in his journalistic work. Peter Hope's question, 'Why should not the paper as a whole appeal to her?' can be read multiple ways: either declaring that the female reader may find the paper as a whole interesting, or framing 'appeal' as a more active verb. In other words, one reading of this statement declares that the paper should be making a more concerted effort to attract female readers throughout its pages, rather than dedicating a particular page for women only. *To-Day* did have a women's page, from its first issue in 1893, although it also had a corresponding men's page, called 'Club Chatter'.

In a way, *Tommy and Co.* serves as a coda to the 'Idler's Club' column. If the 'Idler's Club' column depicted the magazine as a club, *Tommy and Co.* insists that it is superior to one. Women certainly played an important role in the historical *Idler*, but to *Good Humour*, women are central and instrumental. Tommy calls *Good Humour* into being through the parental ambition she reignites in Peter Hope. As the subeditor, she looks after the financial wellbeing of the paper by seeking advertisements, proofing the copy, and mentoring the staff. In Peter's original dream, she comes to be the editor of the paper. The descriptions of her literary success do not specifically mention whether that dream comes to pass, but they stress her role in the literary community. Barr and Jerome both worked to welcome women to the real 'Idler's Club' column, but they created more prominent roles for women journalists in these works of fiction.

Notes

1   First stories: Jerome K. Jerome, 'The Temptation of Miss Ramsbotham: The Love Story of an Unmanageable Woman', *Saturday Evening Post* 175, no. 21 (22 November 1902): 1–2, 19–20, 22. 'The Temptation of Miss Ramsbotham', *Cassell's Magazine*, Christmas 1902 (26 November 1902): 54–62. Subsequent chapters appeared in *Windsor Magazine*. See Jerome K. Jerome Society.

2   Jerome, 'The Temptation of Miss Ramsbotham', *Saturday Evening Post*; 'The Temptation of Miss Ramsbotham', *Cassell's Magazine*.

3   As Linda Hughes puts it, she 'customarily wore a mask'. Hughes, review of Ella Hepworth Dixon, *The Story of a Modern Woman*, 1.

4   Dixon, *The Story of a Modern Woman*, 224.

5   Sharp, *The Making of a Prig*, 118.

6   Barr, *Jennie Baxter*, 3–4.

7   Shannon, *Dickens, Reynolds and Mayhew on Wellington Street*, 14.

8   Barr, *Jennie Baxter*, 1.

9   Barr, *Jennie Baxter*, 4.

10 Barr, *Jennie Baxter*, 162.

11 Barr, *Jennie Baxter*, 163.

12 Barr, *Jennie Baxter*, 318.

13 Barr, *Jennie Baxter*, 322–3.

14 Jerome, *Tommy*, 1.

15 Jerome, *Tommy*, 4.

16 Jerome, *Tommy*, 5.

17 Jerome, *Tommy*, 5.

18 Jerome, *Tommy*, 5.

19 Jerome, *Tommy*, 6–7.

20 Jerome, *Tommy*, 14–15.

21 Sayers, 'Are Women Human?', in *Unpopular Opinions*, 108.

22 Sayers, 'The Human Not-Quite-Human', in *Unpopular Opinions*, 116.

23 Sayers, 'Are Women Human?', 109.

24 Jerome, *Tommy*, 29.

25 Jerome, *Tommy*, 29.

26 Jerome, *Tommy*, 26.

27 Jerome, *Tommy*, 186.

28 Jerome, *Tommy*, 11–12.

29 Garber, *Vested Interests*, 170.

30 Jerome, *Tommy*, 50.

31 Jerome, *Tommy*, 30.

32 Jerome, *Tommy*, 48.

33 Jerome, *Tommy*, 73.

34 Jerome, *Tommy*, 74.

35 Jerome, *Tommy*, 235.

36 Jerome, *Tommy*, 239.

37 Jerome, *Tommy*, 232.

38 Jerome, *Tommy*, 240.

39 Jerome, *Tommy*, 246, 247.

40 Jerome, *Tommy*, 257.

41 Jerome, *Tommy*, 280.

42 Jerome, *Tommy*, 133.

43 Jerome, *Tommy*, 136.

44 Jerome, *Tommy*, 150.

45 Jerome, *Tommy*, 158.

46 Jerome, *Tommy*, 176.

47 Jerome, *Tommy*, 176–7.

48 Ashton, 'Stannard'.

49 Jerome, 'The Temptation of Miss Ramsbotham', 19.

50 Jerome, 'The Temptation of Miss Ramsbotham', 22.

51 Jerome, *Tommy*, 146–7.

52 Jerome, *Tommy*, 287–8.

53 Jerome, *Tommy*, 299.

54 Jerome, *Tommy*, 300.

55 Jerome, *Tommy*, 300.

56 Jerome, *Tommy*, 303.

57 Jerome, *Tommy*, 307.

58 Jerome, *Tommy*, 307.

59 Jerome, *Tommy*, 308.
60 Jerome, *Tommy*, 308–9.
61 Jerome, *Tommy*, 311.
62 Jerome, *Tommy*, 312.
63 Damkjær, 'Awkward Appendages', 482.
64 Jerome, *Tommy*, 312.
65 Jerome, *Tommy*, 314–15.
66 Jerome, *Tommy*, 316.
67 Jerome, *Tommy*, 317.
68 Jerome, *Tommy*, 318.
69 Jerome, *Tommy*, 318.
70 Jerome, *Tommy*, 320.
71 Jerome, *Tommy*, 320.
72 Jerome, *Tommy*, 321.
73 Jerome, *Tommy*, 321.
74 Jerome, *Tommy*, 332.
75 Jerome, *Tommy*, 330.
76 Jerome, *Tommy*, 330.
77 Jerome, *Tommy*, 332.
78 Jerome, *Tommy*, 332.
79 Jerome, *Tommy*, 322–3.
80 Jerome, *Tommy*, 333.
81 Jerome, *Tommy*, 337.
82 Atkinson, 'Jerome, Jerome Klapka (1859–1927)'.
83 Jerome, *Tommy*, 30.
84 Barr, *Jennie Baxter*, 3.
85 Barr, *Jennie Baxter*, 17.
86 Barr, *Jennie Baxter*, 17–18.
87 Jerome, *Tommy*, 162.
88 Jerome, *Tommy*, 165.
89 Jerome, *Tommy*, 170.
90 Warne and Colligan, 'The Man Who Wrote a New Woman Novel', 40.

3

The Club Story and Social Mobility: Rules for Readers in Israel Zangwill and Barry Pain

The strongest manifestation of the treatment of clubs in fiction by the *Idler* circle lies in novels and short stories that truly centre on a club, usually a fictional club with a ridiculous premise. The title of the work is the name of the club, and all or most of the action takes place within the club. Such works often begin with a description of the club rules and a description of the club premises. This chapter will address this feature and its role in the larger social work these club stories perform. The insistence on rules and the humour around rules serve as a vehicle for commentary on social exclusion. Humour helps contain – and reveal – some of the paradoxes surrounding social rules. These rules are arbitrary, even silly, but also very real and occasionally capable of dire consequences. To successfully negotiate Clubland, or any social situation, one must understand its rules. Yet part of the joke is that these clubs attempt to codify the uncodifiable, chiefly friendship and gentlemanly conduct. Club rules are literally exclusive: in these works in particular, breaking the club rules leads to exclusion from the club. From the start, the club stories establish the club rules, and social rules by extension, as both utopian and fundamentally untenable.

Israel Zangwill's *The Bachelors' Club* (1891) set the standard for a humorous novel centring around a club with ridiculous, self-defeating rules. It may have inspired the 'Idler's Club' column and doubtless served as a model for the club stories that followed. Although several works make explicit reference to Robert Louis Stevenson's *The Suicide Club* (1878), which features in the next chapter, that work and its central club are decidedly not humorous. This chapter focuses on the works of Zangwill and fellow Idler Barry Pain, who invented quite a number of clubs in the Bachelors' model. As we have seen, Pain and Zangwill were in the closest ring of the *Idler* circle by every measure: they both participated in the first 'Idler's Club' column, appeared frequently in the first volume, and number among the top ten contributors during the collaborative years. Pain took over the editorship of *To-Day* after Jerome's bankruptcy. Zangwill probably met Jerome when both were working for *Home Chimes*, and both served as presidents of the Playgoer's Club.[1] Both Pain and Zangwill are identified as New Humorists, both in their lifetimes and in twenty-first-century biographies.[2] Despite these similarities, each has a very distinct background and posthumous reputation. They began as the most and least privileged in the circle. Pain was the only Oxbridge graduate and nearly the only *Punch* contributor. As a Jew, Zangwill was keenly aware of not only the recent nature of his British civil rights but also the international precarity of what was frequently described as his race.[3] Today the roles have reversed: Zangwill features more prominently in the Victorian canon, principally for his explicitly Jewish writings, and Pain appears far less frequently on syllabi and in studies. Both wrote broadly about social mobility, and clearly both were keenly aware of the influence of social rules and strictures on their own lives and their larger social surroundings.

Despite Zangwill and Pain's differences, they share a style and an approach to clubs and social rules. Their descriptions of the rules seem to come from the inside, written as if by a club member, but not necessarily for the purpose of keeping the reader out. In fact, the reader is explicitly shown into the club rooms and told all the rules up front. Like the Idler's Club, this is the humour of privilege. It may not always be solely for or about those who have privilege. But it invites readers of all stripes to enter the club and put their feet up on the mantelpiece. The humour at the club's expense is the humour of ownership. The ease of the humour claims the club and its privileges. However, the very foundation of these fictional clubs shows the fundamentally arbitrary and untenable nature of the rules on which they depend.

Etiquette books similarly claim to lay out rules of social behaviour, and they are rife with cautionary tales of those who fail to understand or observe the unspoken rules of Society. In these, the misinformed make fools of themselves and are often put back 'in their place' by their social (and, implicitly, moral) betters.[4] *Hints on Etiquette* (1836) reinforces a rule about familiarity with such an anecdote:

If you have been in society with a nobleman, and should happen to meet him again elsewhere, leave it to him to speak first, or to recognise you. . . . An unfortunate Clerk of the Treasury, who, because he was in the receipt of a good salary and being also a 'triton amongst the minnows' of Clapham Common, fancied himself a great man, dined at the B—f S—k [probably Beef Steak] Club, where he sat next to a noble Duke, who, desirous of putting him at ease with himself, conversed freely with him, yet probably forgot even the existence of such a person half an hour afterwards. Meeting his Grace in the street some days after, and encouraged by his previous condescension, the hero of the quill, bent on claiming his acquaintance, accosted him in a familiar 'hail fellow-well-met-ish' manner – 'Ah, my Lord, how d'ye do?' The Duke looked surprised. 'May I know, Sir, *to whom* I have the honour of speaking?' said his Grace, drawing up. 'Oh! why – don't you know? We dined together at the B—f S—k Club, the other evening! – I'm Mr Timms of the Treasury!!' 'Then', said the Duke, turning on his heel, 'Mr Timms of the treasury, I wish you *a good morning.*'[5]

The duke snubs Mr Timms in the street and embarrasses him, but the author of the etiquette book implicitly sides with the duke because Mr Timms has transgressed the rules of etiquette. The author makes Mr Timms look ridiculous by printing his name in all capital letters and by referring to him ironically as 'the hero of the quill'. The duke, meanwhile, is described in mild terms and has the last word in the encounter. Mr Timms is in the wrong because he attempts to rise in class through ingratiating himself with a duke, the highest rank in society.[6] He is not content with merely improving his standing within his class, and the etiquette book urges its readers not to follow his example. *Etiquette, Politeness and Good Behaviour* tells a similar story in which 'an eminent writer, Mr C— D—,'[7] surely Charles Dickens, publicly embarrasses a man who presumes on their slight acquaintance. Just as the books discourage attempting to rise in rank, they frown upon rising by connection with famous men, and they publicly ridicule those who attempt to do so.

Many Victorian etiquette books lay significant stress on the forming of acquaintanceships or friendships. To 'know' someone was a very significant step, which in part made the 'cut direct' so scathing: it proclaimed 'I do not know you.' Many etiquette books then stipulate that in certain circumstances and situations, people may interact without it being understood that they 'know' each other in a permanent way, travel being the most significant. But it is remarkable that the club is positioned as such a space in this interaction. Dining at a club does not necessarily make one a member; Mr Timms – and the duke, for that matter – might have been guests of a member. Thus, this anecdote is telling not only because it uses humour to reinforce (rather than subvert) social rules and their importance, but also because it highlights the ambiguous relationship between a club and friendship. On the one hand, the club might seem – especially to Mr Timms – to be a vehicle for friendship, even a fast track to it, but on the other hand, the club's institutional nature cannot – to the duke – substitute for actual personal vetting. Implicitly, if it were, Mr Timms would not have made the cut. Although the club can be a startlingly democratic space in which a clerk can dine with a duke, class hierarchies are reinscribed through manners. The club and the etiquette book perform a similar negotiation of social rules. As Barbara Black discusses, one etiquette book attributes itself to 'The Man in the Club Window'.[8] The club contrasts with the street, yet the etiquette book itself brings club knowledge into the public domain.

Historical clubs had rules that practically cried out for parody. While many clubs' rationales for selection were rather straightforward – the East India United Service Club, university clubs, etc. – others had more ambiguous criteria, such as the Garrick's emphasis on those affiliated with the theatre (including as patrons) and the Athenaeum's 'specific eminence in or patronage of the arts, science, politics or religion'.[9] Perhaps the most arbitrary was the highly exclusive Travellers' Club, which required 'that all candidates must have travelled at least 500 miles from London to be eligible'.[10] And of course there were the myriad rules, spoken and unspoken, about a member's conduct if he wished to remain in the club, which emerged over the course of the nineteenth century.[11] The extension of these rules by these humorists to the truly arcane, arbitrary or self-defeating (particularly the latter) exposes the ways in which high society seemed, particularly to the upwardly mobile, arbitrarily exclusive, a realm in which the rules kept changing to keep one out. These rules seem made to be broken, and indeed *The Bachelors' Club* sets the precedent of making repeated rule-breaking part of the novel's structure – and part of the joke.

Misogyny or misogamy?

The title of *The Bachelors' Club* highlights the essential element of West End clubs' exclusivity, which posed problems in the Victorian period and since: gender segregation. As James Eli Adams argues, masculine 'secret societies' were increasingly viewed with suspicion as the century progressed. He frames all-male spaces such as the public school as threats to domesticity, saying they 'undermined the sway of domesticity by challenging the family as the boy's primary source of identity'.[12] Amy Milne-Smith, in contrast, characterises the club as an alternate 'form of domesticity': 'clubland was a rival domestic space, in many ways surpassing what the family could hope to provide'.[13] *The Bachelors' Club* pits these forms of domesticity directly against each other. The club clearly loses: it dissolves as its members each succumb to matrimony, one in each chapter. But the ambiguity of Zangwill's humour allows the tension to linger longer, with ramifications for the treatment of gender and exclusivity.

Perhaps because of its humour, modern critics have tended to regard Zangwill's novel as misogynistic. Barbara Black says Zangwill 'has misogynist fun outlining the requirements for membership in its titular organization'.[14] Nicola Humble claims that throughout the novel, 'marriage is plotted as tragedy', insisting that 'Laboriously as the joke is pursued, the central trope – that marriage is a curse, is never challenged on any level of the text.' Given this, she calls the book 'implausibly popular'.[15] By contrast, Milne-Smith contends that the book, ironically, is pro-marriage: 'The narrator bemoans their fallen states, but the humour of the text lies in the fact that although each member publicly justifies his actions as a misadventure, he secretly enjoys his fate. It is only the narrator who is left out of the joke.'[16] Zangwill's light humour prompts these diametrically opposed readings. Indeed, this could have been a feature to allow for multiple readings within a mass public with differing views on 'The Woman Question'.

Contemporary reviews recognised ambiguity in *The Bachelors' Club*, particularly in terms of its views towards women. One in the *Yorkshire Herald* describes the characters as 'misogamist clubmen',[17] suggesting that their antipathy is towards the institution of marriage rather than women as such. Meanwhile, a *Morning Post* review calls them 'supposed misogynists',[18] indicating that at least some of the joke lies in the complexities of the characters' attitudes towards matrimony. The same review comments on Zangwill's approach to humour: 'The author has a manner of touching upon the foibles of the day, full of a playful malice, but quite devoid of bitterness, that is one of the best gifts of the humorist.'[19] Perhaps twenty-first-century critics have focused too much on the issue of marriage, thereby missing the larger humour on 'the foibles of the day'. Indeed, a review published in Devon says the novel 'aims at striking a new vein of bizarre humour, and embodies some topical satire at the expense of the literary, journalistic, and musical worlds'.[20] This suggests that the central thrust of the humour is not about gender at all, but about the peculiarities of Bohemia. Zangwill evokes and produces the same type of clublike knowledge that would become the hallmark of the 'Idler's Club' column.

Zangwill's own biography shows outright advocacy of women's rights. In later life, he was a member of suffrage organisations, including the Men's League and Jewish League.[21] Although Joseph Leftwich claimed that Zangwill was recruited to the cause by his wife, Meri-Jane Rochelson counters that Zangwill married Edith Ayrton because of their mutual 'concern for social justice'.[22] The central joke clearly lends itself to different readings: I'm inclined to agree with Milne-Smith that the joke lies in the inevitability of marriage. The Bachelors' protestations do not in fact preclude them from enjoying married life. The humour quickly becomes the extent to which the repeated marriage plot appears inevitable, not only to readers but also to the characters themselves. The Bachelors' attempts to stave off their approaching fate are comically exaggerated. As with much of Zangwill's individual epigrams, it can be difficult to decide whether the surface meaning or the reverse predominates. The main effect is to highlight the easy reversibility of words and Zangwill's own wit.

The dissolution of the Bachelors' Club can be read as a rebuttal of the fundamental premise of many actual clubs: exclusivity by sex. In fact, there was a real Bachelors' Club in London, founded in 1881, in which all candidates had to be bachelors and would lose membership after marriage. But while the real Bachelors' allowed married men to reapply as honorary members, Zangwill plays this logic out to a fittingly ridiculous conclusion and, perhaps for that reason, Zangwill claimed that he did not use the real club as a model.[23] In each chapter a Bachelor marries, and by the end the club collapses under the weight of its own rules. The very structure of the novel demonstrates the untenability of single-sex society, even within the confines of a club. In that sense, *The Bachelors' Club* ridicules the premise of male exclusivity – and perhaps exclusivity on other terms as well – although in the process of enacting the joke, the novel to a certain extent replicates it.[24] Ultimately, the structure of the novel suggests the fundamental undesirability of perpetual bachelorhood.

Nevertheless, the novel depicts the club as a pleasant place, particularly because of its sociability. The banter that takes place within the club is its chief pleasure, and the club members even remark on each other's penchant for cracking jokes. One member is 'nettled at [another's] taking the epigram out of his mouth. One does not lead up to jokes for the sake of one's friends.'[25] Yet this very enjoyment of face-to-face sociability makes the driving plot of the novel, the gradual dissolution of the club through marriage, poignant as well as funny. The book's narrator is the last club member and bachelor to succumb; he publishes the book *The Bachelors' Club* in a half-hearted attempt to stave off matrimony. One might say the club is killed into the book, to adapt Gilbert and Gubar's more serious phrase.[26] The premises become a newspaper office; like Jerome, perhaps Zangwill sees the newspaper as the club's mixed-sex successor.[27] The enjoyable sociability of the Bachelors becomes (and always was) literary sociability, not subject to the exclusive demands of the club. The joke is on the attempts to keep this sociability confined within the framework of a club.

Rules for bachelors (and readers)

The first section of *The Bachelors' Club* is entitled: 'Prologue: Of the Bachelors, Their Beliefs and By-laws', and begins: 'The Bachelors' Club was a Club in which all members, without exception, were Bachelors. But this was its only eccentricity.'[28] As with many aspects of the club parodies, the Bachelors' Club's rules, and even their presentation, do not exaggerate greatly from their real-life counterparts. Clubs produced a great deal of print culture: fliers or programmes for dinners, various material related to lectures, and often year books or other sorts of proceedings. The *Year Book for the Boston Club of Odd Volumes* (1922) begins by listing the rules of the club.[29] In this introductory section, the rules of the club are enumerated (literally in some cases) and gone over in great detail, peppered with humour. Beginning a novel this way suggests verisimilitude and invites the reader into the knowledge base of the club. Paradoxically, these rules that can exclude can also serve to include.

The crux of the club appears in Zangwill's characteristically slippery humour: 'The principles of the Club may be summed up in its axiom that marriage was a crime against women for which no punishment, not even exclusion from the Club, could be sufficiently severe.'[30] This line invites the types of contradictory critical readings discussed above. The notion of marriage as a crime against women seems obviously disingenuous in this context. Yet from a certain feminist perspective, marriage is 'a crime against women', in that the terms of marriage were still, even after the Married Women's Property Act, disadvantageous, even criminally offensive, to women. But the idea that this argument might be put forward by an organisation calling itself the Bachelors' Club seems ludicrous. Instead it seems misguided chivalry – the joke is, on one level, about the undesirability of tying oneself for life to a man – packaged in self-interest: particularly in the context of a club, it seems as if the only reason to be a bachelor would be one's own self-interest. Clubs are not generally known for their altruism. A club is, at bottom, an indulgence perpetuated by those who can afford such luxuries. As Amy Milne-Smith points out, there was an extensive discourse around the club as a threat to marriage, with women bemoaning the hours their husbands spent in 'selfish retreat' at clubs.[31] Reading can similarly be described as a 'selfish retreat', including from marriage.[32]

The rules of the Bachelors' Club do seem to codify what it means to be a bachelor, with their 'principles' occasionally seeming to override their narrow self-interest: 'The conditions of membership were four. No member must follow a profession involving celibacy. No member must have ever had a disappointment in love. No member must be under thirty. No duly-elected member must use a latch-key.'[33] This last seems to indicate the notion of freedom that accompanies bachelorhood – but it also has class connotations.[34] The lack of a latch-key denotes the ability to have one's door opened by a servant.

These rules are explained, but not immediately: they are allowed to linger in their seeming arbitrariness, such as references to the 'Celibate Catechism', which seems to take a written form.[35] These forms, also called 'certificates of non-marriage', must be submitted by a 'respectable married householder'.[36] In other words, the club equates marriage with respectability, which runs counter to its so-called 'principles'. Moreover, this procedure indicates that bachelorhood is always dependent in some way upon marriage. One of the questions hints at this: 'Has there ever been any matrimony, or tendency to matrimony, in his family?'[37] Actual children of unwed parents would probably not be welcome in a social club of this kind. While other questions from the 'catechism' are discussed in detail, this one seems to be left alone.

The arbitrariness of the rules is clear in their over-explanation: 'It had been originally determined to frame a condition to exclude those who had ever taken part in the marriage-ceremony, but on reflection it was decided not to keep the best men out of the Club, nor to fail in respect for the Cloth.'[38] In this case, over-explanation provides an opportunity for a pun on 'best man'. The list continues for quite some time: the general principles of the club, the requirements for candidacy, and the rules of the club itself (the admittance of 'strangers' or non-members: no married men; no unmarried ladies). Another rule limits the Bachelors' numbers to twelve in order to avoid the number thirteen. These rules begin to resemble Lewis Carroll-type nonsense, taking logic to extremes and ultimately making the joke on the notion of rules themselves.[39] Just as the line between sense and nonsense can be surprisingly fine, so, too can the line between social structures and parodies. The play on rules signals the arbitrary nature of the larger social structure and the difficulty of trying to quantify relationships, especially male friendships.

One of the rules explicitly guards against the confusion between members and club waiters:

> To distinguish the waiters from the members, who many a morning turned up in evening dress, it was insisted upon that they should belong to the lower caste of married men. The head-waiter owed his supremacy over the rest of the staff to having served a term of years for bigamy, though, on the other hand, the under-waiter had the consolation of feeling that *he* was nearer to the bachelor caste than his superior. The steward was a dusky Indian who had married at the age of three.[40]

The anxiety about differentiating between club members and servants is somewhat typical of anxieties about servants being distinguishable from their 'betters', but existing scholarship has generally focused on this in women.[41] Compounding the class anxiety is a strain of Orientalist jokes – the use of 'caste', the allusion to 'a dusky Indian', and, slightly earlier, a reference to marriage 'whether in Oriental simultaneity or in Occidental sequence'.[42] Zangwill may be trying to mask his own potential connection to the East in such a move.[43] The line between members and servants proves quite porous. Later in the chapter, the first Bachelor to fall not only marries the victim of the head waiter's bigamy – described as his 'widow' – but also becomes a waiter at the club himself.

This first marriage of a club member highlights the pathetic side of the Bachelors' club-or-marriage rule. It's a surprisingly complex scene, complete with all sorts of paradoxical jokes (the modified Wildean paradox serving as Zangwill's weapon of choice): 'Being Bachelors, they were not used to being defied and having their sacred emotions trampled upon.'[44] This is a misogynistic joke – or at least a misogamist one – but it also has a core of pathos: the Bachelors' Club is being held up here as an institution comparable to but better than marriage. The Bachelors understand each other: their alternate domesticity has a more emotionally even keel. The stating of so many explicit rules seems antithetical to marriage, yet at this time the notion of marriage was changing, in part because of the changing role of women.[45] As married couples were asked to be friends and equals as well as everything else, the idea of the club as a model for companionate marriage might not seem far-fetched. Marriage and clubs have more in common than one might think: Zangwill refers to the club rules as 'vows', which connotes marriage as well as monastic vows.[46]

In addition to enumerating the club rules, *The Bachelors' Club* sets a precedent for the club stories to follow by describing the club premises early in the narrative. If, following Chapter 1, we view clubs as a metaphorical space for reading, this physical description invites the reader into the space of the club. Close in space and style to the description of the rules, the evocation of the space makes the rules seem similarly orienting: 'The apartments of the Club were situated in Leicester Square, so that the Alhambra and the Empire music-halls were within easy walk, at least during the early part of the evening.'[47] Many fictional clubs are assigned locations in actual London streets, where they overlay on readers' internal maps of London, populated by other print sources and possibly also personal experience.[48] In this case, the relation to two real music halls cements an association with the theatre and enables one of the embedded, tangential jokes characteristic of this section, if not the entire novel. After this work of location comes a physical description:

> The premises were neither palatial nor inadequate. They consisted of two rooms, communicating with each other by rather loud remarks. The one you entered first, if you had been careful to ascend two flights of stairs instead of one, was the smoking room; but the members always smoked in the other and smaller room, because a pipe was more of a luxury there on account of the placard proclaiming 'No smoking allowed'.[49]

This section, peppered with short jokes, situates readers fairly literally. The use of the second person and the walk-through organisation not only sets the scene but invites the reader into the club rooms. Both of these techniques become typical of club stories: giving readers a virtual tour of the club and symbolically inviting them into the club's space.

In *The Bachelors' Club*, the description of the club premises also carries embedded jokes that argue both sides of the central issue of matrimony. For instance, when all the members spend time in the smaller room that isn't for smoking, instead of the smoking room, 'the better half of the Club was always deserted by the members – as was perhaps only consistent'.[50] This joke takes aim squarely at the Bachelors' attitudes towards matrimony, perhaps helping balance out the many jokes at the expense of matrimony – or women in general. Various 'misogamous texts' adorn the 'better' room.[51] Zangwill describes these as 'the most hateful aphorisms',[52] which could connote judgement or merely describe the attitude of the Bachelors in writing them. Certainly the waiters, the married men, seem unperturbed; they spend most of their time in the room and dust the aphorisms. Yet Zangwill reproduces a long list of these 'hateful' slogans or jokes. Most of them are misogynistic – most notably 'Genius should only marry genius; and no woman is a genius'[53] – but not all. Some play on the idea of marriage itself, such as 'Marriages are made in heaven; but this brand is not exported.'[54] The closest the list comes to a joke on men is 'The truest chivalry to the woman who loves you is to leave her a spinster.'[55] Like one interpretation of the joke about marriage being a crime against women, this implies that marriage to a man will make a woman unhappy. Zangwill seems to adopt the 'golden apple' approach to jokes (of which Samuel Johnson accused Shakespeare): diverting from his path or stooping to chase the opportunity regardless of content.[56] The very excessive nature of Zangwill's style imparts an air of triviality, even to the essential premise of the club. Furthermore, the club's ultimate dissolution indicates that premise's untenable nature. Even though its premise – a club for bachelors – resembles the reality of Clubland more than other fictional clubs in this study, the details of the rules make it appear silly and arbitrary. And that is precisely the point.

No one draws the old maid

The practice, which Zangwill established, of titling the book with the name of the club, conflates club membership and (imagined) reading community. The club is the readership of the book. This phenomenon becomes even more pronounced in Zangwill's sequel, *The Old Maids' Club*, which builds explicitly on readership of Zangwill's prior novel both within and without its fictional world. Unlike the Bachelors' Club, which begins the book fully stocked and gradually dissolves, the Old Maids' Club never officially acquires an additional member. Lillie Dulcimer founds the club as an alternative to marrying Lord Silverdale because, in a fit of logic, she convinces herself that although she loves him and he claims to love her, it is a 'mathematical' improbability that he loves her in return.[57] As Lillie tries to form her club, Silverdale is at her side, and the novel ends with their marriage.

Zangwill acknowledges the foregone conclusion with a series of metatextual jokes. Lillie's father allows her to form the club because 'Having read "The Bachelors' Club", he thought it was the surest way of getting her married.'[58] Lillie sets her club up in conscious contrast to the Bachelors' Club; she embroiders cushions with 'counterblasts to their misogynistic maxims'.[59] As a sequel, this book could take place in the fictional world Zangwill created in the first book, in which the club exists but the book was also published, but all references seem applicable to the book alone. When Lillie declares, 'I hate puns. They spoiled the Bachelors' Club,' she could mean the club or the novel.[60] The practice of titling novels after their central clubs adds to the conflation between the club membership and the book. Zangwill's metatextual reference to his puns not only gives his previous work a self-deprecating puff but also highlights the blending of oral and literary sociability, infusing jokes and other elements of oral culture into print culture. Furthermore, focusing on Lillie as a reader of *The Bachelors' Club* emphasises the unseen presence of women readers in fictional male-only clubs.

The Old Maids' Club carries forward its predecessor's metatextual references to literary Bohemia – in fact, it carries them further. The novel is punctuated by Lord Silverdale, Lillie's suitor, reading her his journalistic submissions (probably in part as a means for Zangwill to incorporate his own): 'That day Lord Silverdale appropriately intoned (with a banjo obligato) a patter-song, which he pretended to have written at the Academy, whence he had just come with the conventional splitting headache.'[61] More of the *Old Maids' Club* takes place outside the doors of the club, including an episode in which Lord Silverdale attempts to interview a journalist for the fictional *Moon*, named Wilkins, who 'did nine-tenths of the interviews in that model of the new journalism'.[62] When Wilkins realises who Silverdale is, they begin trying to interview each other. Another journalist is herself a candidate for the Old Maids' Club, 'about to establish a paper called *The Cherub*, after her popular story *The Cherub That Sits Up Aloft*.'[63] Of course the *Idler*, in which some of the material from *The Old Maids' Club* originally appeared, had a similar etymology, from Jerome's book *Idle Thoughts of an Idle Fellow*. One such piece, originally published as 'The English Shakespeare', features the Society for Mutual Depreciation. As we saw in Chapter 1, contemporary reviews compared that fictional club to the New Humorists and, by association, the *Idler* itself.

The Old Maids' Club ends with a rather too serious moral delivered by Lord Silverdale:

This Old Maids' Club of yours is a hollow mockery. You are playing round the fringes of tragedy. . . . You are young and rich and beautiful – Heaven pity the women who have none of these charms. Life is a cruel tragedy for many – never crueller than when its remorseless laws condemn gentle loving women to a crabbed and solitary old age. To some all the smiles of fortune, the homage of all mankind – to others all the frowns of fate and universal neglect, aggravated by contumely. You have felt this, I know, and it is as a protest that you conceived your club. Still can it ever be a serious success? I love you, Lillie, and you have known it all along. If I have entered into the joke, believe me, I have sometimes taken it as seriously as you. Come! Say you love me, too, and let us end the tragi-comedy.[64]

This attempt at serious treatment of women's inequality perhaps demonstrates why Zangwill generally opted for lighter approaches to the subject. It is particularly awkward for a man to be expounding this to a woman in the context of a marriage proposal. For women, marriage is not a straightforward happy ending. But the lack of marriage is even worse. As his *Idler* editors did with *Tommy and Co.* and *Jennie Baxter*, Zangwill struggles with the question of what kind of ending to give women. The ending of this passage in particular recalls Tennyson's *The Princess*: 'Indeed I love thee: come.' (In W. S. Gilbert's rewriting, the line moves from the Prince to the Princess.)[65] Behind this, in turn, perhaps lurks Petruchio's 'Come on, and kiss me, Kate.' The comparison to the Princess relates the Old Maids' Club to Ida's women's university, and the Prince's statement marks its dissolution. Heterosexual marital domesticity replaces the single-sex domesticity afforded by the university. But the essential difference between *The Princess* and *The Old Maids' Club* is that the Old Maids' Club has never existed, never achieved that degree of domesticity or even conviviality.

Lillie sets up the club space, complete with embroidered mottoes to rival those of the *Bachelors' Club*, but she never really accrues members. While *The Bachelors' Club*'s central device is of the club membership dwindling to zero, *The Old Maids' Club*'s conceit is that almost no members are actually accepted. When two applicants appear at the same time, they immediately insult each other – and then leave together for a double date. In fact, the novel features more men's clubs, including the Mutual Depreciation Society. The only real gathering of the members, or potential members, of the Old Maids' Club occurs at the very end of the book, at the wedding breakfast for Lillie and Lord Silverdale. There the members appear with their friends and husbands. As with *Tommy and Co.*, a mixed-sex social gathering is best. Without the pressures of matrimony, the women can relate to each other and to the men in a state of clubbable conviviality. For, as Zangwill knows, 'old maid' and 'bachelor' are not, in fact, synonymous, because of the power differential between the two.

The Proposal Club

The rules of Barry Pain's Proposal Club, outlined in the story 'Clubs and Hearts' (1914 in *Stories without Tears*), similarly turn on marriage. But although this club theoretically promotes it, as the Bachelors and Old Maids theoretically abhor it, the club and the story actually present quite a dim view of marriage. The premise of the club is not romantic as such, but an answer to the problem of 'odd women', which George Gissing (an 'Idler's Club' contributor) highlights in his novel of that name (1893). The club's premise is that members draw lots to propose to a 'woman . . . chosen for the improbability that under any other circumstances she would ever receive a proposal at all'.[66] For that reason, the club members must all be bachelors 'and by the rules of the club must be unmarried, sound in health, able to support a wife, and not quite intolerably ugly'.[67] The conceit of the club rules purports to formalise the larger social rules surrounding marriage. But human behaviour is not reduced so easily.

Despite its altruistic rationale, the Proposal Club members take an overall unfavourable view of marriage, the opposite of the Bachelors who theoretically abjure marriage but end up in it despite themselves. The club's founder and president makes his case in theoretical terms:

> Lord Northberry urged the beauty of it all with great enthusiasm. There was no chivalry, he would say, in loving and protecting a woman whom one wished to love and protect. There was no merit in giving one's heart where it was quite impossible to keep it. But there was merit and there was chivalry in the man who was prepared cheerfully to sacrifice himself for some woman to whom Nature or the Fates had not been kind.[68]

Like Zangwill, Pain plays on the late-century changes to the practical and cultural terms of marriage. Northberry argues against marriage for love on abstract terms, in a similar fashion to Lillie, but in this case relying on masculine chivalry and self-sacrifice. However, at the meeting of the club narrated in the story, member Colonel Seventree presents a different view – that the club consists of the ultimate gamble: 'It was a brilliant idea of Northberry's to copy the notion of Stevenson's Suicide Club, but to make the stakes rather bigger.'[69] As we will see in the next chapter, Robert

Louis Stevenson's *Suicide Club* (1878) involves a similar lottery for members to aid each other's suicide. The notion that the stakes are higher here, that marriage is a fate worse than death, is the logical extension of Northberry's argument of self-sacrifice, but hardly sounds appealing to either party.

Like the Suicide Club, the Proposal Club accentuates the close relationship between clubs and gambling. The story follows a conversation between Colonel Seventree and Richard Tower during the selection (by lot) of who will be forced to propose to the woman the club has chosen for him. The Colonel's apprehension and relief in being passed over is almost comical in its extreme. But it is not atypical: 'On most of the other faces [besides the President's] there was a look of anxiety, and even of fear.'[70] Notably, the president himself is exempt from the drawing pool, despite his arguments in favour of the scheme. The Colonel declares simply, 'I am a gambler.'[71] He claims he will resign his membership if he is only spared, but when it comes down to it, he says, 'I think . . . I must risk one more meeting. It's the feeling of relief afterwards – there's nothing like it. But after next meeting – '[72] Obviously, the Colonel relies on the club to provide an intense sensation – a high, if you will.

The Colonel's exaggerations nearly come to pass as his 'young friend',[73] Tower, is selected to propose. He knows the woman selected for him, making his proposal seem plausible, and, while he dislikes her, 'there was very little chance of a refusal'.[74] Unfortunately, he has just become secretly engaged to another girl. As a result of the lottery, he breaks off his engagement and proposes to the other woman. In fact, he has a plan to make the stakes of his mandated proposal life-or-death: 'he had decided on some painless form of suicide', complete with a 'last letter' to his beloved, 'explaining all and trusting that now and then she might have a kind thought for the man who had loved her and died for her'.[75] In an extreme gesture, Tower fulfils Northberry's idea of self-sacrifice – except that the object of his sacrifice is his beloved and his method of sacrifice is death, not marriage. Naturally, this plan is far removed from the original idea of the club: neither woman will gain the 'protection' of marriage, and the only real gain will be to the late Tower's sense of honour.

Fortunately, a comic twist averts this fate. Miss Lamley writes back noting her preference for him, but declaring, 'I belong to a society of women – in fact, I am the president of it – who have been struck by the numerical preponderance of our sex over yours, and have agreed to sacrifice themselves for their sisters. In a word, we are pledged to remain unmarried, and the penalties for breaking the pledge are of a kind that I dare not face.'[76] One silly society cancels the other out, and no harm is done. Lamley's club is a realised version of the Old Maids' Club – and a much more practical solution to the Odd Woman problem than the Proposal Club. As we shall see elsewhere in Pain, here a female club unwittingly trumps or negates the machinations of a male club with a silly (or misguided) premise. It is striking that while female clubs do not occur frequently in this genre, and rarely in focus (with the major exception of the Old Maids' Club, which never really gets off the ground), they are often a benign if not positive force.

Zangwill and Silverdale understood that an old maid was not actually the equivalent of a bachelor: marriage remained an unequal institution. In fact, the state of the Proposal Club is quite similar to the position usually held by women – at any given moment they could be informed that they will marry someone for whom they have not the slightest bit of affection. Indeed, another story in *Stories without Tears*, 'The 'Eighty Seven', describes a father who has initially denied his daughter's request to marry a relatively impecunious man, but is convinced through the mellowing agent of the personified, eponymous port. If forced marriage – or even celibacy – is a fate worse than death, it is one historically more suffered by women. The Proposal Club is one that men opt into as a form of 'chivalry', but it resembles the general lot of women in the period.[77] A Punishment Committee for them is not necessary. They may experience ruin as a natural consequence of refusing a proposal, which may entail becoming an old maid.

In which there are surprisingly few actual problems

Barry Pain's full-length novel *The Problem Club* presents a more stable club than the Bachelors' or Old Maids'. The novel ran as a serial in the *Strand* from December 1917 to November 1918 and appeared as a book in 1919. The First World War is never mentioned in the main text – although the serial appeared alongside Arthur Conan Doyle's account of the Battle of the Somme (as well as P. G. Wodehouse's story 'Jeeves and the Chump Cyril'). The preface added for the book describes it as 'an account of some of the pre-war meetings of the club'.[78] The war radically changed the social, political, emotional and artistic landscape of Britain, not to say the world, and with it the context for the club and club stories. As later chapters will discuss further, many post-war club stories associate club life with the pre-war social structure, for better or for worse. *The Problem Club* is one of the more conventional club stories and contains much less implicit critique of the club system or the class structure it represents. This may be partially because of Pain's comparative insider status, but it may also be because the social order was already so manifestly altered through the war. To its wartime and immediately post-war readers, *The Problem Club* presents the club in part as a comforting structure which solves manageable, pleasantly trivial problems.

Amid so much upheaval, *The Problem Club* continues in the form established by *The Bachelors' Club*, barring the dissolution of the club. The club's rules are particularly emphasised, explicitly forming the meat of the 'Prefatory Note'. The chapters, which tell the stories of the club, are framed as an addendum: 'It is permitted to add an account of some of the pre-war meetings of the club, various natural precautions being taken to prevent the discovery of the identity of members.'[79] The rules are the main thing.

Pain begins by situating his fictional club in the wider, non-fictional world of print culture. The novel begins, 'The general public knows little about the Problem Club.'[80] This is certainly true, as Barry Pain has just made it up. But Pain's reference to 'The general public' makes one wonder who the audience of the book is meant to be. Are we the 'general public' who are now being informed? Or are we an insider audience, about to become privy to facts not generally known? He purports to correct 'references to it which have appeared from time to time in the Press', particularly 'a paragraph in a recent issue of a society paper (which, it may be admitted, is generally well informed)'.[81] This contextualisation in a larger fictional textual world follows common practice, as when Doyle's 'The Adventure of the Final Problem' has Watson claim to be responding to, and correcting, accounts of Moriarty published by his brother.[82] More specifically, this reference implies that the club is important enough to be commented on in a society paper but secret (exclusive) enough to be misrepresented. In this case, the paper is being held up against the club and found wanting.

But the novel goes on to reproduce the newspaper's errone-ous claims: 'It says that the club has its premises underground in Piccadilly, that a former Premier is a member of it, that all the members are required to swear a most solemn oath to act with scrupulous honor in the monthly competitions, and that high play frequently goes on.'[83] Pain then purports to disclose, 'The actual truth is that there are no club premises. The famous but old-fashioned restaurant that reserves two rooms on the first floor for the club's monthly meetings is not situated in Piccadilly.'[84] In purporting to clarify, Pain mystifies, augmenting the air of exclusivity through secrecy: dropping hints and indicating the prestige of the restaurant, and defining the geographic area only by exclusion. Perhaps the most important emphasis in Pain's 'correction' is not a rule, but the absence of a rule: 'The story of the solemn oath is even more absurd. After all, the members are gentlemen. They would as soon think of taking a solemn oath not to cheat at cards or at golf. The "scrupulous honor" is taken for granted.'[85] Among 'gentlemen', with its obvious class and gender connotations, explicit statements of some rules violate the unspoken social codes that undergird the club.

After specifically debunking the newspaper's claims, Pain frames his own work as a competing entrée into public discourse: 'Silly misrepresentations of this kind have caused some annoyance, and it is now thought that a discreet but authorized account of some part of the proceedings of the club would be preferable.'[86] Like *The Bachelors' Club*, the novel claims to be a record originating from the club itself, but while Zangwill uses first-person narration by a club member, *The Problem Club* applies the impersonal voice of the institution – or indeed a journalistic voice. The narrator also in this section makes reference to what 'the minute-books of the club show',[87] which not only locates authority within the club and speaks to the notion of being 'authorized' by the club itself, but also recalls the premise Dickens uses in *The Pickwick Papers* of purporting to work from literal papers compiled by a club member (including one passage when he interrupts the text to tell us that the notes become incoherent).[88]

Unlike other clubs, the Problem Club's premise is not inherently silly, although the club activities are distinctly leisure and to be undertaken by men with significant resources in both money and time:

The club consists of twelve members, and the annual subscription is one hundred and thirty-four pounds. Of this sum twenty-four pounds is allotted to the club expenses, including the club dinners which are held on the first Saturday in every month. Each member in turn acts as chairman at one dinner in the year, afterwards adjudicating upon the problem competition for that month; while at the other eleven meetings he is himself a competitor, the remaining one hundred and ten pounds of his subscription being treated as eleven entrance fees of ten pounds each. The problems are not of a mathematical nature, and were for some time invented and propounded by Leonard, the ingenious head-waiter of the restaurant. The winner receives the whole of the entrance fees, amounting to one hundred and ten pounds; if there is more than one winner this amount is divided equally between them.[89]

This description makes the Problem Club sound rather straightforward; the problems sound like trivia or other on-the-spot puzzles. But the chapter titles tell another tale. The very chapter that contains the prefatory material is entitled 'The Giraffe Problem'. A glance at the table of contents reveals such intriguing chapter titles as 'The Kiss Problem', 'The Win-and-Lose Problem', 'The Alibi Problem', 'The Q-Loan Problem' and 'The Pig-Keeper's Problem'. This promises to be interesting.

The description of the club rules heavily stresses the pecuniary arrangements. That might seem ungentlemanly; one of the charges from which the narrator wished to defend the club was allegations of 'high play'. Yet even this is a vice of the upper classes, and a mark of exclusive clubs. Although the narrator notes that 'any betting on the results is prohibited',[90] the entire premise essentially constitutes a bet. Odd bets characterised non-fictional club life, and many clubs kept betting books in which to record them.[91] The idea of using club subscriptions as betting money, however, is novel. And this does amount to very 'high play'. The 1897 *Who's Who* lists entry fees and annual subscriptions for many of the prominent West End clubs, but none approaches £134. The most expensive entry fees are for the United University and Naval and Military clubs, at £42 each.[92] But each of these only has an annual subscription of ten pounds and ten or eight shillings, which is typical for the higher end of the club subscription. The Authors' Club, to which Pain and other Idlers belonged, had an entry fee and annual subscription of four guineas in 1897.[93]

The Problem Club has the same number of members as the Bachelors' Club (when that novel begins): twelve. The rationale differs: the number of club members corresponds to the number of months in the year because each one has to be chair for one monthly meeting. In fact, we find out later that the club has 'a long waiting list'.[94] Twelve members sit on a jury, and the number provides an ample array of characters while retaining a cosy atmosphere. The reason for this common number in literary clubs, however, is probably because it means one member per chapter of a year's run in a monthly journal – beginning, as the *Problem Club* did, with the popular Christmas number, then getting out of the way for the next December issue to introduce new serials.

This is a true club novel in that each chapter is a meeting of the club; no action takes place outside the club-room, although the conversations report on actions that have. It is the consummate example of the men-sitting-around-and-talking book, a larger genre in which the Idlers often worked.[95] The structure also unifies all the short anecdotes: in each chapter, each club member reports on his success or failure – his attempts or lack thereof to solve the problem. Despite all the novel's structures, the conversational aspect renders it diffuse and gives it the affect of gossip. The order of reporting differs each time, as Pain notes at the onset: 'There was, indeed, a marked absence of formality at the Problem Club. There was no order of precedence.'[96] He establishes early on that 'all the members were smokers'[97] and, throughout the novel, the specifics of what a member is smoking or drinking are mentioned along with the dialogue, such as when Mr Matthews, acting as chair, 'lit with care and a cedar-wood spill a cigar that can only be obtained by the favour of the planter'.[98] This contributes to the ambience of luxury and facilitates the vicarious reading community of smokers discussed in Chapter 1.

Despite the premise and organisation of the club, it remains principally a social club. The first chapter sets the pattern of establishing that the dinners are excellent and undisturbed by talk of the problem: 'Any reference to the competition to be settled is by an unwritten law forbidden until the chairman has opened the proceedings.'[99] Like etiquette books, these club novels write the unwritten rules, initiating their common readers. Pain's depiction instead stresses departures from conventional etiquette: 'members seated themselves informally in a semicircle of easy-chairs'.[100] Formal seating might have followed rules of precedence. Likewise, Pain emphasises the informality of the proceedings: 'The chairman did not rise when he spoke, nor did members rise when they answered him.'[101] The posture of these club members may resemble the Idlers with their feet on the mantel, but the invocation of formality suggests that they know some of the conventional social rules but choose not to abide by them.

The Problem Club, like several other club stories, raises the issue of the porousness of the boundary between servants and masters. Instead of a club member becoming a waiter, as in *The Bachelors' Club*, Leonard, the head waiter who has set the problems, becomes a member – a radical move. The final problem he sets requires club members to discover his own identity – and he turns out to be the sixth Baron Herngill, grandson of the founder of the club.[102] Furthermore, the novel actually ends with this cryptic suggestion that draws exclusivity into focus:

> And here the chronicles of the Problem Club must come to an end. The story of how Willy Bunting became a member of the club and subsequently retired from it, and how the solution of one problem brought the Rev. Septimus Cunliffe into the police-court, and how the solution of another made Mr Matthews miss his dinner, and how a negro failed to get into the club, and how a girl of seventeen was actually elected – these things with many others must remain hidden in the club archives.[103]

To a modern reader especially, this passage highlights the disagreeable side of exclusivity, in terms of race as well as gender. In some ways, what's remarkable is not that these kinds of boundary-reinforcing jokes exist in these books, but that they are the exception rather than the rule.

Common readers may not be explicitly invoked in the Problem Club, but an embedded club evokes the reading experience. The novel's final problem is 'to buy a copy of the current issue of *The Pig-Keeper's Friend*'.[104] This periodical turns out to be 'principally devoted to the cryptic record of the many strange activities of the Impersonation Society',[105] a society which gives its members an immersive experience with a slightly different twist. Its members live other people's lives:

> [The founder's] theory was that the ordinary holiday is a mistake, and that what a tired man or woman wants is not only a change of place but a change of personality. In order to get a complete rest you must, for the time being, be somebody else. You must dress and live like the character you have assumed and you must even try to think like him.[106]

Pain doesn't make an explicit connection to the reading experience, but this club resembles an organisation from G. K. Chesterton's *The Club of Queer Trades*, which, as we shall see in Chapter 4, specifically does. Jimmy stumbles upon a pile of *The Pig-Keeper's Friend* at a tobacconist's shop with an unusual worker:

> Tobacconists may do a lot of funny things, but they don't read the *Agamemnon* of Æschylus in the original Greek, which is what this blighter was doing. Nor do they have manicured nails and an Oxford intonation – his attempt at a Cockney accent was one of the most pathetic failures I've ever met.[107]

This Impersonator turns out to be the headmaster of a boys' school, and he reveals himself to Jimmy through his failures at assimilation, particularly in the social valences of his reading. This Impersonator leaves his usual life, then escapes further into a book. The actual impersonation isn't explicitly tied to the desire to extend or replace the reading experience, but couldn't it be said, paraphrasing Chesterton, that if the modern man wants to be someone else, he reads a book?[108] Actors in this period were sometimes said to 'impersonate' characters; might readers do the same?

Gender problems

Unlike Zangwill's club novels, *The Problem Club* does not make gender an explicit feature, yet both gender and class manifest as contested areas in many of the problems. The members of the problem club are, in general, quite distinguished. Several are members of the aristocracy. Leonard, in his true identity as the sixth Baron Herngill, is by far the most exalted. Other titled members include the Hon. James Feldane and Sir Charles Bunford. Sir Charles may be a knight or a baronet; he is described as 'an elderly gentleman of distinguished appearance'.[109] Half of the members belong to respected professions, and they are often introduced (or reintroduced in new chapters) with letters after their names: Mr Wildersley, A.R.A., Mr Quillian, K.C., Mr Harding Pope, M.P., Dr Alden, Major Byles, and the Rev. Septimus Cunliffe. The remaining members are Mr Matthews, described as 'the richest man in a club where nobody was very poor'; Mr Pusely-Smythe, 'a man of middle age, with dark, cavernous eyes and an intellectual forehead [and] less solemn than he seemed', marked early on for being the record-holder for the most wins in a year; Mr Hesseltine, a younger member, friends with Jimmy (who is the youngest member); and Austin, also an artist.[110] All three of these last are tightly connected to another member, with whom they either collaborate (Hesseltine and Feldane, Austin and Wildersley) or spar (Pusely-Smythe and Quillian – who end up accidentally collaborating on the Win-and-Lose Problem). Much of the novel's humour depends on these respectable gentlemen making fools of themselves in pursuit of the month's problem. Essentially, the club rules have distinguished gentlemen acting like schoolboys, playing pranks on each other and/or various innocent passers-by. It's like a riddle to which only the members of the club hold the key.

The club members engage in behaviours which can be perfectly understood by those in the know – members of the club and the 'eavesdropping' readers – but are unintelligible to friends, family and other acquaintances. Wildersley wins the Handkerchief Problem by buying 104 handkerchiefs, making them over to a club member (the chairman, who adjudicates the problem; in this case, Jimmy) by Deed of Gift, then stealing them from his doorstep, saying, 'It's always easier to steal a thing if the owner doesn't know he's got it.'[111] Although this would seem to be an internal matter, it requires the services of his solicitor, who views the matter as extremely bizarre: 'I told him what I wanted, and the shock nearly killed him. When he got better, I explained that it was a joke. . . . He does not understand jokes and will believe anything about them.'[112] Wildersley implies he deceives the solicitor in describing the context as joke, preserving the secrecy of the club. But the manner of the theft and the choice of the chairman constitute a kind of practical joke – especially given Jimmy's elaborate precautions to secure his handkerchiefs: 'For the past month every handkerchief I've used has been attached to the interior of the pocket by a steel chain and swivel, and those not in use have been locked away in a safe. My valet thinks I've gone off my head, of course, but then he'd have been bound to have thought that sooner or later, anyhow.'[113] For the non-competitors, the club members' actions seem inexplicable – or the symptom of another kind of problem.

Occasionally the joke is on the other side: the members sometimes find themselves victims of ridicule by virtue of the silly things they do that non-members don't understand. The book's frontispiece

(Fig. 3.1) shows a bus conductor cracking a joke at the expense of Rev. Cunliffe as he attempts to solve the Threepenny Problem ('to offer a half-crown for a threepenny bus-fare, and to receive the change wholly in threepenny-bits'):[114] 'If you want all them three-pennies, you'd better get them out of the blanky offertory-bag next Sunday!'[115] The bus conductor and a fellow passenger are laughing at the joke, but the reverend remains straight-faced, his pursed lips either indicating disapproval or holding in a laugh. However, although the joke seems to be on him, the reverend knows something the others don't: the larger reason for his request. Are we as readers meant to laugh with the bus conductor, like the fellow passenger, who looks at him and smiles, or to sympathise with the reverend, whose discomfited expression we can well understand

Figure 3.1 Arthur Garratt, frontispiece for Barry Pain, *The Problem Club*. Rare Book Collection, Louis Round Wilson Special Collections Library, University of North Carolina at Chapel Hill.

(once we've read the book)? This particular joke has a class angle: the bus conductor is a working man, not to be included in the club, but perhaps closer in class to the actual readers of the book. Moreover, readers may not be in complete sympathy with the bus conductor because of the nature of his joke, which not only besmirches the reverend's cloth but also contains profanity (assuming he does not actually say 'blanky').

Yet the discrepancy between the club members' distinguished professions and their schoolboy-prank actions (on which, in part, the frontispiece joke depends) also forms jokes from within the club. Most of the illustrations, like that of the frontispiece, depict happenings outside the club walls which are related during the meetings that comprise the text. But one illustrates the club proceedings directly, and, like the frontispiece, it features Rev. Cunliffe (Fig. 3.2). The circumstances resemble each other closely: another character cracks a joke at his expense, in which a third character, an onlooker, laughs. In fact, the faces of the two onlookers are remarkably similar between the drawings, except that instead of spectacles, the club member wears a monocle, a sign of his superior class standing and formal level of attire: the club members all dress for dinner (in contrast to Pain's Failures, as we will see in the next section). In this case, the joke has to do with the Handkerchief Problem. Jimmy, as chairman, has just asked, to save time, 'Will any member who claims to have beaten Hesseltine's score kindly hold up a hand?'[116] When Cunliffe as well as the eventual winner, Wildersley, do so, Jimmy replies, 'What? . . . Our padre is in the sneak-thief business? Has he no respect for his cloth? Leonard has a lot to answer for.'[117] The illustrator has taken the penultimate sentence as the line, and there's indeed an element of truth in it: it hangs over this illustration.

Unlike the frontispiece, this illustration does not depict a benign, virtuous-looking, long-suffering clergyman who has just made a humble, if not particularly common, request for change to a bus conductor. Instead, Rev. Cunliffe clamps a cigarette holder in his mouth and is flanked by wine glasses and a bottle. He steeples his hands in front of him and raises an eyebrow, gazing at the viewer with a look perhaps of supercilious amusement. Jimmy delivers the line deadpan, with an aristocratic sneer. With a monocle, cigar and immaculate dinner outfit, he seems the consummate clubman. Cunliffe here shares in the joke – perhaps he even smiles because he knows that he's succeeded at this challenge

'"Has he no respect for his cloth?"'

Figure 3.2 Arthur Garratt, illustration for Barry Pain, *The Problem Club*. Rare Book Collection, Louis Round Wilson Special Collections Library, University of North Carolina at Chapel Hill.

more than his peers. This problem, more directly than most, pits the members against each other, but all do in some way; that's the nature of the premise.

Like Zangwill's Society for Mutual Depreciation, the official animosity belies real fellowship. These men seem genuinely to enjoy each other's company. Pain makes the point that these official meetings are only a part of the monthly club dinners, which also include the meal before and, increasingly emphasised, a game of bridge afterwards – itself a friendly competition for monetary stakes. Fundamentally, this image differs from the frontispiece: this is a joke in which everyone can share. The Rev. Cunliffe is positioned between Jimmy and the moustached club member: he laughs with them. His smoke mingles with that of the laughing member (in a softer version of Zangwill's 'masculine substitute for a kiss'):[118] they're on the same side, sharing a smoke, sharing a joke. But he also gazes at the viewer, inviting them in. If he is indulging in an additional joke to lob back at Jimmy, he's inviting the reader to share. The upturned eyebrow may indicate competition, but it's within the context of friendship. Rev. Cunliffe rationalises his attempts at this and other problems (including the Kiss Problem, which he wins) with dexterous reasoning. Indeed, in this case, he has a point: he is no ordinary thief, but playing with fellow club-members by the rules of the game, although the novel's final paragraph refers to a problem bringing the clergyman 'into the police-court'.[119]

A number of the problems flirt with the illicit, and a number require members to enlist the unwitting participation of women. The Kiss Problem typifies this trend: 'It is required within the space of one hour to kiss upon the cheek ten females of the age of courtship and not cousins or any nearer relative of the kisser, without giving offence to any one of them.'[120] Mr Pusely-Smythe, with his characteristic 'air of saturnine melancholy',[121] makes a number of deadpan jokes about the scandalous nature of this problem, first recounting the protests lodged against it at previous meetings (by Major Byles and Rev. Cunliffe):

> 'A vote being taken, it was found – to the eternal shame of the club, if I may say so – that there was a considerable majority in favour of the problem being retained.'
>
> Every member being well aware that the chairman himself had voted with the majority, there was some hilarious interruption.
>
> 'Gentlemen,' said the chairman severely, 'this is not the spirit in which to approach stories of wrecked homes and blasted reputations, and these stories we must now hear.'[122]

Although Pusely-Smythe plays this for laughs, a core of truth remains: the stakes for everyone's reputations – particularly the women's – are high. As the club's youngest members, Jimmy and Hesseltine, begin to recount their stories, Pusely-Smythe refers to their acts in ironically melodramatic language: 'loathsome confessions' and 'hideous secret'.[123] Jimmy and Hesseltine have indeed taken the challenge at face value: at a dance, they proceeded to kiss various young women (and one mother), some friends of their childhood and some in the context of flirtation.

Yet this straight approach to the problem reaps no rewards. Jimmy's attempts at rakishness jostle with his own sense of 'decency' and he fails to 'raise' the necessary number: 'I was done in by the time limit. You can't in decency kiss a girl and then do an immediate bunk. You must keep on telling her how maddeningly beautiful she is for a few minutes. . . . Still, I claim a score of six.'[124] As Gayle Rubin classically describes, these women are only being used as bargaining chips to enable these men to 'score' off each other.[125] However, no serious consequences seem to have followed, except perhaps for Hesseltine: 'I might add that, being rather carried away, I got engaged to two different girls in the course of the hour, and though it's all right now, I don't monkey with a buzz-saw again.'[126] Hesseltine frames his engagements as dangers to himself rather than the women involved. His engagements occur in the passive voice, like Bertie Wooster, to whom engagements also seem to happen.

A major victory in the Kiss Problem falls to a female club. Dr Alden visits his 'married sister' on the night she's 'entertaining the girls of her Tennyson Club'.[127] As part of an elaborate plan, he claims to be able to detect face powder through kissing a cheek and proposes a test:

> Let them blindfold me. Then twelve times in succession let a cheek touch my lips. In each case I would state whether or not face-powder had been used, and would employ no other means of detection. I was so certain of it that I would gladly contribute a guinea to the charitable fund of the Tennyson Club for every mistake that I made.[128]

But Alden is in turn tricked by the club: they present him not with a succession of young girls to kiss, but with his sister repeatedly: 'Sometimes she had touched my lips with her cheek, on which there was face-powder, and sometimes with the back of her hand, on which there was none.'[129] The adventure costs him nine guineas for his incorrect guesses, his shot at his club's prize, and the humiliation of being the object of the girls' 'merriment'.[130]

Another older member, Mr Matthews, also plans an elaborate scheme – in this case, to disguise himself as 'an elderly lady'[131] interviewing candidates for a companion, 'it being his abominable intention to kiss each applicant as he said good-bye to her'.[132] But he is foiled not by trickery but by his own instincts. As the first applicant goes to leave, before he kisses her, she drops her handkerchief:

Now Mr Matthews had from the nursery upwards been taught habits of politeness, and his decent upbringing now proved his undoing. Forgetting that he was supposed to be an elderly lady and the girl's prospective employer, he flew to pick up that handkerchief. And as he stooped his hat and wig fell off. For a few awful moments he remained stooping, waiting for Miss Porter's scream. But no scream came. She had realised that Mrs Elsmere Twiss wore a wig, but not that she was a man. And the tactful Miss Porter had retired from the room.[133]

Note that Matthews's masculine betrayal is not descried as inherent but the result of his 'habits' and 'upbringing'. The beginning of the story sounds quite predatory, potentially: a man setting out to deceive women and take advantage of them. But Matthews's chivalry stops him. The narrator tells us it is not explicitly Matthews's better instincts that surface, but that 'his nerve was gone'.[134] Nevertheless, we were told at the outset that there are certain assumptions made about club members being true 'gentlemen' acting with 'scrupulous honour'.[135] So being a gentleman and acting honourably are not merely matters of principle here, but of training: automatically picking up a woman's handkerchief while plotting to use her as a bargaining chip in a game with other men in a way that she would probably not consent to (hence the need for an elaborate deception). Pain's clubmen do not always act in the spirit of gentlemanly behaviour.

This moment of cross-dressing is less revolutionary than that in *Tommy and Co.* Although it's played for laughs, it also gets at the fundamental issues of what makes men and women different. In contrast with pantomime dame tradition, the humorous surprise here is not the degree to which the cross-dressing doesn't work, but the degree to which it does. Even when the wig falls off, the disguise holds. Pain does, however, highlight the discrepancy between feminine dress and masculine habits. As Matthews drives back from his costuming, 'A passer-by who had happened to glance into the cab might have observed a sweet-looking old lady smoking a large cigar.'[136] But even this is hypothetical. Arthur Garratt's illustration, which takes the caption only 'a sweet-looking old lady smoking a large cigar' (Fig. 3.3), exaggerates the humour that's played with surprising subtlety in the text itself. At the same time, it returns to the notion that this might be the behaviour of an actual woman.

P.C.   *Page 37*
'A sweet-looking old lady smoking a large cigar.'

Figure 3.3 Arthur Garratt, illustration for Barry Pain, *The Problem Club*. Rare Book Collection, Louis Round Wilson Special Collections Library, University of North Carolina at Chapel Hill.

Overall, women come out rather well in this problem: the good-natured friends of the family who allow Jimmy and Bobby to kiss them, the women who outsmart Alden, and the 'tactful' would-be companion who, although she is fooled by Matthews, still manages to emerge unscathed. None is seriously harmed, although they are threatened, and several are triumphant. These women share in a bit of the fun, but certainly not all of it. And not on equal terms – though they are sometimes the victors.

In fact, the winner of the Kiss Problem does not prey upon women, or even kiss them. Rev. Cunliffe reframes the problem into an innocuous one: he kisses ten female cats belonging to his aunt. As he points out, 'Leonard does not say women. He does

not say girls. He says females.'[137] He also frames his victory as a
moral one:

> It has pained me to hear to-night aspersions on the character of our
> admirable Leonard. I admit that when I first heard the problem I was
> myself inclined to misjudge him. But on examining it more closely
> I saw that never had he risen to a higher pitch of austere, though
> cynical, morality. I saw that he intended that this prize should be won
> by the most high-minded member of the club – by the man whose
> mind was the least obsessed by thoughts of frivolity or flirtation.[138]

Although delivered within a humorous context – Pusely-Smythe
quickly tells him to 'stop throwing bouquets to yourself'[139] –
there is nevertheless a level on which this works straight. Virtue
is indeed rewarded here – or at least seduction and deception are
not. As Cunliffe claims for Leonard, so we might claim for Pain: a
moral lurks here.

The Kiss Problem appears in the second chapter; the first, 'The
Giraffe Problem', is also about manipulating women: 'It is required
to induce a woman who is unaware of your intention to say to
you, "You ought to have been a giraffe".'[140] The gender of the
speaker turns out to be key: one member is disqualified because,
by dint of a high collar and a conversational gambit, he gets his
brother-in-law instead of his sister to say it. He tries to claim a
win, saying, 'Still, for some purposes – bankruptcy and things of
that kind – a man and his wife count as one, don't they?'[141] But
the chair disallows it.

Why do these problems involve women? Because conversation
between men and women is necessarily more stilted? Because it
would be comparatively easy to get a man to make this declaration?
Because of all the spoken and unspoken rules that govern the interactions between men and women? Because of the high consequences
for both if the rules are misunderstood? Dr Alden hints at such a situation in a story he does not tell: 'I made an attempt. It has probably
cost me the esteem of an excellent woman; these excellent women
never think you're serious except when you're joking. I gave her the
chance to tell me I ought to have been a giraffe, but she never took
it. Enough said. Try the next man.'[142] This also plays on the notion
that men and women have different senses of humour (or, less charitably, that women have no sense of humour). The Bachelors have
a similar problem, divorced from gender: one of their members,

Israfel, develops a reputation as a sentimental parlour singer based on a parody that his audience takes seriously.[143] Jokes are fraught with peril for social interactions.

One problem that turns more than usually on betting endangers a member's domesticity both at home and at his club. 'The Win-and-Lose Problem' requires complex mathematical bets: 'It is required to win an even bet of one pound, resulting in a net loss of one pound to the winner; and to lose an even bet of one pound resulting in a net gain of one pound to the loser. No competitor is to make more than two bets.'[144] Many of the club members make reference to their other clubs when describing this problem, perhaps because of the close association between betting and clubs. Major Byles becomes so preoccupied with his attempts to work out the arithmetic of the problem that he befouls his domesticity in both locations:

> I spent the first fortnight at home, and at the end of it I had contracted insomnia, headache, and what you might call pardonable irritability. At the end of that time my wife said that of course she had noticed the change, and that I seemed to be doing sums all day, and that if we were ruined I had better say so and she would face it bravely. I reassured her and came to town on important business. I used tons of the club notepaper for my calculations, put an undue strain on the club wastepaper-baskets, quarrelled with two of my best friends, was sarcastic in addressing club servants, and am expecting a letter from the committee to ask for my resignation.[145]

Because of the Problem Club's code of secrecy, he cannot include his wife in the true nature of his problem, and so causes her unnecessary anxiety. His other club proves not a respite from domesticity but another arena in which domesticity can be ruined. While restoring order to his home requires only that he 'reassure' his wife, the 'strain' he places on the club involves the infrastructure and servants as well as friends – and he (at least in jest) envisions consequences both harsher and more official, emanating from the committee. The member who successfully makes the bet goes to his club to seek out likely takers – and ends up making the bet with another member of the Problem Club (who is, presumably, also a member of this other, unnamed club). Unwittingly, although the member wins, so does his mark – they each won and lost a bet. Therefore they split the prize money.

In a sort of reconciliation between the club and the institution of marriage, the novel ends with a kind of marriage plot. The final problem turns on Jimmy's being engaged. He finds the solution to the problem not by intention, but through being absent-minded: he forgets his cigarette case and stops at a tobacconist's, which happens to be one of the only places which sells *The Pig-Keepers' Friend*. Of course, there's a larger plot resolution that has to do with the club itself: like the Identity Problem which revolved around Leonard's identity, this problem tells us more about Willy Bunting, the editor of *The Pig-Keepers' Friend* (there is inconsistency in the placement of the apostrophe; it also appears as *The Pig-Keeper's Friend*)[146] and introduces the Impersonation Society and the current setter of the club's problems. So the resolution of the plot is about the discovery of yet another problem-setter's identity – and we are told in the tantalising final sentence that he, like Leonard, later becomes a member of the club. But the resolution is also a marriage plot. The identity of the girl is not disclosed – though Jimmy's friend Hesseltine 'think[s he] know[s] her name'[147] – and Jimmy had not planned to tell the club. Rather, Leonard, who is acting as chairman, deduces it from Jimmy's tale – in just about the only act he commits as club member that demonstrates the acumen he presented as head waiter and problem-setter. When Jimmy demands how he knew, Leonard retorts, 'In many ways, and I'll tell you one. Only one thing on earth could have made you forget your cigarette-case.'[148] Unlike the Bachelors' Club, marriage is not prohibited in this club – in fact, several of the members are married. Still, the masculine pleasure of smoking is juxtaposed with connubial bliss. The club members demonstrate their friendship by rejoicing in Jimmy's engagement and by knowing him well enough to deduce it.

Failing at failure

Barry Pain's Failure Club imitates *The Bachelors' Club* in clearly satirising a central element of a club, and also in relying on rules not only for structure but also for plot. Similarly, too, the plot depends on a member breaking the rules and being expelled. The short story 'Trouble at the Failure Club', first published in *London Opinion* in 1913 and later collected in *One Kind and Another*, resembles a chapter of *The Bachelors' Club* in length. The club's premise simply reverses the rules of clubs such as the Athenaeum or Savage in Gilbertian topsy-turvy style: the club requires failure. Even more strongly than the Bachelors' Club, the Failure Club promotes fellowship, in this case as an overt compensation for the members' failures. Without the complicated ambivalence towards marriage, the focus is more clearly on the irony of success leading to expulsion from the club.

Following the tightest mould of the club story, 'Trouble at the Failure Club' begins with a description of the club premises and rules, and the entire story takes place within the club. The opening situates the club within print culture:

> The Failure Club is not mentioned in Whitaker's list of the principal London clubs. Proved failure in some art, science, or politics is an essential qualification. Friendliness and simplicity are also required. Swank is abhorred. A gentle melancholy, accompanied by a tendency to see the humour of one's own misery, is a strong recommendation. The subscription is low.[149]

Of course the Failure Club does not appear in Whitaker's because it is fictional. But this reference invites readers into seemingly specialised knowledge: the lack of general knowledge becomes a sign of exclusivity. The club's requirements directly mirror the Athenaeum or Savage: failure must be 'proven' and also must be in a particular category. We find out soon that 'an assured income of two hundred pounds in the case of a bachelor, or three hundred in the case of a married man, amounts to disqualification'.[150] The members are explicitly 'poor',[151] which might make one wonder why they need a club at all. The explicit qualifications have to do with dispositional clubbability: 'friendliness' and a sense of humour. Yet class lies beneath these assumptions. Clearly, not all poor Londoners (or even poor men) could or would belong to the Failure Club – and possibly some would consider an assured income of one hundred fifty pounds to be ample. Thus the Failure Club puts some pressure on the divide between class and wealth, which was disrupting the class structure in the nineteenth century and continued to do so in the twentieth.

Given some of the fundamental differences from other clubs, the physical description of the club is humorously conventional:

> The Club premises consist of three cellars in the Leicester Square neighbourhood. Over the staircase by which you descend is painted

the motto: 'You might as well be dead', but the analogy with the tomb is not further accentuated.[152]

The motto is more sinister than Zangwill's for the Bachelors and Old Maids. 'You might as well be dead' invites analogies to Stevenson's Suicide Club, which features in Chapter 4, and with which Pain was very familiar.[153] The club is otherwise conventional in appearance:

> The members use principally the large room. One end of it serves as a dining-room, and at the other end you may sit round a coke stove of the studio variety, and smoke and talk. There is a small library which is a little unusual in character. It includes no book of which over a hundred copies have been sold. Most of the books are presentation copies from members. The other room is divided up into kitchen and store-room. In one respect, perhaps, the club is a little extravagant. Two shifts of servants are employed, and the club is never closed. But, after all, the extravagance is not very great, for only four servants are employed altogether. There is no hall-porter. The outer door is locked, and every member has a key. That the club should be open at all hours was held by the committee to be essential.[154]

As in the description of the Bachelors' Club, the second person invites readers to enter the club, although in this case to do so is to court failure, imaginatively at least. It is striking how the club is both suited to the poverty and dismal state of its members but also preserves the notion of clubbability. Although the club consists mainly of a large room with a sawdust floor, the members call it a dining room and have effectively turned the other end into a smoking room. Its few resources focus on the creation of community. The library situates the members in a larger community of failures: although 'most' of the poorly selling books result from the members' failures, others are unaffiliated.

The club provides compensation for failure through fellowship, and failure becomes an aesthetic. Pain stresses that the members eschew 'artificial simplicity', which he illustrates by choice of pipe.[155] The ubiquitous smoking, which Chapter 1 linked to metaphors of reading, again accompanies aimless conversation. After a meal, the club members 'lit their pipes and discussed a topic which was very frequently discussed at the club. Almost every member was an authority on it. They discussed the best means for securing success.'[156] Of course, they lack the 'authority' of having achieved success itself. But in this case, as in all convivial club chatter in these works, ignorance of the material is no barrier to conversation.

As in the first episode of *The Bachelors' Club*, this story tells of a member who also acts as a waiter – the same Horace Lawes-Webster whose later success leads to his failure as a Failure:

> On one occasion he had broken the unwritten law of the club by appearing there in evening dress. Noting the coldness of his reception, he explained that he merely wore it professionally. Asked if he had obtained a post in a theatre orchestra for which he had been looking, he shook his head sadly. He had obtained some temporary work as a waiter.[157]

As in the Problem Club, Pain stresses the 'unwritten law[s]'. Evening dress is too clear a sign of success – except when it's a sign of the fall into the servant classes. As Zangwill did in the *Bachelors' Club*, Pain raises the idea of confusing members and waiters – although here a member is actually a waiter. Also, while the Bachelors are forbidden from using latch-keys for their homes, all the Failures use latch-keys to enter their clubs.

When Horace achieves a measure of success, he must leave the club. His emotions are comically mixed: '"I had always hoped that this would happen," he said mournfully.'[158] His fellows dismiss him from the club but tell him, 'Outside the club we shall hope to remain your friends.'[159] The bond of membership is a loss: their external friendship remains a fragile hope. His success is that he has 'become a tobacconist' by using a legacy to set himself up in business.[160] His fellow member, Wilder, says, 'You got the idea out of Robert Louis Stevenson,' cementing Pain's own literary links.[161] Instead of merely sitting with his fellow Failures blowing smoke and idly chatting, Horace will make profit from the smoking of others. Horace's metafailure, if you will, demonstrates the pathos of social mobility. Failure has created a community, but to move up in the world necessitates abandoning a community that has defined itself in opposition to traditional success. My argument throughout this study has been that the club story in general and the work of the *Idler* circle in particular are aimed at the readers educated by the 1870 Education Act, the newly literate and upwardly mobile. For readers of the clerk classes, the West

End club represents an aspiration of social and cultural belonging. But those readers, too, may need to leave a community in order to claim success and climb the social ladder. Leaving the Failure Club can be a sad occasion.

The pathos of social mobility

From the Bachelors' Club to the Failure Club, these clubs themselves are destined to fail. The rules that make the club possible also seed its destruction. The upfront declaration of rules puts everyone on an even footing, an equalising move. Yet many of the stories' plots turn on the violation of the rules and the attendant consequences for members. The cosy affect of the club and its abrupt exclusionary function work against each other. The humour exaggerates the background logic of the club. West End clubs derived their social cachet from the double valence of exclusivity: the club is made special because of the people (and the ways) it excludes. It bears repetition that *The Bachelors' Club* takes aim at the most ubiquitous and fundamental assumption behind Clubland: its opposition to marriage, which, as Zangwill highlights, often shades into an opposition to women, who are excluded as a matter of course from most historical and fictional West End clubs. Zangwill bakes into his structure the notion that a club based on exclusivity by sex cannot endure.

Zangwill's template structure also emphasises the pathos of social mobility. Just as the Failures must leave the club through their change in social state, so too must the Bachelors. And who better to understand the double-edged sword of social mobility than a path-breaking Anglo-Jewish celebrity?[162] During this time, Zangwill kept one foot in the Jewish and mainstream presses, writing for the *Idler* and his own *Puck* as well as the *Jewish Standard*. *Children of the Ghetto* made him an international bestseller in 1892, the *Idler*'s first year. Although the West End club and the ghetto seem to fall on opposite ends of social exclusivity, the ghetto, in a way, is a club formed out of a shared experience of exclusion. Leaving the ghetto, like leaving the Failure Club or engaging in drastic social mobility, is a loss as well as a gain.

The Jewish community appears in one episode of *The Old Maids' Club*. Notably, the narrator is a Christian who inadvertently wanders into a shivah service, a ritual of mourning that

occurs at the home for the seven days after a burial. Jewish practices here are seen from the outside by a man who only gradually
figures out what's going on. The comic situation arises from the
Jews' desire to make up a minyan, the minimum number of people
required to say Kaddish, the essential element of the mourning
service. Traditionally, ten adult Jewish men are required, consti-
tuting a club of sorts. As they discuss the difficulty of finding a
minyan on a weekday, some members of the gathering question
the rules, one suggesting that Fanny, a Jewish woman present,
could 'count in quite as well as any man', which she herself dis-
misses as 'irreligious'.[163] Fanny provides the link to the Old Maids'
Club. This story, undoubtedly first conceived as a stand-alone
journalistic piece, makes its way into the novel by Lillie claiming to
have rewritten Fanny's statement of application to the club, divin-
ing her suitor's true identity. Lillie also disqualifies Fanny from
membership in the Old Maids' Club by virtue of her 'race'. When
Lord Silverdale exclaims, 'You surely are not going to degrade
your Club by anti-Semitism,'[164] Lillie explains that Fanny's orthodox desire to marry within her faith lowers her value as an Old
Maid: 'Already by her religion she is condemned to almost total
celibacy.'[165] The small number of Jews in the population at large
renders being an Old Maid less remarkable. Zangwill satirises his
own culture's exclusivity, including the prohibition on interfaith
marriage, which here bumps up against the Old Maids' Club's
own exclusive rules.

As Zangwill well knew, rules that seem arbitrary and nonsen-
sical from the outside – like etiquette or halacha (Jewish law) –
can provide a strong sense of community within a group. Pain's
Problem Club in particular highlights that aspect: the most stable
club in this chapter, its rules dictate behaviour puzzling to an
external observer. The clubs in the following chapter take this
theme to a different level, one that stresses the mystery of the club
and the ways in which it contrasts with more organic friendship.
In a way, the clubs in this chapter are surprising not in their dissolution but in the positive affect that they convey. Both authors,
Zangwill especially, combine that positive affect with social critique. In keeping with the 'Idler's Club' and *Tommy and Co.*, the
question of women's inclusion features prominently. Although
the ambiguity of their humour makes several readings available, women in general come out rather well. The Old Maids'
Club may never form, but Pain's female clubs counterbalance

his male clubs. At the most conservative, women appear here as a salutary counterpart to silly men. Yet it hardly seems a stretch to see the rule excluding women portrayed as the silliest of all.

Notes

1 Findon, *The Playgoers' Club 1884 to 1905.*
2 Cloy, *Muscular Mirth*, 7. Rochelson, *A Jew in the Public Arena*, 14.
3 Zangwill wrote about the pogroms, most famously in *The Melting Pot* (1908), which strongly argued against limitations on immigration.
4 Kent Puckett connects the etiquette book to the novel through studies of form. In an American context, John F. Kasson discusses the relationship between etiquette and democracy. Kasson, *Rudeness and Civility*; Puckett, *Bad Form.*
5 Day, *Hints on Etiquette*, 44–6.
6 American Resident in the United Kingdom, *'Good Form' in England*, 21. A duke is, of course, below royalty, but 'Royalty is not *in* society, it is *above* it' (20).
7 Observer of Men and Things, *Blunders in Behaviour Corrected*, 21.
8 East London Editor, *The Habits of Good Society*, 13. Barbara Black discusses this example. Black, *A Room of His Own*, 12.
9 Milne-Smith, *London Clubland*, 45, 49.
10 Milne-Smith, *London Clubland*, 45.
11 Milne-Smith, *London Clubland*, 63.
12 Adams, *Dandies and Desert Saints*, 64.
13 Milne-Smith, *London Clubland*, 111.
14 Black, *A Room of His Own*, 21.
15 Humble, 'From Holmes to the Drones', 97–8.
16 Milne-Smith, *London Clubland*, 149.
17 'New Books', *Yorkshire Herald, and the York Herald*, 17 June 1891, *19th-Century British Library Newspapers: Part II* (14 May 2015).
18 Review of Zangwill, *Bachelors' Club*, *Morning Post*, 24 June 1891, *19th-Century British Library Newspapers: Part II* (14 May 2015).
19 Review of Zangwill, *Bachelors' Club*.
20 *The Devon and Exeter Daily Gazette* (Exeter, England), Monday, 11 May 1891, p. 7; Issue 13890. *British Newspapers, Part III: 1780–1950.*

21   Rochelson, *A Jew in the Public Arena*, 146.

22   Rochelson, *A Jew in the Public Arena*, 138.

23   Milne-Smith, *London Clubland*, 162.

24   In this way, it resembles what Carolyn Williams calls 'gender parody' in the context of Gilbert and Sullivan. The duo, particularly Gilbert, have often been criticised for conservative gender politics, but Williams points out the flexibility of their representation and the multiple readings inherent in it. Williams, *Gilbert and Sullivan*.

25   Zangwill, *Bachelors' Club*, 109.

26   Their phrase is 'killed into art'. Gilbert and Gubar, *The Madwoman in the Attic*, 18.

27   Zangwill, *Bachelors' Club*, in *Celibates' Club*, 293.

28   Zangwill, *Bachelors' Club*, 1.

29   *The Club of Odd Volumes Year Book for 1922.*

30   Zangwill, *Bachelors' Club*, 1.

31   Milne-Smith, *London Clubland*, 154. (See also 157–8.)

32   Janice Radway describes it in this way, framing a feminist politics of reading as escapism. Radway, *Reading the Romance*, 57.

33   Zangwill, *Bachelors' Club*, 1–2.

34   *The Latchkey* is also the name of a contemporary journal of New Woman studies.

35   Zangwill, *Bachelors' Club*, 2.

36   Zangwill, *Bachelors' Club*, 2.

37   Zangwill, *Bachelors' Club*, 2.

38   Zangwill, *Bachelors' Club*, 3.

39   Inspired in part by Jean-Jacques Lecercle's reading of Carroll, although he might not agree with the last turn. Lecercle, *Philosophy of Nonsense*.

40   Zangwill, *Bachelors' Club*, 5.

41   Valverde, 'The Love of Finery', 183.

42   Zangwill, *Bachelors' Club*, 3.

43   Michael Rogin traces this logic in terms of Jewish blackface, particularly by Al Jolson. Rogin, 'Blackface, White Noise', 434.

44   Zangwill, *Bachelors' Club*, 10.

45   Marcus, *Between Women*.

46   Zangwill, *Bachelors' Club*, 23.

47   Zangwill, *Bachelors' Club*, 5.

48   See Fiss, '*The Idler*'s Club', 417.

49   Zangwill, *Bachelors' Club*, 6.

50   Zangwill, *Bachelors' Club*, 6.

51 Zangwill, *Bachelors' Club*, 6.
52 Zangwill, *Bachelors' Club*, 6.
53 Zangwill, *Bachelors' Club*, 7.
54 Zangwill, *Bachelors' Club*, 7.
55 Zangwill, *Bachelors' Club*, 7.
56 'A quibble is the golden apple for which he will always turn aside from his career or stoop from his elevation.' Johnson, 'The Preface to Shakespeare', 1224.
57 Zangwill, *Old Maids' Club*, in *Celibates' Club*, 312–13.
58 Zangwill, *Old Maids' Club*, 314.
59 Zangwill, *Old Maids' Club*, 317.
60 Zangwill, *Old Maids' Club*, 320.
61 Zangwill, *Old Maids' Club*, 588.
62 Zangwill, *Old Maids' Club*, 386.
63 Zangwill, *Old Maids' Club*, 426.
64 Zangwill, *Old Maids' Club*, 624.
65 W. S. Gilbert, *Princess Ida*, in *The Complete Annotated Gilbert and Sullivan*, 547.
66 Pain, *Stories*, 74.
67 Pain, *Stories*, 74.
68 Pain, *Stories*, 74.
69 Pain, *Stories*, 74.
70 Pain, *Stories*, 73.
71 Pain, *Stories*, 74.
72 Pain, *Stories*, 78.
73 Pain, *Stories*, 73.
74 Pain, *Stories*, 78.
75 Pain, *Stories*, 80.
76 Pain, *Stories*, 80.
77 Pain, *Stories*, 74.
78 Pain, *Problem Club*, 6.
79 Pain, *Problem Club*, 6.
80 Pain, *Problem Club*, 3.
81 Pain, *Problem Club*, 3.
82 Doyle, 'Final Problem', 559. See Langbauer, *Novels of Everyday Life*, 152.
83 Pain, *Problem Club*, 3–4.
84 Pain, *Problem Club*, 4.
85 Pain, *Problem Club*, 4.
86 Pain, *Problem Club*, 4.
87 Pain, *Problem Club*, 6.

88   Dickens, *The Pickwick Papers*, 86–7.
89   Pain, *Problem Club*, 5.
90   Pain, *Problem Club*, 4.
91   Milne-Smith, *London Clubland*, 92.
92   This is the subject of ongoing work in collaboration with Troy Bassett.
93   Sladen, *Who's Who* (1897), 29–31. For Pain's membership, *Who's Who* (1904), 1173.
94   Pain, *Problem Club*, 11.
95   Jerome in particular has many volumes that essentially consist of the records of inconsequential conversation among friends, including *Novel Notes* and the mixed-sex *Tea Table Talk* (1903). Even *Three Men in a Boat*, which is nominally a travelogue, derives much of its delight from the conversation among the eponymous three men (to say nothing of the dog).
96   Pain, *Problem Club*, 8.
97   Pain, *Problem Club*, 7.
98   Pain, *Problem Club*, 67.
99   Pain, *Problem Club*, 7.
100 Pain, *Problem Club*, 8.
101 Pain, *Problem Club*, 8–9.
102 Pain, *Problem Club*, 122.
103 Pain, *Problem Club*, 235.
104 Pain, *Problem Club*, 218.
105 Pain, *Problem Club*, 233.
106 Pain, *Problem Club*, 230.
107 Pain, *Problem Club*, 227.
108 The passage that this paraphrases will be treated in detail in the next chapter.
109 Pain, *Problem Club*, 8.
110 Pain, *Problem Club*, 13, 16–17, 6.
111 Pain, *Problem Club*, 99–100.
112 Pain, *Problem Club*, 99.
113 Pain, *Problem Club*, 88.
114 Pain, *Problem Club*, 187.
115 Pain, *Problem Club*, 188.
116 Pain, *Problem Club*, 94.
117 Pain, *Problem Club*, 94–5.
118 Zangwill, *Bachelors' Club*, in *Celibates' Club*, 70.
119 Pain, *Problem Club*, 235.
120 Pain, *Problem Club*, 24.

121   Pain, *Problem Club*, 23.
122   Pain, *Problem Club*, 24.
123   Pain, *Problem Club*, 26.
124   Pain, *Problem Club*, 28.
125   Rubin, 'The Traffic in Women', 392–413.
126   Pain, *Problem Club*, 28.
127   Pain, *Problem Club*, 30.
128   Pain, *Problem Club*, 31–2.
129   Pain, *Problem Club*, 34.
130   Pain, *Problem Club*, 34.
131   Pain, *Problem Club*, 36.
132   Pain, *Problem Club*, 37.
133   Pain, *Problem Club*, 37–8.
134   Pain, *Problem Club*, 38.
135   Pain, *Problem Club*, 4.
136   Pain, *Problem Club*, 36–7.
137   Pain, *Problem Club*, 39.
138   Pain, *Problem Club*, 39.
139   Pain, *Problem Club*, 39.
140   Pain, *Problem Club*, 9.
141   Pain, *Problem Club*, 16.
142   Pain, *Problem Club*, 10.
143   Zangwill, *Bachelors' Club*, 147.
144   Pain, *Problem Club*, 67.
145   Pain, *Problem Club*, 74.
146   Pain, *Problem Club*, 218.
147   Pain, *Problem Club*, 226.
148   Pain, *Problem Club*, 235.
149   Pain, *One Kind*, 272.
150   Pain, *One Kind*, 273.
151   Pain, *One Kind*, 273.
152   Pain, *One Kind*, 272.
153   Stevenson, *Arabian*, 26.
154   Pain, *One Kind*, 273.
155   Pain, *One Kind*, 273.
156   Pain, *One Kind*, 274.
157   Pain, *One Kind*, 277.
158   Pain, *One Kind*, 282.
159   Pain, *One Kind*, 282.
160   Pain, *One Kind*, 277.
161   Pain, *One Kind*, 278.

162 *Children of the Ghetto* is often described as the first Anglo-Jewish bestseller. Biographer Meri-Jane Rochelson points out that 'Zangwill's obituary appeared on the front page of the *New York Times*.' Winehouse; Rochelson, *Jew in the Public Arena*, 17.

163 Zangwill, *Old Maids' Club*, 479.

164 Zangwill, *Old Maids' Club*, 489.

165 Zangwill, *Old Maids' Club*, 489.

4

The Mysteries of Male Friendship: Uncovering the Club in Stevenson, Doyle, Chesterton and Sayers

This chapter features novels and short stories with a different approach to the club and its rules. These works, by Robert Louis Stevenson, Arthur Conan Doyle, G. K. Chesterton and Dorothy Sayers, all feature clubs within the emerging genre of detective fiction. In many of them, the club itself is the solution to the mystery: seemingly inexplicable behaviour becomes explicable thanks to the arbitrary, silly rules of the club. The frame of the mystery brings the question of club rules into slightly different focus, aligning them with some of the classic perspectives on 'reading the city'. This chapter presents a different approach than its predecessors to the presentation, rules and affect of the club. In a way that may be more familiar to common narratives of the *fin de siècle*, the club appears sinister rather than jovial.[1] This is the club as secret society, as looming force, which recent criticism features more than the club as friendly gathering place.[2] Yet these two approaches are closer than might at first appear. Both strongly value friendships between men. In the works in this chapter, friendship dyads exist outside the club, rather than within it. These male friendships are, to redirect Laurie Langbauer's phrase, 'the real mystery'.[3] While in Chapter 3, the clubs tried to codify male friendship with rules, here clubs threaten more organic male friendship dyads.

Many of the texts in this chapter lend themselves to the general *fin-de-siècle* narrative of danger and degeneracy in urban environments, in which reading the city and its inhabitants becomes a matter of physical and moral self-preservation. Stevenson and Doyle form part of the now classic canon of imperial Gothic, emphasising fears of reverse colonisation.[4] Unlike the organisation of the club stories from the previous chapter, this type of organisation views the club from the outside, not the inside. Although the presentation of the club rules differs, some of the fundamental points remain the same. These club rules are in general as arbitrary and ridiculous as those of the Problem Club or the Bachelors' Club, but they grow distinctly less humorous when not stated explicitly. When we see the club not from the perspective of a club member but a bystander – someone like a conversation partner of a Problem Club member trying to win the Giraffe Problem – it seems much more sinister. Like the more jovial club stories, these critique the imposition of arbitrary social rules. In so doing, they accentuate the extent to which clubs differ from 'real', spontaneous friendships between men.

In a sense, club rules formalise broader social expectations, such as 'gentlemanly' behaviour, in both its ethical and class connotations. Thus parodies of the club rules speak to larger social issues, as we have seen. One of the functions of a club is to facilitate friendships between its members. All club members share a certain bond: they may not automatically become friends by virtue of belonging to the same club, but it brings them a step closer. As we have already seen, even in a convivial club the institution – and especially the rules – of the club can get in the way of friendships, even ones it helped bring about or nurture. All the Bachelors and one of the Failures are forced through breaking a rule to leave the club, and the pain of separation from their friends tests those friendships. Even in the Problem Club, the problems pit the members against each other, and they use their friendships outside the clubs for their own gain. In these mysteries, friendship dyads exist outside the confines of the club, and the club thus serves as their foil.

If, according to the logic of the 'Idler's Club' column, a book or periodical is like a club, then the distrust of clubs' ability to institutionalise friendship reflects back onto the relationship these texts cultivate with readers. Detective fiction as a genre differs from light humour in its approach to the reader as well as its affective colour palette. The 'puzzle' aspect of a mystery involves a reader more or less overtly in attempting to solve the mystery, in collaboration or competition with the fictional detective. In the more humorous of these examples (not all are tremendously humorous), the metatextual appeal of humour combined with the metatextual appeal of detective fiction bend the fourth wall, placing increasing attention on the text's relationship with its reader. The mystery approach to the club calls certain aspects of reading into question, implicitly or explicitly, especially the approach to collectivity. Of all the friendships in these texts, none are more mysterious than those formed by readers.

From cream tarts to suicide

Robert Louis Stevenson's *The Suicide Club* (1878) is the earliest work in this study to fit some of the criteria of a club story. The club plays a different role in this short novel than in works such as *The Bachelors' Club* or *The Problem Club*. It is also not particularly funny. Stevenson's brief but brilliant career has taken on different emphases since his early death, but few regard him as a humorist. Nevertheless, Stevenson certainly could be humorous: as I have argued elsewhere, *A Child's Garden of Verses* contains subtle humour, and *The Wrong Box*, co-written with his stepson, Lloyd Osbourne, wears its humour prominently in its preface.[5] This late work, though not precisely a club story, features a tontine, which resembles a club. *The Suicide Club* is only funny until the nature of the club is revealed. At that point, the emphasis shifts to eliminating the club and its interference in the friendships between men.

Stevenson was an aspirational contact of the *Idler* circle. He published in both the *Idler* and *To-Day*, but not for the 'Idler's Club' column – although he did write an entry for 'My First Book', and *To-Day* carried an interview with him.[6] Several members of the *Idler* circle, particularly fellow Scotsmen Arthur Conan Doyle and J. M. Barrie, touted their connections to him – for instance, Barrie corresponded with him.[7] Stevenson's essay 'An Apology for Idlers' (*Cornhill* 1877) may have influenced the Idlers' views of idling. It begins with an epigraph dialogue between Johnson and Boswell, indicating Johnson's continuing association with the title *The Idler*. Jerome's 'Idle Thoughts' essays adopt a similar tone to this essay's style: light and combining the ironic with the nearly archaic, such as beginning a sentence with 'Nay'.[8] The substance of Stevenson's essay is an argument in favour of idleness, 'which does not consist in doing nothing, but in doing a great deal not recognised in the dogmatic formularies of the ruling class'.[9] Turning conventional wisdom on its head, he declares, 'Extreme *busyness*, whether at school or college, kirk or market, is a symptom of deficient vitality; and a faculty for idleness implies a catholic appetite and a strong sense of personal identity.'[10] This is not quite a Wildean epigram, but it has a similar logic to the reversals that Wilde and Zangwill favour.

Unlike the *Idler*, which clearly depicts reading the magazine as a sign of idling, Stevenson invokes books only as counterexamples. He contrasts idling with 'industry', in which he includes reading in its didactic sense: 'Books are good enough in their own way, but they are a mighty bloodless substitute for life. It seems a pity to sit, like the Lady of Shalott, peering into a mirror, with your back turned on all the bustle and glamour of reality.'[11] We shall see this type of sentiment again in the voice of one of Chesterton's characters. It may seem ironic that the message is delivered via print. Reading the *Cornhill*, however, hardly falls under the category of education (at least for Victorians); instead, it might be the type of truancy that Stevenson goes on to laud. As Nicholas Dames points out, W. M. Thackeray represented a schoolboy reading as a 'lazy idle boy'[12] – a depiction that was first published in the *Cornhill*.[13]

Certainly, some of the situations in which Stevenson calls for 'idleness' might be times when one might pick up a little light reading. For Stevenson, the lack of idleness is not activity: 'There is a sort of dead-alive, hackneyed people about, who are scarcely conscious of living except in the exercise of some conventional occupation. . . . If they have to wait an hour or so for a train, they fall into a stupid trance with their eyes open.'[14] Clearly, doing absolutely nothing does not count as proper idleness here. What else might someone do while waiting for a train? Pick up a book from a bookstall! Stevenson repeatedly uses the example of down time required by the railway, whose bookstalls made the fortunes of W. H. Smith: 'a mind vacant of all material of amusement, and not one thought to rub against another, while they wait for the train'.[15] Following Dames's theory, perhaps idle reading would provide those thoughts, comprising the reverie portion of attentive reading, for which a book itself is unnecessary.[16]

Stevenson's own fiction provided fodder for idleness. Fanny Stevenson describes *The Suicide Club*, which appeared the year after 'An Apology for Idlers' as a serial in *London: The Conservative Weekly* and later in book form in *New Arabian Nights*, as 'light fiction'.[17] It is not as light-hearted as some of Stevenson's other works, nor as clearly humorous; it falls more in the genre of adventure. The funniest part of it lies in the beginning, the curious incident that leads to the uncovering of the eponymous club. The narrative centres on the friendship between Prince Florizel of Bohemia and 'his confidant and Master of the Horse, Colonel Geraldine'.[18] Florizel resembles the bored Prince Orlofsky in Johan

Strauss's *Die Fledermaus* (1874): he must go out of his way to find amusement. Visiting London, enjoying the city's sights incognito, the pair encounter a young man going through a restaurant offering each patron a cream tart. If refused, he eats the tart himself. This seems like it could be the antics of a member of the Problem Club trying to be mistaken for someone else, or other such high jinks.

Initially the humour of 'The Young Man with the Cream Tarts', which is the title of the first chapter, seems to be the seriousness with which he approaches this ridiculous endeavour: '"Sir," said he, with a profound obeisance, proffering the tart at the same time between his thumb and forefinger, "will you so far honour an entire stranger? I can answer for the quality of the pastry, having eaten two dozen and three of them myself since five o'clock."'[19] When he offers Florizel a tart, the Prince questions him, and he says he offers them in 'the spirit . . . of mockery',[20] but he does not say whom or what he mocks. His grandest gesture consists in divesting himself of his final tarts so he can accept Florizel's invitation to supper:

> 'on this great day for me, when I am closing a career of folly by my most conspicuously silly action, I wish to behave handsomely to all who give me countenance. Gentlemen, you shall wait no longer. Although my constitution is shattered by previous excesses, at the risk of my life I liquidate the suspensory condition.'
>
> With these words he crushed the nine remaining tarts into his mouth, and swallowed them at a single movement each.[21]

The young man's elevated diction does indeed make his consumption of the tarts seem 'silly', and his claim to risk his life seems unquestionably hyperbolic. Yet it quickly emerges that this is indeed a matter of life and death.

As it turns out, the incongruity lies not in the young man's seriousness, but in his levity. During their supper, Florizel and Geraldine perceive, 'The young man was fluent and gay, but he laughed louder than was natural in a person of polite breeding; his hands trembled violently, and his voice took sudden and surprising inflections, which seemed to be independent of his will.'[22] He has not enough money to marry the girl of his choice, largely through 'squander[ing]'[23] his small inherited income through frivolities and gambling. He describes his life with bitter irony, stressing his 'manly accomplishments'[24] and their insufficiency for

practical purposes: 'From the whole tone of the young man's statement it was plain that he harboured very bitter and contemptuous
thoughts about himself.'[25] The intense irony in the young man's
speech comes close to humour except for its high stakes and proximity to more painful emotions.

This young man's thwarted love and self-loathing have driven
him to plan suicide, but, unwilling to do it himself, he proposes to
join the Suicide Club. His tart escapade liquidates his cash save for
a forty-pound subscription. Geraldine and Florizel pretend to be
'in the same condition'[26] of suicidal ideation in order to elicit his
story. He introduces the club as the outgrowth of modern technology, as exemplified by the railroad and the telegraph:

> There was one more convenience lacking to modern comfort; a decent,
> easy way to quit that stage; the back stairs to liberty; or, as I said this
> moment, Death's private door. This, my two fellow-rebels, is supplied
> by the Suicide Club. Do not suppose that you and I are alone, or even
> exceptional, in the highly reasonable desire that we profess. A large
> number of our fellow-men, who have grown heartily sick of the per-
> formance in which they are expected to join daily and all their lives
> long, are only kept from flight by one or two considerations. Some
> have families who would be shocked, or even blamed, if the matter
> became public; others have a weakness at heart and recoil from the
> circumstances of death. That is, to some extent, my own experience.
> I cannot put a pistol to my head and draw the trigger; for something
> stronger than myself withholds the act; and although I loathe life, I
> have not strength enough in my body to take hold of death and be
> done with it. For such as I, and for all who desire to be out of the coil
> without posthumous scandal, the Suicide Club has been inaugurated.[27]

Although the Suicide Club has no explicit gender requirements,
these terms are distinctly masculine. In fact, they show men wres-
tling with their own masculinity. The young man frames his inability to commit suicide without aid as a deficiency in strength, yet
the struggle with 'something stronger than [him]self' might be
a positive force. His weakness, in this case, might be seen as a
strength. The text as a whole hardly advocates suicide, particularly
by these means.

Parallels to Pain and Zangwill's club descriptions are not coincidental, as Pain explicitly imitates Stevenson. The description
of the club's rules and procedures renders it both legitimate and

mysterious by placing it within the context of Clubland, imagined and imaginary. This club, it emerges, has rules, procedures and premises like its fictional and non-fictional fellows. After paying their forty-pound subscription, men who, like the eponymous young man, cannot support themselves, can live at the club. At each nightly gathering a ceremony occurs, centring on an ordinary deck of cards, from which every member draws. The ace of spades marks the member for death. Whoever draws the ace of clubs administers that death at the precise direction of the club and its president. At the first meeting the Prince and Geraldine attend, there are eighteen members, a gathering the President describes as 'middling'.[28] The President interviews prospective members before allowing them to join – or even admitting that the club exists. The young man knows about it through late members: 'More than one of my friends has preceded me, where I knew I must shortly follow.'[29] Although dead members cannot propose candidates, a logic of friendship and recommendation remains, in a macabre form.

Unlike the fictional clubs of previous chapters, this is hardly a cheerful place. The members seem more thrown together than clubbable: 'As in all other places of resort, one type predominated: people in the prime of youth, with every show of intelligence and sensibility in their appearance, but with little promise of strength or the quality that makes success. Few were much above thirty, and not a few were still in their teens.'[30] Again, the drive to the Suicide Club (if not to suicide itself) is described in terms of weakness. Indeed, the gathering is far from pleasant:

> There was little decency among the members of the club. Some boasted of the disgraceful actions, the consequences of which had reduced them to seek refuge in death; and the others listened without disapproval. There was a tacit understanding against moral judgments; and whoever passed the club doors enjoyed already some of the immunities of the tomb. They drank to each other's memories, and to those of notable suicides in the past. They compared and developed their different views of death – some declaring that it was no more than blackness and cessation; others full of a hope that that very night they should be scaling the stars and commercing with the mighty dead.[31]

The club operates under its own social rules, which starkly differ from ordinary 'decency', but which afford the members some 'enjoy[ment]'. Florizel thinks, 'If a man has made up his mind to kill himself, let him do it, in God's name, like a gentleman.'[32] Clearly, Florizel frames this courage in terms of class and gender, implying that the club is not for 'gentlemen'. The text thus does not completely repudiate suicide.

But some club members frame the club in terms of amusement or pleasure, more like the terms of a conventional club. When the club's president interviews the prospective new members, the Prince gives his reason for being tired of life as 'unadulterated laziness'. When challenged, he continues, 'I have no more money. . . . That is also a vexation, without doubt. It brings my sense of idleness to an acute point.'[33] Geraldine seeks out the one older, seemingly calmer member, a victim of paralysis, and discovers he's a type of 'honorary member'[34] who has been coming to the club at intervals for two years. The aptly named Mr Malthus describes it as a cheap thrill:

'If my enfeebled health could support the excitement more often, you may depend upon it I should be more often here. It requires all the sense of duty engendered by a long habit of ill-health and careful regimen, to keep me from excess in this, which is, I may say, my last dissipation. I have tried them all, sir,' he went on, laying his hand on Geraldine's arm, 'all without exception, and I declare to you, upon my honour, there is not one of them that has not been grossly and untruthfully overrated. People trifle with love. Now, I deny that love is a strong passion. Fear is the strong passion; it is with fear that you must trifle, if you wish to taste the intense joys of living. Envy me – envy me, sir,' he added with a chuckle, 'I am a coward!'[35]

For Malthus, the club is a way of experiencing 'strong passion'. He enjoys the gambling aspect of the club, in the way that Pain imitates in his Colonel at the Proposal Club.

But Malthus's sensory enjoyment also manifests as extreme bodily discomfort. When it comes time to draw the cards, 'The members were all very quiet and intent; every one was pale, but none so pale as Mr Malthus. His eyes protruded; his head kept nodding involuntarily upon his spine; his hands found their way, one after the other, to his mouth, where they made clutches at his tremulous and ashen lips. It was plain that the honorary member enjoyed his membership on very startling terms.'[36] Even the Prince 'was conscious of a growing and almost suffocating excitement;

but he had somewhat of the gambler's nature, and recognised almost with astonishment that there was a degree of pleasure in his sensations.'[37] But indeed he is not to enjoy the sensations for long, as the young man with the cream tarts draws the ace of clubs, signifying he is to be the 'club's agent'. Malthus draws the ace of spades, marking him for death: 'but when Mr Malthus turned up his card a horrible noise, like that of something breaking, issued from his mouth; and he rose from his seat and sat down again, with no sign of his paralysis. It was the ace of spades. The honorary member had trifled once too often with his terrors.'[38] The horror rather than the comic certainly predominates here – for both men, as the young man with the cream tarts 'remained frozen with horror, the card still resting on his finger; he had not come there to kill, but to be killed'.[39] In a sense, the rendering of the first victim of the Suicide Club – and the only one to actually be killed – as unwilling, rather than the willing if ambivalent young man of the cream tarts, makes the tale more straightforwardly a thriller, more a murder.

The president of the club is distinctly the villain of the piece. Part of the club's problem is its top-down organisation: the President never competes himself, and he is represented throughout as a conniving, sinister figure who preys on the unfortunate. It is he, not the young man with the cream tarts, who is judged responsible for Malthus's death (in addition to the risk-seeker himself), and the young man is granted a happy ending. The club itself only lasts for the first chapter, but the President remains. In the third and final chapter, the Prince kills him in a duel.

The club nearly forms the Prince's undoing but is bested by the central friendship dyad. On the second meeting of the Suicide Club, the Prince draws the fatal ace of spades, but Geraldine rescues him by disobeying a direct order. The members of the club are collected and brought before the Prince, who promises to dispense justice and help. Addressing the members collectively, he says,

> Foolish and wicked men . . . as many of you as have been driven into this strait by the lack of fortune shall receive employment and remuneration from my officers. Those who suffer under a sense of guilt must have recourse to a higher and more generous Potentate than I. I feel pity for all of you, deeper than you can imagine; to-morrow you shall tell me your stories; and as you answer more frankly, I shall be the more able to remedy your misfortunes.[40]

The conclusion of the tale reveals that the eponymous young man *'is now a comfortable householder in Wigmore Street, Cavendish Square'*.[41] Presumably, the Prince gives him the wherewithal to marry, and his 'comfort' seems to extend to moral absolution for his murder.

The true bond between men beats the false one. The Prince is capable of true friendship, both with the young man with the cream tarts and with Geraldine. Geraldine rescues him, in an act of class-inflected friendship (for we are consistently reminded that he is the Prince's subordinate), and all becomes well. As the Prince faces his doom, he tells himself, 'Come, come, I must be a man.'[42] And when Geraldine saves him, 'The Prince threw himself upon the Colonel's neck in a passion of relief.'[43] This is certainly an intense friendship, whether or not it contains the 'homoerotic secret' Barbara Black reads in *The Suicide Club*'s second chapter. Indubitably, their friendship emphasises the breaking of rules.[44] Yet certain social rules remain unbroken, including Geraldine's fundamentally subordinate relationship to his social superior.

Baker Street vs the clubs

Sherlock Holmes and John Watson form the most iconic friendship established through and in relation to a series of mysteries – and indeed their friendship shapes the mystery as a genre. Particularly early on in the series, several of the mysteries involve obscure clubs or clublike structures, most of which are sinister. The clubs and the havoc they wreak on the relationships between their members highlight the enduring friendship between Holmes and Watson: an unequal duo against the shadow world.

Clubs or secret societies seem to appear in the Holmes stories around key moments in Holmes and Watson's relationship, including the eponymous group in *The Sign of the Four* (in which Watson meets his future wife), many of the early adventures that establish their relationship, and 'The Adventure of the Empty House', in which Holmes seemingly returns from the dead. The latter story's mystery (other than the obvious one about Holmes's escape from Reichenbach Falls) centres around the murder of Robin Adair and, in typical fashion, the killer, Sebastian Moran, is caught before we find out the reason for the murder. Adair had caught Moran cheating at cards and planned to expose him: 'The exclusion from his clubs would mean ruin to Moran, who lived by his ill-gotten card-gains.'[45] Club membership and the breaking of rules that enforce gentlemanly behaviour are literally a matter of life and death to these clubmen. Viewing Watson as a stand-in for the reader has become a critical commonplace, yet it bears stating that these pivotal moments in Holmes and Watson's friendship are also pivotal moments in Holmes's relationship with the reader. In many accounts of Doyle's career, Holmes seems to take on a life of his own that competes with Doyle's own, leading Doyle to describe 'The Final Problem' in his diary as 'Killed Holmes'.[46] Readers responded personally to Holmes's 'death': one letter to Doyle began 'You brute', and tales abound of the public wearing black armbands and possibly assaulting Doyle in the street with umbrellas.[47] The contrasting of Holmes and Watson's relationship to a club may have helped inculcate this feeling. As the stories' popularity persists, some readers may have experienced their own relationships with the story and its central character as a dyad; others have responded through forming their own clubs, most famously the Baker Street Irregulars.

'The Red-Headed League', the second story in *The Adventures of Sherlock Holmes* published in the *Strand* in August 1891, establishes Holmes and Watson's relationship in contrast to a club-like structure. The League of Red-Headed Men is not precisely a club, but it has a similar logic and similarly arbitrary rules. As Holmes unravels this 'three-pipe problem', he discovers that the entire League is a fabrication designed to get Jabez Wilson out of his workplace during the day so that a gang of criminals can dig a tunnel from his office to a nearby bank for the purposes of robbing it, a plan which Holmes foils.[48] Because both Wilson and one of the gang members have red hair, they concoct a false League, place an advertisement in the newspaper, and Wilson's assistant (a member of the gang) points it out to him.[49] Watson, Holmes and the reader are presented with the advertisement first to heighten the mystery. Like many sections in the paper – especially the 'agony' column, which features in so many Holmes stories – this advertisement is circulated to a mass audience but intended for a single reader within that larger community. Yet the Red-Headed League is funny, at least to Holmes and Watson. When their client recounts finding the notice of its dissolution, they laugh: 'Sherlock Holmes and I surveyed this curt announcement and the rueful face behind it, until the comical side of the affair so completely over-topped every other consideration that we both burst out into a roar of laughter.'[50] Although their client, the erstwhile club member, finds their laughter offensive, laughter at the club's expense bonds Holmes and Watson, even though the latter still lacks the key to the mystery.

Doyle's most famous club – and perhaps the best-known of all the fictional clubs in this study – is the Diogenes. The club actually plays a small part in 'The Adventure of the Greek Interpreter' – Sidney Paget's illustrations for the story do not show its interior – but it looms much larger in adaptations of the Sherlock Holmes stories. The Diogenes first appears when Holmes introduces Watson to his brother, Mycroft: 'The Diogenes Club is the queerest club in London, and Mycroft one of the queerest men. He's always there from quarter to five to twenty to eight.'[51] Holmes clearly links Mycroft and the club when he promises 'to introduce [Watson] to two curiosities'.[52] This introduction of Mycroft makes his primary association to Sherlock seem to be one of club membership.

Watson (and the reader) first meet Mycroft in the Stranger's Room of the Diogenes Club. Stranger's Rooms were common in West End clubs – a stranger being a non-club member[53] – and in the Diogenes it is the only room that allows talking. Mycroft and Holmes are connected through membership to a club in which Watson is a stranger, and a club whose members are ironically connected through their antisociability. This club can thus also be seen as one which serves as a foil to a close male friendship dyad. The Holmes brothers clearly share a bond: they survey passers-by through the Diogenes Club's bow window (à la Beau Brummel), in which Mycroft proves Sherlock's assertion that he exceeds his detective brother in deduction. Yet it is Watson with whom Sherlock chooses to live, whom he finds most useful to his work, and with whom he is uniquely close.[54] The logic of the club groups men together by their commonalities – such as theatrical activities in the case of the Garrick Club – but Holmes and Watson's friendship is based on their opposite, complementary qualities.

The Diogenes Club highlights these contrasting qualities, particularly in terms of emotion. 'The Greek Interpreter' begins with Watson's description of Holmes's social isolation, particularly his habit of not mentioning his family: 'This reticence upon his part had increased the somewhat inhuman effect which he produced upon me, until sometimes I found myself regarding him as an isolated phenomenon, a brain without a heart, as deficient in human sympathy as he was pre-eminent in intelligence.'[55] When Holmes first brings Mycroft up, Watson is surprised because he had not realised that Holmes had a brother. Holmes is also not entirely unemotional. In 'The Adventure of the Three Garridebs', first published in the January 1925 number of the *Strand*, Watson receives a bullet to the thigh during a confrontation with a criminal, and Holmes expresses deep concern, which gratifies Watson:

> It was worth a wound – it was worth many wounds – to know the depth of loyalty and love which lay behind that cold mask. The clear, hard eyes were dimmed for a moment, and the firm lips were shaking. For the one and only time I caught a glimpse of a great heart as well as of a great brain. All my years of humble but single-minded service culminated in that moment of revelation.[56]

The juxtaposition of 'heart' and 'brain' hearken back to the opening of 'The Greek Interpreter'. Holmes may be more like Watson than first appears. Still, after so many years of acquaintance, Holmes remains a bit of a mystery to Watson – as well, perhaps, as to the reader. But there can be no doubt of their friendship's intensity, which needs no rules or official club premises to cement it.

Yet the Diogenes Club, as described by Holmes, is fundamentally a club for readers:

> There are many men in London, you know, who, some from shyness, some from misanthropy, have no wish for the company of their fellows. Yet they are not averse to comfortable chairs and the latest periodicals. It is for the convenience of these that the Diogenes Club was started, and it now contains the most unsociable and unclubbable men in town. No member is permitted to take the least notice of any other one. Save in the Stranger's Room, no talking is, under any circumstances, allowed, and three offences, if brought to the notice of the committee, render the talker liable to expulsion.[57]

Without the *Idler* context, this notion of a club for 'unclubbable men' seems uncharacteristically funny for Doyle. Like Zangwill and Pain, Doyle fundamentally addresses one of the ironies of real London clubs: they may have seemed to be about engaging in social interactions with one's peers, but they could often be antisocial in a number of ways. Yet the Diogenes *is* social, in ways that may not be obviously apparent. The allure of the club is 'comfortable chairs and the latest periodicals'. In other words, the Diogenes Club is a space of reading. Engaged in literary sociability, they shut out their immediate companions.[58] Holmes expresses the pleasure of membership: 'I have myself found it a very soothing atmosphere.'[59] Although Watson generally serves as the reader's avenue to Holmes, silent reading gives readers membership to a club in which Watson is a stranger. Holmes is at home in a group of silent readers.

Queer trades, queer city

Of all the works in this chapter, G. K. Chesterton's *The Club of Queer Trades* is the most conventional club story and the funniest. It was originally serialised in the *Idler* in 1904 (with illustrations by the author), but Chesterton was not part of the key social/ professional circle of the *Idler* – for instance, he never wrote for the 'Idler's Club' column. Chesterton's interests and reputation are wide-ranging, even in the context of the other figures in this study: from the Father Brown detective novels to literary criticism to religious philosophy.[60] Given this, it might be surprising just how much *The Club of Queer Trades* appears in dialogue with the club story tradition. *The Club of Queer Trades* forms a kind of hybrid, combining the club as sinister and the club as jovial, and also combining the explicit description of rules and the emergence of rules through detection. The club only seems sinister, according to Chesterton, when its rules are unknown.

The form of *The Club of Queer Trades* combines some elements of the rule-first organisation with the detection model. In both serial and book forms, the novel begins by describing the club, its premises and its rules 'as we afterwards discovered it to be',[61] then proceeds to tell the story of how the narrator discovered the club. The novel is arranged like a series of detective stories: each chapter presents a series of problems or odd incidents to which the club and one of its members' 'queer trades' provides the solution. In each chapter, individuals behave in odd ways that challenge the protagonists' ways of reading the city; then, gradually, the actions are explained in a way that comes back to the eponymous club. In this case, the nature of the club leads to the pattern of repetition. Hence, even though the novel begins with the club's premise, it also reveals the club slowly over its course: a fusion of the treatments of club rules. Like the Diogenes, the Club of Queer Trades is a paradox: a club whose members have in common that they are unique. Specifically, each member has to be the only one who pursues a particular trade. These trades include Professional Detainers, who arrange for the protagonists to miss a dinner engagement so that their client can be alone with a woman to whom he wishes to propose; the Adventure and Romance Agency, which stages elaborate scenarios that mimic sensation novels (a sort of LARP *avant-la-lettre*); and an Arboreal House-Agent, who sells, and lives in, treehouses. Notably, most of the discoveries of the trades derive from a difficulty in reading a social situation, reading the city, and/or reading the character of an individual.

The Club of Queer Trades directly parodies the Holmes brothers' confidence in reading the city. Unlike many of the other club stories, the bulk of the novel is not devoted to the activities and conversations of members within the club, but of a small group of men who keep encountering members of the club engaging in their various professions: a detective, Rupert Grant; his lackadaisical brother, Basil; and a narrator, Charles 'Gully' Swinburne. In contrast to Holmes, Rupert is comically inept as a detective. And although Basil is vastly superior at unravelling the mysteries the Club of Queer Trades presents, he is not infallible. In fact, we are told from the outset that he is insane. The first curious situation leading to a member of the Club of Queer Trades comes to the group's attention through an official case on which Rupert is employed, but the others arise in the course of the men's everyday lives. In several cases, the adventure stems from the question of judging or reading character, either the character of an acquaintance (Professor Chadd or Lieutenant Keith) or of a complete stranger. In the second chapter, Basil notices a man on the street, forms a negative impression of his character, and follows him to his destination, which turns out to be the home of a mutual acquaintance. In the final chapter, Rupert comes to a similar conclusion that a milkman he encounters in the street is up to no good. He and Charlie follow the milkman and investigate the house at which he stops – in this case, with no reliance on a previous acquaintanceship.

In each of these two cases, the brother is wrong. Neither man they identify as suspicious is particularly at fault. The milkman is completely innocuous, and the man whom Basil identifies at first sight as 'the wickedest man in London'[62] turns out to be operating under a rather mild deceit by employing a member of the Club of Queer Trades to both write witty repartee for him and be the butt of his jokes. Pursuing both men through the darkened streets, Basil identifies not the seemingly wicked man but the member of the Club of Queer Trades as a 'scoundrel',[63] knocking him down and rifling through his pockets to solve this mystery – solely for his own gratification.

It turns out, however, that Basil plays an active role in the Club of Queer Trades. In the final chapter, Charlie and Rupert find their way to the club's annual dinner, wherein it emerges that not only is Basil the president of the club, but he also therefore is a practitioner of a 'queer trade', which ends up being the solution to the chapter's mystery (which started with the milkman). When Charlie introduces Basil in the first place, he says that Basil used to be a judge, but 'suddenly went mad on the bench'. In addition to singing a comic song, Basil demonstrates his madness through an unconventional approach to his profession: 'He accused criminals from the bench, not so much of their obvious legal crimes, but of things that had never been heard of in a court of justice, monstrous egoism, lack of humor, and morbidity deliberately encouraged.'[64] At the Club of Queer Trades dinner, Charlie and Rupert discover that Basil has in fact become a judge of these kinds of crimes: 'I offered myself privately as a purely moral judge to settle purely moral differences.'[65] All parties seem to agree to abide by his judgments and his sentencing; the mystery of this chapter ends up being a woman sentenced to solitary confinement for 'breaking off an engagement through backbiting'.[66] She provokes the mystery by refusing to emerge from her prison until Basil gives her permission.

The 'queer trades' themselves frequently relate to reading. The first trade the novel presents, the Adventure and Romance Agency, allows its clients to live out a book. The case that leads to the discovery of the club begins when a client approaches Rupert and suggests that Basil and the narrator, Charles 'Gully' Swinburne, might prove useful (in a very Holmes-Watson fashion). Brown recounts a tale of surprise and excitement: he has had an inexplicable adventure involving cryptic messages spelled out in his favourite flower, riddles pronounced by a seemingly disembodied head, and a mysterious damsel in distress. They trace the source to a business, where a man presents Brown with a bill. Basil deduces that there has been a mix-up, and Brown has been mistaken for someone else. The business is the Adventure and

Romance Agency, which provides the experience of living in a novel: staff writers script adventures, which are then acted out for the subscribers in the course of their everyday lives. Nevertheless, its founder couches his description as a critique of reading, which echoes some of Stevenson's language in 'An Apology for Idlers':

> It has continually struck us that there is no element in modern life that is more lamentable than the fact that the modern man has to seek all artistic existence in a sedentary state. If he wishes to float into fairy-land, he reads a book; if he wishes to dash into the thick of battle, he reads a book; if he wishes to soar into heaven, he reads a book; if he wishes to slide down the banisters, he reads a book. We give him these visions, but we give him exercise at the same time. . . . We give him back his childhood, that god-like time when we can act stories, be our own heroes, and at the same instant dance and dream.[67]

Of course, this manifesto about the 'lamentable' predominance of books as a way of understanding experience itself appears in a book. The desire to live longer in the space of a book is common and takes many forms, such as 'pushing at the boundaries of the book' or 'continual reading'.[68] The humour works on multiple levels, including the clear infeasibility of the business, as the mix-up with Major Brown proves. Because Brown never signed up for the service, he does not enjoy the adventures as reading. He actually lives out the novel without a suspension of disbelief, which leads to his achievement of an actual marriage plot. The actress employed by the Romance Agency accepts his offer because he acted in her defence not knowing the whole affair was a fiction.

Gully first discovers the Club of Queer Trades by reading it – deciphering it, even – on the card of the first member he meets, which he produces as he explains the mix-up with Major Brown: 'It ran, "P. G. Northover, BA, CQT, Adventure and Romance Agency, 14 Tanner's Court, Fleet Street".'[69] His interlocutors enquire as to the acronym CQT, and Northover rejoins, 'Don't you know? . . . Haven't you ever heard of the Club of Queer Trades?'[70] Although the club acronym is cryptic, Northover clearly does not intend it to be so, but rather in keeping with the other initials on his card. Far from a secret society, this club might help its members with personal and professional connections. The members are, after all, tradesmen by definition, and therefore they live off others' readings of their cards.

The second episode in *The Club of Queer Trades* also involves a writer plying his trade on the unsuspecting. Similarly, this writer belongs to the Club of Queer Trades, and his existence and that of his trade provide the solution to an apparent mystery. The caper begins when Basil 'reads' the character of a man he sees from the top of a bus and decides to follow him. Having decided this stranger is a 'the wickedest man in London', Basil poses to Gully the puzzle of why he should be entering the house of 'a very good man'.[71] Yet they leave the house chasing a different character who has seemed to Gully very innocuous: the butt of the wicked man's jokes. Having wrestled him to the ground, Basil reveals,

> This fat old gentleman lying on the ground strikes you, as I have no doubt, as very stupid and very rich. Let me clear his character. He is, like ourselves, very clever and very poor, He is also not really at all fat; all that is stuffing. He is not particularly old, and his name is not Cholmondeliegh. He is a swindler, and a swindler of a perfectly delightful and novel kind.[72]

As it turns out, this man's profession is to write jokes for others – in this case, the seemingly wicked man –to play out at his own expense. When another member of the house party says indignantly, 'that fellow ought to be in jail', Basil returns 'indulgently', 'Not at all . . . he ought to be in the Club of Queer Trades.'[73] The club transforms potentially criminal behaviour, in part by providing an alternate institutional framework.

Many of the Queer Trades involve impersonation, trading on the illegibility of the city. Most strikingly, the Professional Detainers prevent Basil and Gully from attending a dinner, employed by their friend, who wishes to be alone with a woman. They appear to each man separately in identical costume as elderly clergymen and tell a story to keep their subject occupied. Gully's clergyman's story involves another impersonation: five lower-class criminals dress up so well as respectable ladies that they fool the vicar, and then they kidnap him. They reveal that they've chosen him because he's the spitting image of the mother of the man they want to rob. They show him this by means of a photograph, which is later revealed to be mechanically faked:

> As the glass moved, I saw that part of the picture was painted on it in Chinese white, notably a pair of white whiskers and a clerical collar.

And underneath was a portrait of an old lady in a quiet black dress, leaning her head on her hand against the woodland landscape. The old lady was as like me as one pin is like another. It had required only the whiskers and the collar to make it me in every hair.[74]

As in *Tommy and Co.*, this impersonation suggests that gender lies in dress and other external trappings that can be removed or added.

Unlike Jerome, however, Chesterton includes typical jokes that reinforce gender binaries. Some humour lies in the difficulty of detection: 'To every human eye, in every external, we were six very respectable old ladies of small means, in black dresses and refined but antiquated bonnets; and we were really five criminals and a clergyman.'[75] However, the feminine exterior also contrasts with the 'essential' masculinity of the disguised criminals: 'In all the nightmares that men have ever dreamed, there has never been anything so blighting and horrible as the faces of those five men looking out of their poke-bonnets; the figures of district visitors with the faces of devils.'[76] Femininity is used as a pejorative in Gully's reaction when the vicar first appears and says that he's been forced to dress as a woman: 'I thought in my heart that it required no great transformation to make an old woman of him.'[77] The whole thing is played for laughs:

'As Vicar of Chutsey in Essex,' he said, 'I have never been forcibly dressed up as an old woman, and made to take part in a crime in the character of an old woman. Never once. My experience may be small. It may be insufficient. But it has never occurred to me before.'
'I have never heard of it,' I said, 'as among the duties of a clergyman. But I am not well up in church matters.'[78]

The gravity with which they entertain the notion that this might be a common practice is a comic device. Yet the surface meaning here also applies: one never entirely knows the rules. Social rules, like those of the unusual clubs, are constantly changing and surprising. The supposed vicar also suggests, before he realises the truth, that this unusual behaviour might derive from a hitherto unknown club: 'Was it really true, as I had suddenly fancied a moment before, that unmarried ladies had some dreadful riotous society of their own from which all others were excluded?'[79] The club comes to mind as an explanation for otherwise unexplained behaviour.

The first three stories feature marriage plots and trades which adapt narrative strategies. The next two Queer Tradesmen are not out to deceive, but the plots still hinge on reading people – the arboreal house-agent is discovered because Rupert and Basil disagree about the character of their mutual acquaintance Lieutenant Keith, and the case of Professor Chadd hinges on whether or not he has gone mad. In the latter case, Chadd suddenly ceases speaking and begins dancing. This obviously resembles Doyle's 'Dancing Men', which involves a code depicted by images of dancing. Rather than exchanging a prearranged code, however, the professor develops a language based on dance and relies on Basil to decipher it without a reference. Basil must read the language to prevent a misreading of the professor's character (as well as the literal misreading of his language). The professor's livelihood hangs in the balance but, in the end, he receives a research grant recognising the whole affair as a linguistic experiment.

Throughout the novel, Gully and Basil form the central friendship dyad. The central club threatens this friendship, in part because only one of them is a member. Gully, meanwhile, belongs to a plethora of clubs:

> I have a mania for belonging to as many societies as possible. I may be said to collect clubs, and I have accumulated a vast and fantastic variety of specimens ever since. In my audacious youth I collected the Athenæum. At some future day, perhaps, I may tell tales of some of the other bodies to which I have belonged. I will recount the doings of the Dead Man's Shoes Society (that superficially immoral, but darkly justifiable communion); I will explain the curious origin of the Cat and Christian, the name of which has been so shamefully misinterpreted; and the world shall know at least why the Institute of Typewriters coalesced with the Red Tulip League. Of the Ten Teacups, of course, I dare not say a word. The first of my revelations, at any rate, shall be concerned with the Club of Queer Trades, which, as I have said, was one of this class, one which I was almost bound to come across sooner or later, because of my singular hobby. The wild youth of the metropolis call me facetiously 'The King of Clubs'.[80]

The name-dropping of the Athenaeum elevates the rest, as that is not only one of the more exclusive West End clubs, but a club whose requirements hinge on personal achievement rather than birth or wealth. This paragraph also contextualises the Club of

Queer Trades with both this non-fictional club and also a set of fantastical, fictional clubs. Like the untold stories hinted at in the last sentence of *The Problem Club* or the cases Watson refers to but never narrates, these fictional clubs flesh out the fictional world. In addition to the whimsical, this passage evokes the dark side of clubs: 'superficially immoral, but darkly justifiable', like the Suicide Club or the Society for Doing Without Some People (see Chapter 5).

Basil is practically the opposite of the narrator. The narrator collects clubs, but Basil has no need: he treats the world as if it were one giant club. The penultimate chapter begins by describing Basil's unusual sociability:

> Basil Grant had comparatively few friends besides myself; yet he was the reverse of an unsociable man. He would talk to any one anywhere, and talk not only well but with perfectly genuine concern and enthusiasm for that person's affairs. He went through the world, as it were, as if he were always on the top of an omnibus or waiting for a train. Most of these chance acquaintances, of course, vanished into darkness out of his life. A few here and there got hooked on to him, so to speak, and became his lifelong intimates, but there was an accidental look about all of them as if they were windfalls, samples taken at random, goods fallen from a goods-train or presents fished out of a bran-pie.[81]

The narrator mentions some instances in the modern world where it is permissible to strike up conversations with strangers – including 'waiting for a train', that time of idleness – but he does not mention the club, although it played a crucial role in their meeting:

> I had met Grant while he was still a judge, on the balcony of the National Liberal Club, and exchanged a few words about the weather. Then we had talked for about half an hour about politics and God; for men always talk about the most important things to total strangers. It is because in the total stranger we perceive man himself; the image of God is not disguised by resemblances to an uncle or doubts of the wisdom of a mustache.[82]

For those not gifted with Basil's eccentric nature, the club provides the perfect excuse to talk to strangers and the perfect setting for an anonymous, intimate confessional. This proclivity is distinctly gendered masculine here. Moreover, the description of an inter-action with a stranger could also describe an encounter through reading with a character, author or fellow reader, all equally imagined.

The club creates the conditions for Basil and Gully's friendship, yet something else propels it past the interaction between affable strangers. That quality remains undefined, but the intensity of the friendship comes through. When Basil begins confronting the Professional Detainer, who looks to Gully like an innocuous vicar, Gully fears for his sanity:

> And at these words I also rose to my feet, for the great tragedy of my life had come. Splendid and exciting as life was in continual contact with an intellect like Basil's, I had always the feeling that that splendor and excitement were on the borderland of sanity. He lived perpetually near the vision of the reason of things which makes men lose their reason. And I felt of his insanity as men feel of the death of friends with heart disease.[83]

So focused is Gully on Basil that his friend's insanity would be 'the great tragedy of [Gully's] life'. This bond recalls that of Watson and Holmes; it may indeed be a parody, although one that may be read straight. The Club of Queer Trades tests Basil and Gully's friendship in part because, like Holmes with Watson, Basil does not divulge the depth of his knowledge to his friend. As Gully fears the onset of personal tragedy, it gradually dawns on him that the vicar sees the situation differently: 'In fact, the unintelligible truth must be told. They were both laughing.'[84] Basil's first reaction on perceiving the queer trade behind the 'unintelligible' behaviour is frequently laughter, which itself is at first unintelligible to Gully and Rupert.

Like The Old Maids' Club, The Club of Queer Trades ends with a gathering of people who have been introduced separately to the novel, in this case at the annual club dinner. These group-ings underscore the similarity between the club and the novel. Indeed, the club dinner recapitulates the storytelling that has pre-ceded it:

> At last came the moment which I knew must in some way enlighten us, the time of the club speeches and the club toasts. Basil Grant rose to his feet amid a surge of song and cheers.

'Gentlemen,' he said, 'it is a custom in this society that the president for the year opens the proceedings, not by any general toast or sentiment, but by calling upon each member to give a brief account of his trade. We then drink to that calling and to all who follow it.'[85]

For those of his readers unfamiliar with the general procedures of club dinners, Chesterton provides a guide. Northover starts to explain his business, and the novel closes with a formal, metatextual reference: 'Thus our epic ended where it had begun, like a true cycle.'[86] Fully explained, the club is convivial after all, not sinister. Gully and Rupert's friendship can exist within its context, but the club does not replace the friendship.

A joke made horribly real

Born the year between the first issue of the *Idler* and Robert Louis Stevenson's death, Dorothy Sayers belongs to a different generation than the other figures in this chapter – not to mention a different gender. Yet *The Unpleasantness at the Bellona Club* (1928) picks up on many of the underlying ideas about clubs established by previous mysteries. The novel's premise is to render a Victorian joke horribly real: that a member has died behind his newspaper and no one has noticed. The club and its rules, written and unwritten, become a synecdoche for the pre-war social order. Lord Peter Wimsey, Sayers's detective, navigates a range of social contexts, using detection as therapy for his shell shock. The structure of the mystery, now well established, imposes a sense of order for both Wimsey and perhaps also his readers, yet *The Unpleasantness at the Bellona Club* also suggests the limits of this kind of containment.

The joke practically opens the novel: the club is called a 'Morgue' in the opening line, and Wimsey's friend George Fentiman, a First World War veteran with wounds visible and invisible, follows the reference up: 'Place always reminds me of that old thing in "Punch", you know – "Waiter, take away Lord Whatisisname, he's been dead two days."'[87] It's an old joke – the reference to *Punch* makes it seem potentially Victorian, at very least pre-war. Yet the joke is fulfilled: Fentiman's grandfather is discovered, behind a newspaper where all thought he was sleeping, in full rigor mortis. When they discover the body, Fentiman hysterically recalls the joke:

Fentiman laughed. Peal after hysterical peal shook his throat. All round the room, scandalized Bellonians creaked to their gouty feet, shocked by the unmannerly noise.

'Take him away!' said Fentiman, 'take him away. He's been dead two days. So are you! So am I! We're all dead, and we never noticed it!'[88]

With the literal fulfilment of the Victorian joke, the joke changes to a post-war context. To the younger Fentiman, his grandfather's death is indicative of a larger social problem: 'We're all dead, and we never noticed it!' As an absurdist post-war sentiment, this recalls T. S. Eliot's evocation of malaise in *The Waste Land*: 'Are you alive, or not? Is there nothing in your head?'[89] The Diogenes-like body behind the newspaper is revealed to be not merely a body from whence the mind engages in imaginative journeys of reading, but a corpse. Despite carrying the name of the Roman goddess of war, the club represents the previous generation, which doesn't understand the young men who have fought in the war. Or rather, like Macbeth, 'Bellona's bridegroom', they only see the romantic side of war.

The club is so ossified that George's joke registers on a level comparable to his grandfather's death: 'It is doubtful which occurrence was more disagreeable to the senior members of the Bellona Club – the grotesque death of General Fentiman in their midst or the indecent neurathenia [sic] of his grandson. Only the younger men felt no sense of outrage; they knew too much.'[90] If the other young men, who had also presumably been in the war, don't share George's hysterical laughter, they still 'get' his joke. The discovery of the body takes place on Armistice Day: the murder of one old man is darkly contrasted with the war deaths of millions of young men on all sides of the conflict. For much of the novel, George appears guilty of his grandfather's murder, both to a reluctant Wimsey and ultimately to himself. In the throes of a post-traumatic episode, he even falsely confesses.

The novel concludes with the joke that nothing changes in the club. After both Fentiman brothers have been suspected of the murder, Wimsey proves that Robert tampered with the body after death to secure an inheritance, but the doctor who examined the body – also a member of the club – is revealed as the murderer. Wimsey encourages him to write a confession, and another club member provides him a pistol with which to shoot himself in the club library. The novel closes with a longstanding member complaining about a slew of troubles, including both deaths and culminating in corked wine, crying, 'My God! I don't know what's come to this Club!'[91] The dark joke, after all, lies with what has not changed. Older members continue to class murder and war as similar tribulations to corked wine. The unspoken rules, too, lead Wimsey to allow his fellow clubman a gentlemanly exit from the predicament.

Yet elsewhere in her Wimsey canon, Sayers introduces the Egotists' Club, of which Wimsey is a member. Her short story 'The Abominable History of the Man with Copper Fingers' (1928 in *Lord Peter Views the Body*) takes place entirely within the club, including narration of events elsewhere. The story begins with a description of the club's premises and rules that uses the now-familiar second person:

> The Egotists' Club is one of the most genial places in London. It is a place to which you may go when you want to tell that odd dream you had last night, or to announce what a good dentist you have discovered. You can write letters there if you like, and have the temperament of a Jane Austen, for there is no silence room, and it would be a breach of club manners to appear busy or absorbed when another member addresses you. You must not mention golf or fish, however, and, if the Hon. Freddy Arbuthnot's motion is carried at the next committee meeting (and opinion so far appears very favorable), you will not be allowed to mention wireless either. As Lord Peter Wimsey said when the matter was mooted the other day in the smoking-room, those are things you can talk about anywhere. Otherwise the club is not specially exclusive. Nobody is ineligible per se, except strong, silent men. Nominees are, however, required to pass certain tests, whose nature is sufficiently indicated by the fact that a certain distinguished explorer came to grief through accepting, and smoking, a powerful Trichinoply cigar as an accompaniment to a '63 port. On the other hand, dear old Sir Roger Burnt (the coster millionaire who won the £20,000 ballot offered by the *Sunday Shriek*, and used it to found his immense catering business in the Midlands) was highly commended and unanimously elected after declaring frankly that beer and a pipe were all he really cared for in that way. As Lord Peter said again: 'Nobody minds coarseness, but one must draw the line at cruelty.'[92]

Magnanimously, the club is not above accepting new money (that has been dignified by a title) – though it labels that 'coarse' – but it does 'draw the line' at pretension, particularly at those who imperfectly attempt to perform good taste. Like the real Beefsteak Club, 'where everybody talks to everybody without introductions', the Egotists' prides itself on its conversation about things you couldn't 'talk about anywhere'.[93] The opposite of the Diogenes Club, this is a place for sociability and fellowship – but it has a clear hierarchy, one of good taste, if not actual class standing. Like the Failure Club's disdain for 'artificial simplicity', the class distinction that's being drawn is against pretension, but also against aspirational upward mobility. Sir Roger stays in his place, his original class origins, rather than trying to wear the cultural trappings of his new rank.

Unlike the *Idler* circle's jokes about clubs, which question the arbitrary rules of culture or society, this depiction seems to uphold them. The Egotists' Club is not the subject of the joke. Its jokes uphold the notion of exclusivity of taste. Sayers may or may not expect her readers to know that one shouldn't smoke such a cigar with such a beverage, but she certainly expects them to concur with the notion that such a thing deserves social embarrassment. In general, Sayers does not try to democratise or to reach readers of all classes. Her Peter Wimsey novels are peppered with allusions in different languages. *Gaudy Night* (1935) flirts with the notion that a female academic is suffering from a mental delusion, but then foists the offense off on a lower-class servant suffused with rage at the academics she regards as unfeminine. Sayers may question some of the boundary cases, but her work fundamentally upholds class- and taste-based systems of exclusivity.

In 'The Man with the Copper Fingers', the Egotists' Club is a safe haven and an unexpected meeting-place. At first, it seems that Wimsey will not hugely figure in this story at all, despite his prominence in the introduction of the club (because for readers of the series, Wimsey's recommendation makes the club seem suitable, rather than the other way around). A 'stranger' in the club, Varden, tells a story of fantastic mystery. He has been the guest of a sculptor who has been behaving oddly. A mysterious man arrives in the middle of the night to tell him to flee: the sculptor believes Varden has had an affair with his model and plans to murder him. In fact, he reveals that what seemed to be a sculpture of the model really contained her corpse. At the close of Varden's story, some club members dispute its veracity, but Wimsey speaks up to defend him. With a start, Varden recognises Wimsey as the mysterious man who saved him. Wimsey then takes up the tale to describe his confrontation with the sculptor, in the course of which the villain dies in the manner planned for Varden. He becomes the eponymous Man with the Copper Fingers.

Although Varden is shocked to discover his mysterious benefactor in the club, the other club members seem not to be, and neither is the reader, probably: the club seems designed for such fortuitous meetings. Wimsey is reluctant to take up the tale, but is reassured by oaths to respect the sanctity of the clubroom:

> 'it's not really a story I want to get about. It might land me in a very unpleasant sort of position – manslaughter, probably, and murder possibly.'
>
> 'Gosh!' said Bayles.
>
> 'That's all right,' said Armstrong, 'nobody's going to talk. We can't afford to lose you from the club, you know. Smith-Hartington will have to control his passion for copy, that's all.'
>
> Pledges of discretion having been given all round, Lord Peter settled himself back and began his tale.[94]

Nobody seems to consider the possibility that Wimsey might deserve to be charged with murder. His membership in the club serves as his bona fide but Armstrong implies that, even if he was a murderer, the pleasure of his company at the club outweighs abstract moral claims.

Ironically, the least critical depiction of the club in this chapter comes from the author who, by virtue of her gender, would be automatically excluded from the prototypical West End clubs.[95] The only way Sayers can participate in the all-male world of clubs is through fiction – like the majority of her readers. And, as a university-educated woman who was initially denied a degree because of her gender, Sayers was accustomed to inhabiting the edges of exclusivity. In addition to highbrow allusions such as untranslated Latin and French, Sayers incorporates into the Wimsey novels allusions to middlebrow authors, including those contained in this chapter. In *Unnatural Death*, the Wimsey novel that precedes *Bellona*, Wimsey compares himself to Prince Florizel of Bohemia; and in *Murder Must Advertise* (1933), characters compare him to Bertie Wooster.[96] Sayers played her own humorous 'game' with the works of Arthur Conan Doyle, as she explains in the Foreword to *Unpopular Opinions*:

> The game of applying the methods of the 'Higher Criticism' to the Sherlock Holmes canon was begun, many years ago, by Monsignor Ronald Knox, with the aim of showing that, by those methods, one could disintegrate a modern classic as speciously as a certain school of critics have endeavoured to disintegrate the Bible. Since then, the thing has become a hobby among a select set of jesters here and in America. The rule of the game is that it must be played as solemnly as a county cricket match at Lord's: the slightest touch of extravagance or burlesque ruins the atmosphere.[97]

One hopes that at the present time, the notion that Doyle can provide material for criticism is no longer taken as a big joke. Sayers uses her predecessors to demonstrate her own critical prowess – and her membership in 'a select set of jesters', that is to say, a kind of club.

Outside these clubs, Wimsey has two major friendship dyads with men, both of which cross class boundaries. His relationship with Bunter, his manservant, might in fact be too inveigled with class constraints to properly qualify as a friendship – he is, after all, Bunter's employer – but their relationship is unconventional. They have several overlapping roles in relation to each other: Bunter served under Wimsey as his sergeant during the war, and he continues to assist Wimsey's detective 'hobby', principally as a photographer. Furthermore, Bunter helps nurse Wimsey through his shell shock, as seen in *Whose Body* (1923):

> Lord Peter allowed himself to be dosed and put to bed without further resistance. Mr Bunter, looking singularly un-Bunterlike in striped pyjamas, with his stiff black hair ruffled about his head, sat grimly watching the younger man's sharp cheekbones and the purple stains under his eyes. . . . He peered at him anxiously. An affectionate note crept into his voice. 'Bloody little fool!' said Sergeant Bunter.[98]

Bunter steps outside his valet role here, appearing 'un-Bunterlike' and as a sergeant, regarding the sleeping Wimsey with parental affection.

Yet Wimsey's relationship with Charles Parker is more fraught than that with Bunter, perhaps because the class lines are more blurred. Bunter essentially stays in his 'place', although he and Wimsey clearly care for one another, but it is Parker who serves as Wimsey's friend, collaborator in his detective work, and, eventually, his brother-in-law, by marrying Wimsey's sister, Lady Mary. The barriers between Wimsey as moneyed aristocracy and Parker as a working man, despite his promotions, occasionally manifest. In *The Unpleasantness at the Bellona Club* in particular, the differences in their class and approach to detection threaten to strain their friendship. The club itself as an institution of friendship (or even of social status) is not directly the cause, although it does affect Wimsey's approach to the investigation. When the case is first brought to Wimsey's attention by Murbles, the Fentimans' family solicitor, Wimsey demurs slightly in a way that makes Murbles 'look[] up sharply': 'After all . . . I'm a member of the Club . . . family associations chiefly, I suppose . . . but there it is.'[99] When Charles proposes that Wimsey 'might take [him] down to the Bellona in a tactful way', Wimsey replies with a groan: 'I shall be asked to resign if this goes on.'[100] Yet these are largely matters of form, and even Wimsey's friends (and readers) occasionally have difficulty telling when he is joking.

The real difficulty between Parker and Wimsey emerges not because of the club as such, but because of the actual friendships Wimsey has with its members. Robert and George Fentiman both fall under suspicion of the murder. The seriously shell-shocked George looks particularly bad; everyone, including himself, suspects him of the murder at one point or another. Robert and Wimsey even have a violent altercation over Robert's attempts to conceal evidence that seems to point to George, in which Robert calls Wimsey an 'infernal little police spy'.[101] The accusation seems to hit home, as when Wimsey relays the seemingly damning evidence to Parker, 'Parker was aware of a thin veil of hostility, drawn between himself and the friend he valued. He knew that for the first time, Wimsey was seeing him as the police. Wimsey was ashamed and his shame made Parker ashamed, too.'[102] Just as Parker's class background bars him from the Bellona Club, Wimsey's keeps him from fully engaging in police work. In its own way, that is a club to which he cannot fully belong. Nevertheless, this is merely a bump in the road: Parker and Wimsey go on to enjoy many more years (and books) of friendship, and neither Fentiman is a murderer.

Conclusion

The texts in this chapter test the club as a metaphor for readership. They often show the club as key to the changing social landscape thorough an emphasis on the city as social text (incredibly legible to Sherlock Holmes, perhaps, but befuddling to most others). But the mysteries in this chapter also test the argument of the study as a whole, in part because they are at once more canonical and, in general, less funny than most of the other works. The surprise in this chapter, then, may be the extent to which these texts perform similar affective and social work to the club stories. Despite their comparative emphasis on danger and the club as a (varyingly) sinister force, these club mysteries emphasise the positive affects of homosocial bonds, albeit largely in informal dyads rather than clubs.

This tension between the friendship dyad and the club highlights the larger ambivalence about the club as a structure more generally. The humour and good feeling may mask this, but mainstream club stories also contain ambivalence about the club as a structure. *The Bachelors' Club*, of course, presents the club as a project doomed to failure, and even *The Problem Club* represents the tensions the club's demands place on friendships and other relationships both with fellow club members and 'strangers' – including wives. The problem with the club, as the works in this chapter point out, is that it risks replicating the problems of the larger social structures against which some of the clubs explicitly pit themselves. In other words, a fundamental problem with the club is that it is an institution. Explicit rules are one of the starkest ways in which a club differs from a friendship group. But, as Chapter 3 shows, those explicit rules can be clarifying. When a friendship falls under threat, as in Gully's fears of Basil's insanity or Parker's awareness of Wimsey's hostility, the reeling friend might wish to apply to a committee to help adjudicate whether the relationship can continue. Similarly, the community of readership, not to mention the infrastructure of a magazine, helps buttress literary relationships across the page. The club as a metaphor is large enough to encompass authors, characters and even imagined fellow readers. Indeed, many characters in these texts prefer the company of books, from the Diogenes Club members to the patrons of the Adventure and Romance Agency, and surely these mysteries' readers can sympathise.

Notes

1 Works on the *fin de siècle* that portray it as dangerous include, among many others, Brantlinger, *Rule of Darkness*; Showalter, *Sexual Anarchy*.
2 Adams, *Dandies and Desert Saints*, 17; Black, *A Room of His Own*, 191.
3 Langbauer, *Novels of Everyday Life*, 139.
4 The term 'imperial Gothic' comes from Brantlinger, who discusses Stevenson and Doyle, the latter particularly in relation to 'occult phenomena follow[ing] characters from imperial settings home to Britain'. The term 'reverse colonization' was made famous in Arata's analysis of *Dracula*, using Stevenson's *Jekyll and Hyde* as a frame. Arata, 'The Occidental Tourist', 621; Brantlinger, *Rule of Darkness*, 230–1.
5 Fiss, 'Pushing at the Boundaries of the Book', 258–78. For *The Wrong Box*'s humour, the preface reads, '"Nothing like a little judicious levity", says Michael Finsbury in the text; nor can any better excuse be found for the volume in the reader's hand. The authors can but add that one of them is old enough to be ashamed of himself, and the other young enough to learn better.' Stevenson and Osbourne, *The Wrong Box*.
6 Stevenson, 'My First Book', 5–11. 'A Chat with Robert Louis Stevenson', 6–7. A note from the editor reads, 'I have to thank a San Francisco journalist for the following sketch' (6).
7 Birkin, *J.M. Barrie and the Lost Boys*, 18.
8 Stevenson, 'An Apology for Idlers', 83.
9 Stevenson, 'Apology', 80.
10 Stevenson, 'Apology', 83.
11 Stevenson, 'Apology', 81.
12 Dames, *The Physiology of the Novel*, 73.
13 [Thackeray], 'Roundabout Papers'.
14 Stevenson, 'Apology', 83.
15 Stevenson, 'Apology', 84.
16 Dames, *Physiology*, 122.
17 Stevenson, *Arabian*, vii. Each of the three stories appeared in three instalments, from 8 June 1878 to 27 July 1878. Thanks to Troy Basset and *At the Circulating Library* for the serial references.
18 Stevenson, *Arabian*, 3.
19 Stevenson, *Arabian*, 5.

20 Stevenson, *Arabian*, 5.
21 Stevenson, *Arabian*, 7.
22 Stevenson, *Arabian*, 8.
23 Stevenson, *Arabian*, 9.
24 Stevenson, *Arabian*, 10.
25 Stevenson, *Arabian*, 11.
26 Stevenson, *Arabian*, 11.
27 Stevenson, *Arabian*, 15.
28 Stevenson, *Arabian*, 24.
29 Stevenson, *Arabian*, 18.
30 Stevenson, *Arabian*, 25.
31 Stevenson, *Arabian*, 26.
32 Stevenson, *Arabian*, 27.
33 Stevenson, *Arabian*, 21.
34 Stevenson, *Arabian*, 28.
35 Stevenson, *Arabian*, 30.
36 Stevenson, *Arabian*, 33.
37 Stevenson, *Arabian*, 33–4.
38 Stevenson, *Arabian*, 34.
39 Stevenson, *Arabian*, 34.
40 Stevenson, *Arabian*, 44.
41 Stevenson, *Arabian*, 45.
42 Stevenson, *Arabian*, 42.
43 Stevenson, *Arabian*, 42.
44 Black, *A Room of His Own*, 191.
45 Doyle, 'The Empty House', 376.
46 Lellenberg, Stashower and Foley, *Arthur Conan Doyle*, 324.
47 Roberts, 'Introduction', *Sherlock Holmes Selected Stories*, xi; 'The Case of the Resurrected Detective'.
48 Doyle, 'Red-Headed League', 197.
49 Doyle, 'Red-Headed League', 191–2.
50 Doyle, 'Red-Headed League', 196.
51 Doyle, 'Greek Interpreter', 296.
52 Doyle, 'Greek Interpreter', 296.
53 Milne-Smith, *London Clubland*, 31.
54 Steven Moffat and Mark Gatiss have taken this tension as a seed for a greater exploration of the relationship between the three characters in their adaptation, *Sherlock*.
55 Doyle, 'Greek Interpreter', 296.
56 Doyle, *The Complete Sherlock Holmes*, II.1053.
57 Doyle, 'Greek Interpreter', 297.

58 Leah Price discusses the shielding function of 'the repellent book'. Price, *How to Do Things with Books in Victorian Britain*, 57.

59 Doyle, 'Greek Interpreter', 297.

60 Beaumont and Ingleby, *G. K. Chesterton, London, and Modernity*.

61 Chesterton, *Club of Queer Trades*, 4.

62 Chesterton, *Club of Queer Trades*, 58.

63 Chesterton, *Club of Queer Trades*, 82.

64 Chesterton, *Club of Queer Trades*, 8.

65 Chesterton, *Club of Queer Trades*, 268.

66 Chesterton, *Club of Queer Trades*, 269.

67 Chesterton, *Club of Queer Trades*, 46.

68 Fiss, 'Pushing at the Boundaries of the Book'; Han, 'Pickwick's Other Papers', 19–41.

69 Chesterton, *Club of Queer Trades*, 48.

70 Chesterton, *Club of Queer Trades*, 48.

71 Chesterton, *Club of Queer Trades*, 58, 63.

72 Chesterton, *Club of Queer Trades*, 87.

73 Chesterton, *Club of Queer Trades*, 88.

74 Chesterton, *Club of Queer Trades*, 107–8.

75 Chesterton, *Club of Queer Trades*, 110.

76 Chesterton, *Club of Queer Trades*, 113.

77 Chesterton, *Club of Queer Trades*, 97.

78 Chesterton, *Club of Queer Trades*, 96–7.

79 Chesterton, *Club of Queer Trades*, 103.

80 Chesterton, *Club of Queer Trades*, 5–6.

81 Chesterton, *Club of Queer Trades*, 179–80.

82 Chesterton, *Club of Queer Trades*, 180–1.

83 Chesterton, *Club of Queer Trades*, 121.

84 Chesterton, *Club of Queer Trades*, 123.

85 Chesterton, *Club of Queer Trades*, 266.

86 Chesterton, *Club of Queer Trades*, 270.

87 Sayers, *Bellona*, 7.

88 Sayers, *Bellona*, 10.

89 Eliot, *The Waste Land*, 126.

90 Sayers, *Bellona*, 10.

91 Sayers, *Bellona*, 192.

92 Sayers, 'Man with the Copper Fingers', 53–4.

93 Graves, *Leather Armchairs*, xv.

94 Sayers, 'Man with the Copper Fingers', 63–4.

95 Of course, there were clubs for women, most famously the Pioneer, but at least in the Victorian period, there was surprisingly little

cross-penetration between men's and women's club networks, particularly among authors. (This is the subject of ongoing work in collaboration with Troy Bassett.)

96 Sayers, *Unnatural Death*, 17; Sayers, *Murder Must Advertise*, 10, 11.

97 Sayers, *Unpopular Opinions*, 7.

98 Sayers, *Whose Body?*, 134.

99 Sayers, *Bellona*, 14.

100 Sayers, *Bellona*, 117.

101 Sayers, *Bellona*, 151.

102 Sayers, *Bellona*, 153.

5

Through a Club Window Wistfully: J. M. Barrie and the Politics of Social Awkwardness

J. M. Barrie was odd. Contemporaneous press accounts, biographical studies, critical accounts and even current popular culture depict him as eccentric at best and dangerously warped at worst.[1] Most sources, popular and critical, connect Barrie's oddness with *Peter Pan*, childhood and sexuality in various combinations, some more benign than others. This is important work, but as anyone who works in the history of sexuality knows, sometimes you reach a point where questions can't be definitively answered. When we look at Barrie through the lens of the Idlers, an alternative picture emerges, one that can be viewed in parallel with any explanation of Barrie's underlying oddness. Barrie defined himself as unclubbable, insisting that his social awkwardness derived from his disposition. I argue that this pre-emptively foreclosed an alternative explanation: that his inability to fit seamlessly into London society stemmed from his lower-class upbringing in Scotland. Like many of his own unclubbable clubmen, Barrie assumed the class privilege of eccentricity.

As we saw in the introduction, Barrie met Jerome and Zangwill through F. W. Robinson and *Home Chimes*. He met Doyle at an *Idler* At-Home, even though he never contributed to the magazine. Of all the Idlers, he saw the greatest rise in class: his father was a hand-loom weaver, and he died a baronet with over £17,000 in probate.[2] His social belonging also manifested in club membership: over his lifetime he belonged to several clubs including the prestigious Athenaeum, which rewards distinction in an intellectual field; the Garrick, a social club centred on the theatre; the Reform, which began as a political club but became more broadly social; and the Authors' Club, to which many in the *Idler* circle belonged.[3] His baronetcy and posthumous reputation rest largely on his dramatic works but his early career depended on journalism, periodical pieces and novels (many drawn from those periodicals). *Peter Pan* in particular dominates Barrie's posthumous reputation and heavily influences his biographies; even a recent monograph on his cricket team bears the title *Peter Pan's First XI*.[4] Most biographies highly stress the origins of this work in Barrie's relationship with the Llewelyn Davies family, a compelling tale as gripping as fiction. The five sons – George, Jack, Peter, Michael and Nicholas (nicknamed Nico) – lost first their father and then their mother at a young age, at which point Barrie became their guardian. Then came the First World War. The eldest three saw active duty, and George was killed in action in 1915. Ironically, after escaping the perils of war, Michael drowned at Oxford in 1921 in a swimming accident that continues to provoke speculation by biographers and critics.[5] Peter became a publisher and published some of Barrie's late works. He was sorting through Barrie's archive, destroying many documents, when he died by suicide in 1960.[6]

Barrie is in fact peripheral to most of this story's drama, although it often becomes conflated with the sensational story of Barrie's own divorce, in which his wife, *née* Mary Ansell, alleged that he never consummated their marriage. The contemporaneous press made the *Peter Pan* connection, calling him 'the boy who couldn't go up'.[7] Later, critic James Kincaid refers to Barrie as among the 'agreed-upon pedophiles'.[8] Meanwhile, biographer Andrew Birkin cites a later letter from Mary saying the couple had 'normal marital relations'.[9] Yet the characterisation of Barrie as a 'lost boy' or a 'boy who wouldn't grow up' continues – in part because of the compelling nature of the image, which Laura Wilkie uses more widely as a style of masculinity.[10] As the critical appetite for sensational or, as Eve Sedgwick famously put it, 'paranoid' readings of familiar literature has waned, Marah Gubar has viewed children as collaborators as she traces Barrie's working relationships with child actors.[11] The focus on Barrie's relationship with children has shifted the focus to his later work, obscuring his debut in journalism, periodicals and novel-writing.

For understandable reasons, critics have focused on the reasons for Barrie's oddness, but I'd like instead to look at Barrie's use of that oddness in his self-representation, focusing on his early years. Like Jerome and other Idlers, Barrie engaged in a variety of types of publishing, many of which seemed to trade on his authorial persona. This chapter focuses on his early work, mainly from 1888 to 1890, including material from *The Greenwood Hat* (1937), which reprinted his early periodical pieces along with reminiscences of that period. The chapter concludes with *The Little White Bird*, which is best known for introducing Peter Pan, but which largely takes place in a club. Like his fellow Idlers, Barrie created a plethora of fictional clubs, specialising in those for 'unclubbable men'.[12] As with Doyle's Diogenes Club, face-to-face unsociability creates space for the pleasures of mediated contact, although the connections to reading here are more implicit. In his take on the pathos of social mobility, Barrie stresses the loneliness of club membership, but his most compelling group finds community in their shared unclubbability.

The Scotch humorist

The dominance of Peter Pan on Barrie's reputation masks the fact that his early career capitalised heavily on his Scottish identity: he built his career on fiction about Scotland, much of it using dialect. His three first books, all published in 1888, all involve Scotland and Scottish protagonists: *Better Dead*, *Auld Licht Idylls* and *When a Man's Single*. The first and last of these feature later in this chapter, but *Auld Licht Idylls* was the most popular of the three. It collected and linked periodical stories featuring the fictional Scottish town of Thrums. A series of Thrums novels followed, which established Barrie's reputation and attracted the attention of Robert Louis Stevenson, a fellow Scotsman.[13] In an early periodical piece reproduced in *The Greenwood Hat*, Barrie depicts his awkwardness when asked to officiate at an unnamed club's Burns night. The physical comedy of Barrie's attempts to fulfil his social obligations ultimately establish a bond with his reader – and, in a roundabout way, with his fellow diners.

The piece's title, 'Mr Barrie in the Chair', indicates his position in the evening's ritual. Social dinners among men in this period were often presided over by a chairman, as we have seen in *The Proposal Club*. As Barrie struggles with the duties, the conventions become clear. The piece stresses, even to one unfamiliar with the rituals (such as an original reader who had never been to a dinner of this type, or a twenty-first-century researcher), that his effort misses the mark. Barrie appears from the outside. A club member narrates, adopting a style typical of New Journalism, including some humour at the narrator's expense. At the onset, he admits,

'I have not read Mr Barrie's books,' and reports, 'We, or at least I, had looked to see a jovial Scot, full of merry quirk, rollicking, gay.'[14] Originally published in the *Scots Observer*, this remark may have resonated with readers accustomed to encountering stereotypes. But the main humour remains squarely at Barrie's expense.

The chief, extended joke is about Barrie's unclubbability. He is not precisely antisocial, as 'He was evidently anxious to please,' but he seems to be constitutionally, even physically, unable even to go through the motions of normal social interaction.[15] The piece has a number of moments of physical comedy, beginning with a handshake:

> I was introduced to him, and we both held out our hands: having shaken his, I let go. His remained in the air, as if the ceremony was new to him. Several others were introduced, and he gave to all his hand to do what they liked with it. This being over he placed it by his side. We then adjourned with unwonted solemnity to the hall where dinner was to be served.[16]

As in Henri Bergson's argument that laughter derives from a person unexpectedly behaving like a machine, Barrie does indeed seem to merely be going through the motions, even expecting others to power his hand for him.[17] Despite his best efforts, Barrie casts a pall over the gathering, inspiring 'solemnity'. Indeed, Barrie's major 'struggle' in the evening is with laughter:

> When a joke was made, you could see him struggling, not with his face alone, to laugh heartily. It was as if he tugged the strings that work the organs of risibility, but either the strings were broken or he had forgotten to bring the organs. Only once did he manage a genuine smile, but some of us forgot ourselves and cheered, and it fled. . . . Our cheering did not offend him. He took it in the spirit in which it was meant. But he was chiefly engaged in keeping the so-called smile there.[18]

This description suggests something fundamentally wrong with Barrie's make-up, but the humour largely lies in the detailed description.

As physical comedy in written form, this sequence recalls Jerome K. Jerome's style, perhaps most memorably encapsulated in an extended sequence from *Three Men in a Boat (To Say Nothing of the Dog)* (1888) about the eponymous crew's attempts to open a tin of pineapple without a tin-opener:

> We beat it out flat; we beat it back square; we battered it into every form known to geometry – but we could not make a hole in it. Then George went at it, and knocked it into a shape, so strange, so weird, so unearthly in its wild hideousness, that he got frightened and threw away the mast. Then we all three sat round it on the grass and looked at it.[19]

The major distinction between these two excerpts (besides sheer length: this is one of ten paragraphs in the incident of the pine-apple tin) is the use of the collective 'we'. Not only does Jerome describe the collective action of three men, but also the reader might be expected to have encountered a similar problem, on a smaller scale (because the passage's hyperbole is clear). Barrie places the predicament in the third person; the collective 'we' observes and engages. Although Barrie seems almost inhuman in his confusion about social gestures, this very confusion may be familiar to readers. After all, Barrie and the club members are suc-ceeding in communicating their mutual goodwill, without the aid of the usual social signals. Barrie tries to use these social signals and conventions, though he seems to fail. But even the effort pro-duces something like the desired effect. These conventions might be silly, but they can indeed convey an earnest desire to please, even when followed badly.

By the end of the evening and the sketch, some of the joke is on the extent to which Barrie's manoeuvres fail. He painstakingly performs the duties of a chairman – indeed, there's an extended riff on the attention he pays to the programme – but the spirit falls flat:

> He proposed the toast of the Queen in those words.
> He had to call upon the various speakers and singers, and as soon as he had uttered their names, he fell back with the recoil.
> His own health was proposed, and we sung determinedly that he was a jolly good fellow. When we asked each other who could deny it, he sat and scowled. His speech in reply consisted of fifty words at least, but it was probably intended to be confidential in nature, for it never crossed the table; and though it has been repeated to me, I scorn to betray a secret.[20]

This description makes clear that a good chairman is more than a programme, more than a way of orchestrating the proceedings. The inescapable conclusion is that the evening was not fun for the participants: as they in turn go through the motions of 'For He's a Jolly Good Fellow', the joke seems to be that they stray dangerously close to literally challenging each other to 'deny it' – which would seem to be speaking the truth. Paradoxically, in writing this article Barrie gains social traction with his readers through painting a picture of himself as intensely socially awkward. In particular, he stresses his taciturnity, yet his jokes are funny in their length, like Jerome's. In contrast to the club members, the readers of this piece likely have a good time.

Barrie's twentieth-century commentary on this story largely focuses on his habit of passing such pieces off as third-person journalism – all anonymous, of course. Gleefully, he reports that most took its authorship at face value. However, he does claim that the event itself happened: 'It was true, too, that I had presided at the Greenock dinner referred to. This must have been my first public appearance in any chair, for in the days of Mr Anon I was so afraid of oratory that rather than make a speech I would have fled the country.'[21] He then dilates upon a later piece he wrote claiming to be an interview with his butler, boasting that he baffled his butler with its appearance. Like 'Mr Barrie in the Chair', the piece is not especially flattering and emphasises the notion that Barrie is unsocial: the premise is that the interviewer talks with the butler because Barrie makes an appointment with him, then flees. Although Barrie impersonates his butler in his authorship, the frame exaggerates the class distinctions between Barrie and his butler and attributes his social awkwardness to unclubbability rather than class upbringing.

My search for biographical connections between Barrie, Jerome and Zangwill led me to the following paragraph from the Dundee *Evening Telegraph* in 1891, which was published months before the first issue of the *Idler* and centres on a gathering of the *Home Chimes* circle:

Mr F. W. Robinson, the genial author of 'Grandmother's Money', and other excellent novels, was the hero of a pleasant little gathering at the Criterion Restaurant the other evening. Among the guests was Mr J. M. Barrie. To the toast of his health, proposed by Mr Zangwill, the Scotch humourist made a characteristic and original reply. In the course of his speech, the author of 'The Bachelors' Club' had asked the author of 'Auld Licht Idylls' how the title of that remarkable work was pronounced, and when, after his health had been drunk amid enthusiastic cries of 'Barrie', the languid genius rose to respond, his speech consisted of five words. They were, 'It is "Auld Licht Idylls".' It was a lesson alike in pronunciation and brevity.[22]

Given Barrie's claims to have written multiple pieces of this sort about himself, it seems likely that he authored it: as a Scotsman, he seems the most likely of the group to be interested in publishing in Dundee. Like 'Mr Barrie in the Chair', it plays on his taciturnity and overly literal responses to social conventions. Among this group of friends, Barrie is unclubbable but not unpopular: his friends cry 'enthusiastically' for him to speak. The incident stresses his Scottishness: not only does it label him 'the Scotch humourist', but also the substance of his reply is 'a lesson . . . in pronunciation' – one that completely fails to carry over to the print medium but is perhaps unnecessary for a Scottish audience. Regardless of the authorship, Barrie controls this joke, represented as 'the languid genius' among friends, not a fish out of water.

External accounts by the *Idler* circle confirm the notion that Barrie acquitted himself well at this type of social gathering. As we saw in the Introduction, Arthur Conan Doyle wrote of Barrie's participation in the *Idler* At-Homes in his memoirs and wrote to his mother of his early friendship with Barrie and Jerome.[23] Jerome writes much of Barrie in his memoirs, including his role at a group dinner:

> I recall a dinner given me on the eve of my setting out for a lecturing tour through America. Barrie was in the chair, I think – anyhow in one of them. In the others were Conan Doyle, Barry Pain, Zangwill, Pett-Ridge, Hall Caine – some twenty in all. Everybody made a speech. I am supposed to be rather good at after-dinner speaking, but forgot everything I had intended to say that night.[24]

The idea that Barrie would take the chair in this sort of gathering seems antithetical to the image of him as an unsociable, unclubbable, emotionally stunted man. Jerome's very lack of memory as to whether or not Barrie occupied the chair suggests that it would not have been extraordinary if he had done so. Of course, this passage primarily hones Jerome's own self-representation. He, too, aspired to upward social mobility, though, as we have seen, he was less successful in that regard than Barrie. Perhaps Jerome's attempts to frame himself as a 'rather good' speaker were less effective in managing his social rise than Barrie's more exaggerated self-deprecation.

Barrie's friendship with Jerome formed his primary connection to the *Idler* circle. In their late-career memoirs and autobiographies, Jerome makes more of the connection than Barrie does, but by the 1920s and '30s Barrie was a wealthy baronet, whereas Jerome's *Times* obituary marked him as a has-been. In his 1926 memoir, *My Life and Times*, Jerome makes frequent reference to Barrie, especially emphasising their friendship's origins when both men wrote for F. W. Robinson's monthly magazine *Home Chimes*:

> Swinburne, Watts-Dunton, Doctor Westland Marston and his blind son Philip, the poet, Coulson Kernahan, William Sharp, Coventry Patmore, Bret Harte, and J. M. Barrie, were among my fellow contributors to *Home Chimes*. Barrie has left it on record that his chief purpose in coming to London was to see with his own eyes the editorial office from which *Home Chimes* was broadcasted to the world. He had been disappointed to find it up two flights of stairs in a narrow lane off Paternoster Row. He had expected that, if only as a result of his own contributions, Robinson would have been occupying more palatial premises.[25]

In his 1937 memoir and reprinting of early periodical essays, *The Greenwood Hat*, Barrie presents a different narrative of his early days, one that emphasises Frederick Greenwood, not Robinson, as the editor who made his career – and whom he was most eager to see when he came from Nottingham to London. Of course, Jerome engages in some hyperbole, and it is difficult to tell precisely where it begins. *Home Chimes* was instrumental to Jerome's career (it serialised *Three Men in a Boat*), while the *St James* not only played a more crucial role in Barrie's career – being one of the primary places he published the 'Auld Licht' stories that would go on to form the basis for much of his early novel career – but was also a more prestigious publication.[26]

Conversely, Barrie only mentions Jerome once in his own memoir, as we saw in the introduction. *The Greenwood Hat, Being a Memoir of James Anon 1855–1887*, explicitly treats

Barrie's early journalistic days in London and features his early periodical writing. His third-person stand-in character is so named because of the anonymous system of publication at the *St James's Gazette* and elsewhere at the time: 'This book consists merely of some old newspaper articles tied together with a string of memories which the re-reading of them has evoked. They are samples of hundreds I wrote (as Mr Anon) in my first two years in London in the late 'eighties.'[27] Throughout, Barrie refers to himself as 'James Anon' to evoke the anonymous publication. His introduction evokes the notion of 'idleness' that Jerome made famous: 'To be more candid, I question whether I make this memoir of Anon to uplift my friends so much as in idleness to recall myself.'[28] In keeping with Barrie's unclubbable persona, the memoir contains much less name-dropping than Jerome's or even Doyle's.

Barrie is very funny about his own naivete and Greenwood's eminence. The eponymous hat is one that he wears when going to see Greenwood: 'The Hat, of course, was bought for the subjection of Greenwood. He [James Anon] understood that without a silk hat he could not advance upon a lordly editor, and from first to last it was used entirely for this purpose every few weeks. It never fitted him . . . He had, however, a religious faith in it.'[29] Through the hat, Barrie marks himself as an outsider in terms of geography, class and, not insignificantly, disposition. Despite having been a baronet for over twenty years (since 1913), Barrie writes in *The Greenwood Hat* that he 'does not know his size in hats to this day'.[30] Having achieved literary, monetary and class success, he almost aggressively maintains the personal quirks of an outsider. This kind of unclubbability is thus reframed not as a demographic ineligibility but as an integral part of the kind of personality that enabled Barrie to achieve his various successes.

Barrie's most prominent (and well publicised) avenue of organised sociability was his cricket team, which saw him at the head of a sporting endeavour but also at the nexus of a social network. Both roles ran counter to Barrie's general persona, leading to the impression, recounted in Kevin Telfer's monograph on the team, 'that Barrie's cricket team was actually just an elaborate joke'.[31] Indeed, the team's name is a joke, as we saw in the introduction, that contains self-deprecation as well as irreverent cultural appropriation. Cricket is especially a sport of the upper classes, and its play affords plenty of time for socialising. Telfer argues that, for Barrie, cricket was 'far more than just a game, it was also a symbol of opposition to the modern urban values of dour progress, profit margins, and colonial expansion'.[32] A different political interpretation is that cricket indicated both a connection to the aristocratic tradition (as Wodehouse's Mike discovers, to play as a full-time team member rather than as a 'pro' coaching others, one must be independently wealthy), outdoor activity and, above all, quintessential Englishness. All these might be seen as a joke coming from Barrie with his outsider status – both intrinsic (like his Scottish origins) and cultivated. As with the 'Idler's Club', one level of the joke may be that these humorists with varied backgrounds could be considered cricket players at all.

Whatever personal satisfaction Barrie may have gained from his role at the helm of a cricket team, it was also profoundly enmeshed in his professional image. Like a club, it allowed him to cultivate relationships at the nexus of the personal and the professional, pursuing friendships out of business contacts that might in turn become professionally advantageous. Many literary men played on Barrie's team, as we saw in the Introduction, including writers and illustrators for the *Idler* and *Punch*, which overlapped, especially through Bernard Partridge.[33] Many of the figures in this study were Allahakbarries at one time or another, from Jerome to Wodehouse. Barrie's team was one of a loose network of affiliated teams that took on different configurations over the years along personal and professional lines. The same loose group around the Allahakbarries played in some themed matches, notably Artists v. Writers and Married v. Single, as well as on other teams, including the 'Idlers' and Undershaw XI, both captained by Doyle.[34] Doyle was the best cricket player in the group, and while he was serving as a doctor in the Boer War, many of the Allahakbarries played as 'Arthur Conan Doyle's IX'.[35] The Allahakbarries thus essentially constituted a club whose premise is a joke, comprised of humorists who depicted clubs with ridiculous premises.

The Allahakbarries' effect was not confined to Barrie's immediate social circle: the team had a wider print culture presence. Several of the matches had press coverage, including the Artists v. Writers match,[36] and Barrie discusses the team in *The Greenwood Hat*. Given the number of writers and artists, cricket aided their image-building, connecting them to the leisured classes, a real-life equivalent of the Idler's Club. Underlining the connection between their personal and professional interests, Barrie had two short books privately printed for his cricket team, as he states in *The Greenwood Hat*, which itself was privately printed in 1930 before being published for the general public in 1937: 'Anon twice made little books about the "Broadway Week", the first consisting of four pages, but the second was swollen to thirty.'[37] The second volume, *Allahakbarries C.C.* (1899, 1950), is an inside joke: it is not surprising that it was not publicly printed in Barrie's lifetime, unlike *The Greenwood Hat*, and it has never been in wide circulation. Unlike the 'Idler's Club' and other club stories, it is not aimed at a wide public, but a very specific group of friends for a specific occasion: a particular cricket match. The volume contains some material that might be circulated more widely, chiefly pieces by the writers and illustrators on the team, caricaturing themselves, Barrie and their teammates. Barrie includes one of these, a poem by team member Owen Seaman, in *The Greenwood Hat*.[38] But much of the rest of the text, written by Barrie, is full of comic 'predictions' of how the match will play out, which are difficult for a common reader to follow. Barrie even leaves a blank page for the score to be recorded.[39] Clearly, this volume has pragmatic and entertainment use at a particular time for a particular group. It is an example of a true coterie text, which serves to illustrate by contrast the ways in which many of these humorists' print participations in clublike structures were foundationally presentations of their public personae.

A comedy of anonymity

Barrie's experiences in journalism, and especially his concern with anonymous publication, doubtless influenced *When a Man's Single* (1888, serialised 1887 in *British Weekly*). Despite the double marriage plot, the novel's true energy comes from the literary fellowship around the newspaper. Characteristically of Barrie, this does not rise to the clublike comfort of *Tommy and Co.*'s *Good Humour* office. The newspaper office fuels the humour, and different sorts of newspaper jokes also appear: those that readers might have recognised as being reused from Barrie's periodical pieces, such as someone proposing with a thimble, and a few jokes recycled from *My Lady Nicotine*.[40] The newspaper provides the Scottish protagonist, Rob Angus, with class mobility: he rises to become a leader writer, which as a salaried position enables him to marry a landed colonel's daughter. As he navigates this rise, he learns the implicit rules of both his profession and his new social milieu. Distinctions between the two, particularly dealing with anonymity, drive the novel's plot and humour.

Parallels to Barrie's own life abound. Framed in Thrums, the novel opens with a sad episode. Despite the light-hearted title, alluding to a phrase that ends 'he lives at his ease',[41] Rob becomes 'single' upon the accidental death of his young niece and ward, Davy – possibly an allusion to the childhood death of Barrie's older brother, David, which Birkin identifies as a profound influence on his life and work.[42] Ironically freed, Rob moves from Scotland to a fictional Midlands manufacturing town called Silchester – perhaps based on Nottingham, where Barrie went after he left Scotland – and from thence to London.

The novel's romance is rooted in journalism. Rob's relationship problems stem from a poor review he wrote for the joy of flexing his muscles but later regrets when he meets Mary Arbinger, who wrote the offending novel. Thus, his romance is complicated by literary sociability: the distinction between reviewing a book in the abstract and thinking of a review as a work in circulation and something that affects a live person whom he might meet. To add to the humour of the situation, the same periodical had published a prior review that was very different in spirit. This also becomes a joke on the nature of the newspaper as a business and the absurdity of ascribing a single view to a newspaper (a tempting practice in which scholars still engage today).

The dinner party where Rob meets Mary is full of jokes about his social faux pas stemming from his lack of familiarity with social conventions:

> The dinner had already begun, but the first thing he realized as he took his seat was that there was a lady on each side of him, and a table-napkin in front. He was not sure if he was expected to address the ladies, and he was still less certain about the table-napkin. Of such things he had read, and he had even tried to be prepared for them. Rob looked nervously at the napkin, and then took a covert glance along the table. There was not a napkin in sight except one which a farmer had tied round his neck. Rob's fingers wanted to leave the napkin alone, but by an effort he forced them toward it. All this time his face was a blank, but the internal struggle was sharp. He took hold of the napkin, however, and spread it on his knees. It fell to the floor imme-diately afterwards, but he disregarded that. It was no longer staring

at him from the table, and with a heavy sigh of relief he began to feel more at ease. There is nothing like burying our bogies.[43]

The physical comedy recalls Barrie's account of his own performance at the Burns dinner, and the underlying humour remains similar: that of a fish out of water. Yet Rob here is unfamiliar with the social conventions, whereas Barrie seemed to understand them but be physically unable to fulfil them. Each is also clearly marked as Scottish and consequently misread by his dinner companion: the woman who sits next to Rob 'was interested in a tame Scotsman'.[44] He does his best to oblige, and here the joke is more overtly on English misperceptions of Scotland and its people.

Furthermore, Rob has another problem at this dinner party. He's trying to avoid Colonel Abinger because of a previous meeting in which Rob 'unconsciously'[45] flouted actual laws (rather than social or professional convention) by poaching in the Colonel's stream. A humorous scene details how the Colonel discovers Rob poaching but ends up engrossed in the drama of landing the fish on his line: 'Then he [Rob] apologized, offered all his fish in lieu of his name and address, retired coolly so long as the furious soldier was in sight, and as soon as he turned a corner disappeared rapidly. He could not feel that this was the best introduction to the man with whom he was now on his way to dine.'[46] As it turns out, he is saved from this embarrassment at the party itself as he circumvents his host.

The dinner party highlights Rob's difficulty in negotiating the social environment of Silchester, particularly the relationship between actual sociability and literary sociability. Some of this rests on the notion of journalistic anonymity. Part of the confusion with Mary has to do with the anonymity of his review – and of course the anonymity of Mary's original publication; she publishes the book under the pseudonym 'M'. The favourable review refers to her as a man, but Rob's slam assumes she is a woman.[47] Mary's friend Nell spends much of the previous chapter trying to figure out Rob's identity, chiefly by entrancing a schoolboy friend, Greybrook, and getting him to ask at the newspaper's office. But Rob reveals his own identity to her after a little flattery. In a social setting, and new to the business, he is unable to do what his editor did under pressure from Greybrook: protect journalistic anonymity. The idea that Nell could be professionally interested in the literary world does not occur to him because of her gender.

When Rob moves to London, he is similarly confronted with the mysterious distinction between print sociability and face-to-face contact, particularly through the joint anonymities of journalism and the London street: 'A certain awe came upon Rob as he went down Fleet Street on the one side, and up it on the other. He could not resist looking into the faces of the persons who passed him, and wondering if they edited the *Times*.'[48] The narrator makes clear that Rob misreads many characters: 'Rob did not recognize a distinguished poet in a little stout man who was looking pensively at a barrowful of walnuts, and he was mistaken in thinking that the bearded gentleman who held his head so high must be somebody in particular.'[49] To cap it off, he himself is misread: 'Rob observed a pale young man gazing wistfully at him, and wondered if he was a thief or a sub-editor. He was merely an aspirant who had come to London that morning to make his fortune, and he took Rob for a leader writer at the least.'[50] Conversely, in Silchester, Rob reverses the street encounter: 'Rob had written many leaders, and followed readers through the streets wondering if they liked them.'[51] Here Barrie firmly connects the experience of passing someone in the street with that of encountering their words on a newspaper page – in both directions. In both cases, many things about the other person are unknown and unknowable; however, a definite sort of contact is made, but one that is difficult if not impossible to bridge into a more intimate type of sociability. Therein lies Rob's problem. Although the flip side is that in Silchester the print world is less anonymous and less removed from the social world than Rob initially thinks.

In fact, in Silchester, many of the jokes about newspapers have to do with the imprinting of individual personalities. The newspaper may seem to be an impassive record, but Barrie delights in showing the human factor. For instance, a politician's speech is not only set in type as it comes in, but the full summary is printed before the speech concludes. Likewise, a review of a concert is set before the concert ends: 'they seldom waited for the end of anything on the *Mirror*'.[52] One of the *Mirror*'s staff is nicknamed Umbrage because of a mistake he once made interpreting a telegram reading 'Zulus have taken Umbrage'[53] into the headline 'LATEST NEWS OF THE WAR; CAPTURE OF UMBRAGE BY THE ZULUS'.[54] His mistake jams the machine of the press, inadvertently inserting him into the headlines; his nickname reinforces that idea. When lovestruck Rob forgets to write his piece about Colonel Abinger's speech, he discovers that it has been done for him – presumably by a member of the staff who guessed at its contents. But this further irritates the Colonel because the notice is so brief – and he assumes that Rob wrote it.

When Rob does find a close friend in 'Noble Simms' (later revealed to be Dick Abinger, Mary's brother), the two develop their friendship through notes that Simms sends up their mutual staircase to Rob: 'Rob found these suggestions valuable, and often thought, as he passed Simms's door, of going in to thank him, but he had an uncomfortable feeling that Simms did not want him. Of course Rob was wrong. Simms had feared at first to saddle himself with a man who might prove incapable; and besides, he generally liked those persons best whom he saw least frequently.'[55] In other words, Simms has his own version of unclubbability. Part of this professional instruction involves the defence of anonymous publication: '"I would gladly say 'Use my name'," Simms wrote, "but it is the glory of anonymous journalism that names are nothing and good stuff everything. I assure you that on the press it is the men who have it in them that succeed, and the best of them become the editors."'[56] In *The Greenwood Hat*, Barrie emphasises that Greenwood enjoyed the speculation that the anonymous pieces were written by known stars but also delighted in revealing that popular articles were by relative unknowns.[57] Nevertheless, Simms's use of gendered language is telling: anonymity plays differently for him than it does for his sister. This is not yet the milieu of Tommy and Jennie Baxter.

Simms's skill in journalism comes at the expense of his personal relationships. When Rorrison introduces Simms to Rob, he tells him that Simms can make 'copy' out of anything and supplies several anecdotes about incidents in their friendship that turned into articles – including one anecdote that already appeared in *My Lady Nicotine* (with another object substituted).[58] But the way Rorrison describes it, it sounds like their friendship suffers as a result. He frames the practice to Rob, saying Simms 'would have had an article out of you before he had talked with you as long as I have done.'[59] The formulation, which recurs frequently, of taking an article or 'copy'[60] 'out of' a friend without notice or permission sounds uncomfortable and invasive. One occurrence stresses Simms's financial motives: 'When I play on his piano I put scraps of paper on the notes to guide me, and he made his three guineas out of that.'[61] Beyond the fictional world, an unfavourable review of Barrie's *Edinburgh Eleven* in the *Glasgow Herald* compares him to his own character: 'Doubtless he is right in thus using the men whom he has in one way or another come across; like Mr Noble Sims [*sic*] in his own novel "Whcn a Man's Single", he would make an article out of anything or anybody.'[62] In some ways, Barrie encouraged autobiographical readings of his works, although, as we have seen, he also blurred the line in the other direction between fiction and life-writing.

As Simms (or rather Dick) introduces Rob to London literary society, he takes him to literary clubs:

> The Wigwam is one of the best-known literary clubs in London, and as they rattled to it in a hansom, the driver of which was the broken son of a peer, Rob remarked that its fame had even travelled to his saw-mill.
>
> 'It has such a name,' said Simms in reply, 'that I feel sorry for any one who is taken to it for the first time. The best way to admire the Wigwam is not to go to it.'
>
> 'I always thought it was considered the pleasantest club in London,' Rob said.
>
> 'So it is,' said Simms, who was a member of half a dozen; 'most of the others are only meant for sitting in on padded chairs and calling out "sh-sh" when any other body speaks.'[63]

As in Chapter 4, the club throws Rob and Dick's friendship into relief, rather than furthering it. Dick, particularly considering his actual social status, wields the power of unclubbability. 'A member of half a dozen' clubs, Dick uses them for social cachet: he has the social power to spurn famous clubs. The Wigwam was the name of a real London club, featuring in 'Idler's Club' contributor Joseph Hatton's *Club-Land* (1890).[64]

A mixed-sex club elicits a similar reaction:

> Rob did not altogether enjoy the Symphonia, which is a polite club attended by the literary fry of both sexes ; the ladies who write because they cannot help it, the poets who excuse their verses because they were young when they did them, the clergymen who publish their sermons by request of their congregations, the tourists who have been to Spain and cannot kcep it to themselves. The club meets once a fortnight, for the purpose of not listening to music and recitations; and the members, of whom the ladies outnumber the men, sit in groups

round little lions who roar mildly. The Symphonia is very fashionable and select, and having heard the little lions a-roaring, you get a cup of coffee and go home again.[65]

Neither club is lingered in. Both clubs draw out a surprising side of Dick: in the first, he uncharacteristically sings a comic song critiquing the press, and in the second, he wears 'the lion's skin'.[66] This is in keeping with Barrie's theme that clubs impose artificial character traits on their members, thereby urging them towards conformity.

These clubs do not test Dick and Rob's friendship, but another class-associated institution does: marriage. When Rob thinks Mary is engaged to an aristocrat, Dick reinforces that belief because of the difference in their social standings. Despite their friendship, he would prefer not to have his sister marry Rob. But at that moment, their friendship is also most clearly declared:

> Dick did not dare to look him in the face, but Rob put his hand on the shoulder of Mary's brother.
>
> 'I was a madman,' he said, 'to think that she could ever have cared for me, but this will not interfere with our friendship, Abinger?'
>
> 'Surely not,' said Dick, taking Rob's hand.
>
> It was one of those awful moments in men's lives when they allow, face to face, that they like each other.[67]

Like Zangwill's 'masculine substitute for a kiss',[68] this is a moment that acknowledges the fragility and power of male friendships – the extent to which they largely remain unspoken and the power of the moments in which they are. Barrie's use of 'awful' here resonates both humorously as terrible, uncomfortable or awkward, but also seriously as commanding and deserving of awe. In a classic Sedgwickian triangulation, a woman inspires this intimacy between men.[69] As with Zangwill's cigar-sharing, it does not have to be erotic to be significant: a handshake and an explicit relationship discussion can be so momentous as to be frightening.

Dick ends the novel by being intensely 'indifferent'[70] – perhaps a different version of unclubbable. He discovers that he has ceased to love Nell, but he plans to marry her anyway, and imagines they 'shall get on very well together'.[71] Yet he is disturbed by his own lack of feeling:

Except by fits and starts I have ceased apparently to be interested in anything. The only thing nowadays that rouses my indignation is the attempt on any one's part to draw me into an argument on any subject under the sun. Here is this Irish question; I can pump up an article in three paragraphs on it, but I don't really seem to care whether it is ever settled or not. Should we have a republic? I don't mind; it is all the same to me: but don't give me the casting vote. Is Gladstone a god? is Gladstone the devil? They say he is one or other, and I am content to let them fight it out. How long is it since I gave a thought to religion? What am I? There are men who come into this room and announce that they are agnostics, as if that were a new profession. Am I an agnostic? I think not; and if I was I would keep it to myself. My soul does not trouble me at all, except for five minutes or so now and again. On the whole I seem to be indifferent as to whether I have one, or what is to become of it.[72]

Is Dick's journalistic habit of arguing a question pragmatically a symptom or a cause of his larger malaise? The question is exacerbated at the close of the chapter:

Dick rose and paced the room, until his face gave the lie to everything he had told himself. His lips quivered and his whole body shook. He stood in an agony against the mantelpiece with his head in his hands, and emotions had possession of him compared with which the emotions of any other person described in this book were but children's fancies. By and by he became calm, and began to undress. Suddenly he remembered something. He rummaged for his keys in the pocket of the coat he had cast off, and, opening his desk, wrote on a slip of paper that he took from it, 'Scalping Knife, Man Frightened to Get Married (humorous)!'

    'My God!' he groaned, 'I would write an article, I think, on my mother's coffin.'[73]

Like the *Glasgow Herald*, Birkin sees this sentiment as autobiographical on Barrie's part.[74] Regardless, it's distinctly a variation on the larger Barrie theme of unclubbability: in this case, a disposition that hinders the division between the personal and the professional that undergirds many assumptions of club life. To put it another way, Dick cannot stop working, which makes him a poor idler (though similar to the Idlers).

Meanwhile, Rob has become much more socially acceptable; when he meets the Colonel again, 'This was the Angus who had

once been unable to salute anybody without wondering what on
earth he ought to say next. . . . Rob was no longer the hobblede-
hoy of last Christmas. He was rather particular about the cut of
his coat. He had forgotten that he was not a colonel's social equal.
In short, when he entered a room now he knew what to do with
his hat.'[75] These social graces help propel him into a different
social rank: a salary of £800 a year on *The Wire* and the hand of
a landed colonel's daughter. Rob's unclubbability ends up attributed to circumstance, not disposition. Months in the metropolis
have seasoned the Scotsman; also, some degree of unclubbability
may result from his mourning of his niece's death, which time has
softened. The unclubbable journalist is bifurcated by the end of
the book into Rob, unclubbable by demographic reasons which
he overcomes, and Dick, unclubbable by disposition, which he can
conceal, given his well-bred social graces.

Reviewers responded especially personally to this book, which
might not be surprising given the nature of its relationship to
their profession. A reviewer in the *Graphic* not only noted that
'The love is well done, the journalism still better,' but also waxed
almost vehement and possibly autobiographical: 'plenty of men
who have won to the front by means of trampling down difficulties, and have taken their calling grimly, and made themselves
its slaves in order that they might become its masters, will find
but little over-colour even in that curiously-powerful scene where
Dick Abinger suddenly finds himself, by force of habit, mechanically setting down his own spoiled life for humorous copy.'[76] The
Dundee Courier, perhaps especially partisan towards 'the Scotch
humourist', praised the superlatively 'truthful' nature of the novel:
'That he is qualified to write on [the internal working of a newspaper office] is admitted at once, when he tells us of a printing
foreman who had a settled opinion that the sub-editor arranged
with leading statesmen nightly to flood the composing-room with
copy. That printing foreman was no mere creation of the writer's
brain.'[77] The *Pall Mall Gazette* directly contradicts the *Graphic*,
preferring the love over the journalism, which it describes as 'ridiculous caricature'.[78] But most reviews were positive, including that
in *The Times*, which praised Noble Simms as 'the person who
really gives distinction to the book' and claiming he would 'be rec-
ognized as the original of many of Mr Barrie's fugitive sketches'.[79]
As in Barrie's other stories, the blurring of literary and real roles
invites readers to guess at what's 'real' amid the farce.

A highly antisocial society

Debuting between the serial and book of *When a Man's Single*, Barrie's first published book, *Better Dead* (1888), takes a less realistic approach to the theme of a young man coming from Scotland to London. Famously, Barrie later disavowed the book, as Birkin reports: 'When asked of his opinion of it in later years, Barrie's reply was the title.'[80] In *The Greenwood Hat*, he recalls his pride in the book: 'from no other book of his had he such a lively rush of blood to the head as when "Better Dead" was first placed in his hands'. Even in this nostalgic piece, Barrie embeds self-deprecating asides: 'The cover of the book, which is certainly the best of it, shows the then well-known figures of Sir William Harcourt and Lord Randolph Churchill about to turn a street corner where the well-intentioned hero is waiting for them with an upraised knife.'[81] Like 'The Proposal Club' and *The Suicide Club*, *Better Dead* features a club that deals in death, the Society for Doing Without Some People. But unlike the others, this novel treats the club with rather light-hearted fun. The tone throughout is one of frivolity rather than suspense – although the frivolity of the tone in turn creates a menace all its own.

Andrew, this novel's Scottish protagonist in London, shares Rob's lack of familiarity with London social rules, but he has even more chutzpah, as the book's first line indicates: 'When Andrew Riach went to London, his intention was to become private secretary to a member of the Cabinet. If time permitted, he proposed writing for the Press.'[82] In part because he personally calls on cabinet ministers and launches into reading his testimonials, this attempt fails. In a trope familiar from previous chapters, he is introduced to the club when he sees one of its members perform strange actions, then follows him and seeks explanations. In this case, he watches the President follow a man and shove him into the Thames. The rationale of the club, as the President describes it, is this: 'The grand function of the Society is to find out the persons who have a claim on it, and in the interests of humanity to lay their condition before them. After that it is in the majority of cases for themselves to decide whether they will go or stay on.'[83] The novel emphasises those times when the Society ends up acting for the people it has deemed 'better dead'.

It is a society and not a club; still, election works similarly. As the President says when trying to convince Andrew, 'Three black balls exclude.'[84] There is a probationary period of three months, after which time the prospective member submits a thesis, 'generally a paper with a statement of the line of action you propose to adopt, subject to the Society's approval'.[85] Approval means membership; the reverse, it is implied, means becoming one of the Society's victims. The forms of a club – and with a thesis, hints of a university – contrast with calculated extermination. Andrew is warned of a previous young man who went too far: 'It went to his head. He took a bedroom in Pall Mall and sat at the window with an electric rifle picking them off on the door-steps of the clubs. It was a noble idea, but of course it imperilled the very existence of the society.'[86] Clubs come under literal fire here, and the society objects not to the aims but to the scale.

Part of the humour of *Better Dead* lies in name-dropping. The society contemplates killing 'Stead, of the "Pall Mall Gazette"' and 'Idler's Club' column contributors Clement Scott and Andrew Lang.[87] Millicent Fawcett appears and makes an impassioned speech to the Society to consider accepting women to both dimensions of their society: as members, and as people to do without. She demands equality and calls them out for their 'injustice': 'Your president tells me you are at present inquiring for the address of the man who signs himself "Paterfamilias" in the "Times"; but the letters from "A British Matron" are of no account.'[88] Another of the future contributors to the 'Idler's Club' column receives this backhanded compliment: 'Has not Mrs Lynn Linton another article in the new "Nineteenth Century" that makes her worthy your attention?'[89] At least one celebrity took the fictional assassination threat as a compliment. In *The Greenwood Hat*, Barrie recalls, 'Lord Randolph was not only one of the few people who wrote to the author about "Better Dead", but he was also the first.'[90] These celebrity references, antisocial though they are, may have helped Barrie advance his own career.

Andrew ultimately has a great impact on the press, though not in the way he had initially envisioned:

> It was Andrew – though he never got the credit of it – who put his senior in possession of the necessary particulars about the comic writers whose subject is teetotalism and spinsters.
>
> He was unwearying, indeed, in his efforts with regard to the comic journals generally, and the first man of any note that he disposed of was 'Punch's' favorite artist on Scotch matters. This was in an alley off Fleet Street.[91]

Anonymity as a measure of protection takes on a new meaning in this context. Andrew's fury seems to vent itself particularly against the comic press: 'The young Scotchman resented people's merriment over nothing; sometimes he took the Underground Railway just to catch clerks at "Tit-Bits".'[92] In a macabre twist on Rob's imaginings that he might read the reading and writing habits of anonymous figures in the London street, Andrew uses those habits as fuel for murder. True, Rob engages in violent fantasies when his early articles meet with rejection.[93]

Andrew's adventure ends with his separation from the club and return to a surprisingly domestic future. He runs afoul of the Society for excessive zeal, for in his 'thesis' he proposes to the Society that all people be put to death at age forty-five. The president of the Society, who recruited him in the first place, helps him escape. In a happy ending, he returns to Scotland and marries his sweetheart:

> Domesticated and repentant, he has renounced the devil and all her works.
>
> Sometimes, when thinking of the past, the babble of his lovely babies jars upon him, and, still half-dreaming, he brings their heads close together.
>
> At such a time all the anxious mother has to say is:
>
> 'Andrew!'
>
> Then with a start he lays them gently in a heap on the floor, and, striding the room, soon regains his composure.
>
> For Andrew has told Clarrie all the indiscretions of his life in London, and she has forgiven every thing.
>
> Ah, what will not a wife forgive![94]

In a stark contrast to the opening of *When a Man's Single*, potential infanticide is played for a laugh. Andrew's murders are 'indiscretions'. But amidst the patent unreality of it all, Andrew seems to form no real human connections, even within the society. In a way, that remains the most chilling angle of the book.

Sociable unsociability

Conversely, Barrie's most positive model of fellowship lies in an unofficial club whose members find commonality in their unsociability. The Arcadians in *My Lady Nicotine* (1890) are moulded into an unclubbable, unsociable type based on their association with each other. Barrie frames this not entirely by association but through the habit of 'smoking the Arcadia'. [95] As Barrie biographer (also novelist and dedicatee of Wodehouse's *Summer Lightning*)[96] Denis Mackail notes, the production of the book sprang from concerns about periodical anonymity:

> *My Lady Nicotine*, though as usual there had been plenty of careful and skilful revision, consisted of old articles – not all, though certainly most of them, connected with smoking – which he had gathered from the *St James's*, the *Edinburgh Evening Dispatch*, and even from so far away in point of time as the *Nottingham Journal*; and again it is a sign of his increasing escape from anonymity that one of the main reasons why he put the collection together was to establish his title to the contents in the face of pirates and rival claimants.[97]

The structure of loose affiliation between pieces echoes the loose affiliation between the Arcadians. Particularly given the parallels between smoking and reading discussed in Chapter 1, this sense of camaraderie can extend easily across the boundary of the book to include common readers, themselves united without directly interacting.

Like Jerome's *Novel Notes* (which it preceded), the loosely constructed novel follows a group of five young men who form an informal club: those who smoke the Arcadian mixture of pipe tobacco. A haze of nostalgia hangs over the book; the narrator has given up smoking upon marrying because his fiancée 'said that I must choose between it and her'.[98] Yet the speaker's claims to be happy in his choice ring hollow:

> I have now come, as those who read will see, to look upon smoking with my wife's eyes. My old bachelor friends complain because I do not allow smoking in the house, but I am always ready to explain my position, and I have not an atom of pity for them. If I cannot smoke here neither shall they.[99]

In a pattern typical of Barrie's narrators, he insists on a personal belief that his narration consistently undermines. It is unclear whether the narrator is aware of this tension and trying to convince himself of his belief, or if he simply lacks self-awareness. The latter dynamic lends itself to a sustained dramatic irony which resembles humour; the former would mean that the narrator is 'in' on the joke at his own expense.

Barrie's narrator describes the Arcadia as an influence that reduces his group of friends to a distinct social, or rather antisocial, type:

> Before I discovered the Arcadia, and communicated it to the other five – including Pettigrew – we had all distinct individualities, but now, except in appearance – and the Arcadia even tells on that – we are as like as holly-leaves. We have the same habits, the same ways of looking at things, the same satisfaction in each other.[100]

Though unclubbable, unfriendly and unsociable to others, the group of Arcadians enjoys each other's company. This recalls another of Barrie's tales of a club for the unclubbable, 'The Club Ghost', one of the stories reprinted in *The Greenwood Hat*. This narrator is likewise a member of a club that emphasises solitude rather than sociability. The club changes the narrator to make him less sociable. The humour extends into absurdity when the narrator meets a dog who behaves much like a club member. Discussing the matter with a club servant, the narrator discovers that the dog was made an honorary member of the club – and that the club changed him as well. Moreover, Barrie suggests that the dog has actually died and that the narrator has encountered his ghost. The paradox of antisociability as a social trait repeatedly preoccupies Barrie.

The Arcadia makes its mark upon the conversation (or lack thereof) of its smokers: 'If you meet in company a man who has ideas and is not shy, yet refuses absolutely to be drawn into talk, you may set him down as one of us. Among the first effects of the Arcadia is to put an end to jabber.'[101] The effect is almost magical, but Barrie distinctly frames it as not a deficit but a dispositional dislike. It's not that the Arcadian has nothing to talk about (he 'has ideas'); nor is he 'shy'. He is simply 'indifferent' – the same word Dick uses to describe himself in *When a Man's Single*.[102] The novel recounts several amusing anecdotes about instances in which one of the Arcadians allows a mistake to remain uncorrected because it would take too much effort to set things right. In the most dramatic case, the narrator allows an acquaintance to persist in the error of thinking the narrator has two brothers instead of one. The acquaintance's persistence in pursuing this topic leads to greater and greater fabrication and ultimately the loss of the friendship – a mixture of the ridiculous and the pathetic. But it indicates the passivity of the Arcadians and their disregard for conventional sociability.

Barrie's initial description of the Arcadians emphasises the extent to which they go out of their way to avoid conversation at dinner parties, some of which is framed as advice for like-minded readers. Some, but not all, of these conversation partners are women. Barrie reuses a joke from *When a Man's Single* about a compliment paid to a lady that hinges on his having a pipe (or in *When a Man's Single* a walking-stick) prone to falling apart: 'Madam . . . what else was to be expected? You came near my pipe – and it lost its head!'[103] In both cases, the care the narrator takes over setting this compliment up is its own source of humour. In *My Lady Nicotine*, this culminates, 'By the help of a note-book, of course I guard myself against paying this very neat compliment to any person more than once.'[104] This recurring joke on the effort required in social humour recalls Barrie's self-representation in 'Mr Barrie in the Chair' and speaks to the politics of social awkwardness. Barrie's narrator concludes this episode by remarking, 'after I smoked the Arcadia the desire to pay ladies compliments went from me'.[105] He thus chooses to be unclubbable rather than elaborately attempting sociability. One wonders how he met and married his wife – although that seems to be a moot point.

In fact, the novel distinctly privileges the domesticity of the five (or six) friends over marriage. They gather in the narrator's rooms – they all live on the same stair – and each has his accustomed place. Jimmy is known by his first name because he was at school with some of them: this is a domestic group of long standing. One of the most touching testaments to their friendship is when the Arcadians help the narrator smoke his last pipe: the last one before his wedding, honouring his promise to his betrothed to give up smoking. It reads like a deathbed or a wake, which is of course funny at a certain level, but also sentimental at the same time: lauding the strength not only of the narrator's love for smoking and his relationship with his smoking paraphernalia, but also of the deep bonds of this male domestic venue. Pettigrew indicates that one can marry and still remain connected – they allow him as at least partially one of their own, although his marriage as well as his journalistic success make him distinct – but the narrator's departure from smoking forms a more overt break.

To emphasise the connection between the pleasures of smoking and the pleasures of reading, the novel closes not with the scene of the narrator's last pipe, nor even of his wedding or domestic bliss, but rather with his marital habit of smoking vicariously through the neighbour who shares the wall of his flat. The chapter is entitled 'When my wife is asleep and all the house is still'.[106] Although the chapter title seems to indicate that the narrator smokes in secret, that is not quite the case: 'when my wife is asleep and all the house is still, I listen to the man through the wall. At such times I have my briar in my mouth, but there is no harm in that, for it is empty.'[107] Although he has never seen this man, the narrator follows his actions in smoking his pipes carefully and in great detail, deducing from the sounds not only the type of pipe, but certain repairs – and the reason for those repairs. He then uses those inferences to speculate on the man's character and disposition.

The intimacy is intense but also intensely mediated, like the relationship between a reader and a writer. The narrator knows many things about the man that his friends and family might not know but lacks knowledge of other much more basic things, such as his appearance. This might be read as a metaphor for several different kinds of relationship or modes of sociability, including, if you like, an erotic one. As a metaphor for reading, it is striking in its emphasis on the auditory, as opposed to the prevalence of precinematic visual metaphors.[108] Like the narrator and his neighbour, readers and authors have an intimate bond, but it is in many ways a one-way street. Authors don't know how their work will be received; they don't even know who their readers are much of the time. Meanwhile, readers can never, for the most part, hope to meet or have an intimate conversation with the author, although they might feel they know his or her habits, proclivities and character: all rarely shared outside very close friends and family. The intimacy the narrator feels with the man through the wall is so intense that the man might not like it if he knew about it. Yet the act of overhearing, intentionally or unintentionally, is a common fact of urban living. Like street encounters, it combines intimacy with anonymity. The man through the wall has no control of how his actions will be received (or read). And although the narrator learns much about him, he concludes that he cannot tell whether his neighbour is worthy to smoke the Arcadia.

Barrie compares those who smoke the Arcadia to a club in an intriguing direct address to the reader explaining that he could 'give you the only address at which the Arcadia is to be had. But that I will not do. It would be as rash as proposing a man with whom I am unacquainted for my club. You may not be worthy to smoke the Arcadia mixture.'[109] Not only does Barrie highlight the clublike quality of the smokers of the Arcadia, but he also emphasises the limits of his sociability with the reader: of course, he would never propose a reader to his club without knowing him (and female readers would face even more barriers). This passage imagines an interactive relationship between the narrator and addressee, who seems increasingly less like an anonymous reader: 'Even though I became attached to you, I might not like to take the responsibility of introducing you to the Arcadia. This mixture has an extraordinary effect upon character, and probably you want to remain as you are.'[110] Barrie addresses the reader as unitary and acknowledges their lack of contact, but also presents the possibility that he might 'become attached to you', either through the wall of the book or otherwise.

The tendrils of the Arcadian mixture's smoke extend beyond its pages. The narrator of 'Mr Barrie in the Chair' reports, 'I have not read Mr Barrie's books, but I wanted to ask him about that tobacco.'[111] Doyle places an allusion to the tobacco and *My Lady Nicotine* in 'The Crooked Man': 'a few months after [his] marriage', Watson is visited by Holmes, who observes, 'Hum! You still smoke the Arcadia mixture of your bachelor days, then! There's no mistaking that fluffy ash upon your coat.'[112] More than a superficial allusion, this carries the larger dynamics behind *My Lady Nicotine* about the effects of marriage on smoking and male friendship. Holmes and Watson's friendship can survive the competing institution of marriage. Unlike the Holmes stories and other works from Chapter 4, Barrie rarely portrays friendship dyads in his fiction. Dick and Rob serve as an exception, but their bond does not rival that of Holmes and Watson. *My Lady Nicotine*, however, in its ambivalence and stress on the dissolution of the friendship group, accords well with the tradition begun by *The Bachelors' Club*. In fact, it preceded that novel by a year; given Barrie and Zangwill's relationship in that period, it is possible that the 'languid genius' influenced his dining companion.

'The pleasantest club in London'

Barrie's antisocial clubman and curiously constructed clubs overlap with the advent of Peter Pan. The majority of *The Little White Bird* (1902), which introduces Peter Pan, takes place in a club. The novel is so bifurcated that Barrie later excerpted the Pan section and published it under the title *Peter Pan in Kensington Gardens* (1906). But the majority of the novel as written involves a clubman, Captain W—, observing a family out of his club window. W— and the readers alike follow the courtship of Mary, then a nursery governess, her marriage, and the childhood of her son David up to the birth of his younger sibling. W— grows closer to the family, first merely observing, then attempting to help them anonymously, and finally becoming a friend entrusted with occasionally looking after David. Like the narrator of *My Lady Nicotine*, W— seems to be attempting to delude himself. He projects gruffness, pretending not to care about Mary. Many critics and biographers read this family through the lens of the Llewelyn Davies family (before Peter's birth) and read into it both an infatuation with the mother and a rivalry with the nursemaid.[113] Yet the haunting presence of Timothy, a son whose birth and death W— invents in his attempts to deceive Mary and her husband, suggests the mirror image of *My Lady Nicotine*: W— longs for domesticity, which he finds only indirectly in his club. The club window serves as an essential trope in the novel, marking W—'s distance in terms of class and an unclubbable disposition.

The Little White Bird and the club window also link the club with the act of reading. W— watches life unfold outside his club window, in a similar way to how readers watch characters 'through the window of this book', as Robert Louis Stevenson says in another context.[114] Given Barrie's admiration for Stevenson and his interest in writing children's literature, he was probably familiar with *A Child's Garden of Verses*, which was initially marketed to adults as well as children.[115] Stevenson uses the window as a metaphor for the book: the reader can see the action unfold and must grapple with the instinct to try to interact by 'knocking on the window'.[116] W— as reader fulfils the fantasy of interacting with the characters whose lives one observes.

The club window is a crucial part of the club's cultural work and symbology, particularly when it comes to socialisation. Bow windows offered a panoramic view of the street that allowed club members both to observe and to be seen observing. Famously, Beau Brummel judged passers-by on their attire from the vantage of White's bow window.[117] As Amy Milne-Smith observes in the context of the Hyde Park Riot of 1886, the prominent bow windows of clubs served as powerful symbols of the class imbalance that inspired rioters to target those windows with stones.[118] Likewise, Barbara Black invokes the 'Man in the Club Window', the putative narrator of James Hogg's etiquette book *The Habits of Good Society* (1859), who uses his vantage point to 'read' the passers-by in the street – not unlike Sherlock and Mycroft Holmes through the Diogenes Club window.[119] Later, in *Leave it to Psmith*, P. G. Wodehouse has his title character watch a woman through a club window and fall in love with her.[120] As she walks down Pall Mall, Mary 'has had the assurance to use the glass door of the club as a mirror in which to see how she likes her engaging trifle of a figure to-day'.[121] Like Beau Brummel, Mary sees the club window as a source of fashion knowledge, but her judgment is entirely for herself (within the context of internalised beauty standards). The window can turn into a mirror, all the more galling to W— because Mary seems unconcerned with the potential watchers from inside the club.

The idea that Mary's romantic drama unfolds like the action of a book is heightened by the degree to which W— seems to feel proprietary interest: 'I always feel that I have rung for her.'[122] He knows when she will appear. He consumes her with his coffee and liqueur, like a periodical (which the club certainly keeps and for which he doubtless *could* have rung). When describing his habitual action, W— intersperses his own actions: 'with such a sparkle of expectation on her face that I stir my coffee quite fiercely', and her beau's youth 'is so aggressive that I have sometimes to order William testily to close the window'.[123] William becomes implicated in the action: if W— rang for Mary, it would be he who brought her: 'her happiness had become part of my repast at two P.M., and when one day she walked down Pall Mall without gradually posting a letter, I was most indignant. It was as if William had disobeyed orders.'[124] W— seeks to conceal his concern for Mary through his abrasive persona, but there's a larger parallel here: he wishes to control his environment and, having selected Mary as his entertainment, he expects her to deliver.

For W—, the club is a place of solitude, and the relationships he forms there are not with the other members but rather with those of other classes: with Mary, who begins as a nursemaid and becomes the wife of a painter; with William, the club servant; and with Irene, William's daughter, who becomes David's nursemaid. The major mentions of other club members are when W— hopes they will leave him alone to enjoy his voyeurism or when he directly confronts one to make him retract a complaint against William that puts the servant at risk of losing his situation. Yet all of W—'s cross-class relationships contain an inevitable sense of class distance. The irascibility that W— displays towards Mary and Irene appears even more starkly in his relationships with William and might be read not as misogyny or womb-envy, but rather as being about class performance.

Despite his solitude, W— does have some sense of a collective. He describes himself as a 'clubman' as a primary identity category and talks about 'we [. . .] at the club.'[125] The male domesticity pales in comparison with the families that W— primarily sees through his club window. The club's name, the Junior Old Fogies' Club,[126] implies that his fellow members share his unclubbability. When obfuscating a description of himself that David's father acquires, he replies, '"My dear man . . . I know almost no one who is not like that," and it was true, so like each other do we grow at the club.'[127] This is reminiscent of the club in the 'Club Ghost' story: the club is an active force that makes the members grow like each other. Yet no evidence suggests that other members feel W—'s compassion for the other characters, particularly for William. W—'s 'clubman' persona of the worldly-wise cynic is easy to see through and the novel ends with his potential domestication, as he and Mary make their peace and she invites him to one of her tea parties so that she can introduce him to some eligible young women. Like the Diogenes Club and Barrie's other clubs, *The Little White Bird* emphasises the club as a site of loneliness and anti-sociability. Rather than forming alternate domesticity among members, this club contrasts with family domesticity in lower-class characters.

William does play a crucial part in the club's domesticity, such as it is. W— describes him in a chapter whose title, 'The Inconsiderate Waiter', foreshadows his fall from waiterly perfection:

Many a time have I deferred dining several minutes that I might have the attendance of this ingrate. His efforts to reserve the window-table for me were satisfactory, and I used to allow him privileges, as to suggest dishes; I have given him information, as that someone had startled me in the reading-room by slamming a door; I have showed him how I cut my finger with a piece of string. William was none of your assertive waiters. We could have plotted a murder safely before him.[128]

William is not only incredibly self-effacing but also resembles a parent here, particularly when W— shows him his cut. Of course, the idea that W— is doing William a favour in some of these is absurd. William is after all not 'inconsiderate', and W— is the one who does not show concern.

William becomes the source of a different cross-class drama enacted through the club window. When his wife is ill, their daughter Irene comes by the club to tell William how she is doing by means of standing in the street and signalling to her father in the club. W— is first made aware of this problem when William tries to see past him out the window into the street. The description is heavily overlaid with class overtones, and irony on Barrie's part: 'I had to repeat my order "Devilled kidney," and instead of answering brightly, "Yes, sir," as if my selection of devilled kidney was a personal gratification to him, which is the manner one expects of a waiter, he gazed eagerly out at the window, and then, starting, asked, "Did you say devilled kidney, sir?"'[129] Then in trying '[t]o get nearer the window he pressed heavily on my shoulder.'[130] After offering an 'audacious apology', 'this burst from him passionately, "For God's sake, sir, as we are man and man, tell me if you have seen a little girl looking up at the club-windows."'[131] W— projects horror: 'Man and man! But he had been a good waiter once, so I pointed out the girl to him.'[132] William's explicit acknowledgement of his human equality with a club member is a distinct social transgression, but of course also true.

Irene's gestures through the window become more and more pronounced as W— enters their lives as a kindly godfather (though maintaining a bristling distance). Before this culminates in his taking the family to the seaside for the wife's health, Irene's signs grow more elaborate: 'her pantomime was so illuminating' as she communicates her mother's improved appetite, 'licking an imaginary plate in the middle of Pall Mall'.[133] But when W— speaks to Irene in the street, he 'draw[s] her out of range of the club-windows' that his fellow members might not observe him in the same way.[134] Irene's interaction with W— differs significantly from his interactions with Mary, in that Irene views the window as a two-way communication, not as a mirror. She begins by trying to reach William but accidentally gets W— instead. Then she becomes more dramatic. Mary treats the window as a mirror, unaware of her audience – or perhaps affecting unawareness in keeping with her upwardly mobile femininity. In her embrace of her own performance, Irene seems to relish the physical comedy of her 'pantomime' just as she rejoices in her mother's continued health. Like Barrie writing about his antics at the Burns dinner, she is willing to be laughed at.

The Peter Pan material fits imperfectly into the novel, yet the two worlds come together in W—'s characterisation of Kensington Gardens as 'The pleasantest club in London',[135] which also forms a chapter title.[136] Barrie uses the same phrase to describe the Wigwam in *When a Man's Single*: in that case it seems to damn with faint praise.[137] Here, it might form a critique of the club as an institution. Like a magazine, Kensington Gardens is open to the public. In fact, despite its literal gates, it has less gatekeeping: admittance is free and literacy not required. Nevertheless, W—'s tour of the Gardens highlights class distinctions:

> first you come to the Figs, but you scorn to loiter there, for the Figs is the resort of superior little persons, who are forbidden to mix with the commonality, and so is named, according to legend, because they dress in full fig. These dainty ones are themselves contemptuously called Figs by David and other heroes, and you have a key to the manners and customs of this dandiacal section of the Gardens when I tell you that cricket is called crickets here.[138]

Despite the comparison to a club, those who seek to impose the restrictions of a club in terms of exclusivity and class are met with scorn. Some of this is reverse snobbery, reacting to the claims of superiority. The Figs treat the Gardens as a club, not a public place where they might 'mix with the commonality'. The 'dandia-cal' charge and the 'crickets' joke, which may indicate the Figs' unfamiliarity with the sport, have gendered overtones but are also class-based.

The novel's action begins when W— invites David to the club. A short preamble introduces W—'s relationship with David, mislead-ingly referring to David as 'the little boy who calls me "father"'.[139] Then the story begins *in medias res*: 'One day, when David was about five, I sent him the following letter: "Dear David: If you really want to know how it began, will you come and have a chop with me to-day at the club?"'[140] Whimsical time-travel ensues when W— instructs a hansom cab to '[d]rive back six years'.[141] David fears that he will disappear as the time recedes. The chapter ends, 'You can't think how little David looked as we entered the portals of the club,'[142] and the next begins, 'As I enter the club smoking-room you are to conceive David vanishing into nothingness, and that it is any day six years ago at two in the afternoon. I ring for coffee, cigarette, and cherry brandy, and take my chair by the window, just as the absurd little nursery governess comes tripping into the street.'[143] The invitation to lunch at the club constitutes an initiation into manhood: most clubs did not allow children.[144]

However, this is also a scene of social mobility. Bringing David to his club is not only a marker of masculinity but a marker of class. Mary has distinct class aspirations – of which W— approves, though he also uses them to nettle both Mary and Irene, who aspires to imitate Mary.[145] Mary is characterised by a lady-like demeanour and the habit of making bourgeois accoutrements from the cheapest materials. One of the first things W— tells us when she is still a nurserymaid is 'It must enrage the other servants to see her deporting herself as if she were quite the lady.'[146] By virtue of her gender, as well as her membership in the servant classes, Mary cannot afford to be unclubbable. Other methods of class mobility lie open to her, but they depend on such strategies as adjusting her appearance in the club window. While many critics read W— and Mary as competing for David, they conspire together to facilitate his social mobility. This carries with it its own pathos, as we have seen. Mary cannot follow David into the portals of the club, by virtue of class as well as gender, but perhaps she wishes him to go where she cannot follow, except by gazing through the club window.

Unclubbability as class privilege

If Barrie invites W— to be read biographically, this reading served his own class mobility. W—'s dispositional unclubbability signals the class privilege he takes for granted. The club serves as a backdrop to the action. W—'s membership never comes into question – in fact, he is on the committee. Rob and Andrew aspire to club membership and the social belonging it represents; the narrator of *My Lady Nicotine* mourns the loss of his unofficial club; but W— can afford to be unclubbable as only a born gentleman can. Barrie's own arc mimics neither Rob's nor Andrew's: Andrew returns to Scotland (but keeps his core disposition) while Rob assimilates out of his awkwardness as Dick's malaise comes into focus. Barrie adopts the pose of the unclubbable clubman, masking the narrative of his social rise by attributing his awkwardness to his disposition.

Paradoxically, then, unclubbability requires a club. The club serves as a marker of status and affiliation even if it conveys little true community. And unclubbability requires an audience. All of Barrie's unclubbable characters – including himself – acquire a friendship group. Unclubbability can perhaps mean being an acquired taste. As in Zangwill's Society for Mutual Depreciation, or Pain's Problem Club with its friendly competition, a test of friendship is seeing through a prickly exterior.

In its distanced sociability, Barrie's version of unclubbability particularly resembles reading. The Arcadians together in their unsociability, W— observing action unfold through a window or the narrator of *My Lady Nicotine* through a wall: intimacy occurs in traversing boundaries. Even Barrie's layers of ambiguous narration allow the satisfaction of getting to know the narrator – and perhaps the sensation of getting to know the author. By leaning into his oddness, Barrie avoids easy classification – even as 'the Scotch humourist'.

Notes

1 The most intense case of this is Piers Dudgeon's *Neverland*, which seriously accuses Barrie of ruining three familys' lives through murder and mesmerism.
2 Jack, 'Barrie, Sir James Matthew, baronet (1860–1937)'.
3 *Who's Who* (1904), 856, *Who Was Who* (1929–40), 71 (first two listed in 1904; only Athenaeum at death); <http://www.authorsclub.co.uk/>.
4 Telfer, *Peter Pan's First XI*.
5 See Birkin, *J.M. Barrie and the Lost Boys*, 293.
6 Birkin, *J.M. Barrie and the Lost Boys*, 212.
7 Birkin, *J.M. Barrie and the Lost Boys*, 180. Charge of impotence recorded in Jack, 'Barrie, Sir James Matthew'.

8   Kincaid, *Child-Loving*, 212.

9   Qtd in Birkin, *J.M. Barrie and the Lost Boys*, 180.

10   Wilkie, *The Lost Boys of Zeta Psi*.

11   Gubar, *Artful Dodgers*, vii, 182; Sedgwick, 'Paranoid Reading and Reparative Reading', 123–51.

12   Doyle, 'Greek Interpreter', 297.

13   Birkin, *Lost Boys*, 18.

14   Barrie, *Greenwood Hat*, 198.

15   Barrie, *Greenwood Hat*, 199.

16   Barrie, *Greenwood Hat*, 198–9.

17   Bergson, *Laughter*.

18   Barrie, *Greenwood Hat*, 199.

19   Jerome, *Three Men in a Boat*, 196.

20   Barrie, *Greenwood Hat*, 201–2.

21   Barrie, *Greenwood Hat*, 203.

22   'Notes mainly Personal', *Evening Telegraph* (Dundee), 10 June 1891.

23   See Introduction.

24   Jerome, *My Life and Times*, 115.

25   Jerome, *My Life and Times*, 75–6.

26   Varga, 'St James's Gazette'.

27   Barrie, *Greenwood Hat*, 1.

28   Barrie, *Greenwood Hat*, 1.

29   Barrie, *Greenwood Hat*, 19.

30   Barrie, *Greenwood Hat*, 19.

31   Telfer, *Peter Pan's First XI*, 57.

32   Telfer, *Peter Pan's First XI*, 42.

33   Telfer calls Partridge 'the main link that brought in more players from [. . .] *Punch*'. Telfer, *Peter Pan's First XI*, 45.

34   Telfer, *Peter Pan's First XI*, 84, 133–4.

35   Telfer, *Peter Pan's First XI*, 149.

36   Telfer, *Peter Pan's First XI*, 108–9, 128.

37   Barrie, *Greenwood Hat*, 102.

38   Barrie, *Greenwood Hat*, 104.

39   *J. M. Barrie's Allahakbarries C.C.*

40   Barrie, *When a Man's Single*, 18, 150–1, 162. Bob Nicholson and Maria Damkjær have theorised the circulation of jokes in newspapers and periodicals. Damkjær, 'Awkward Appendages', 475–92; Nicholson, '"You Kick the Bucket; We Do the Rest!"'

41   Barrie alludes to this phrase in his preface and calls the title 'curiously inappropriate'. Barrie, *When a Man's Single*, vii. A possible

source of this allusion is a Victorian print by Frederick William
Fairholt, after a painting by John Watson Nicol.

42   Birkin, *Lost Boys*, 3.
43   Barrie, *When a Man's Single*, 82.
44   Barrie, *When a Man's Single*, 83.
45   Barrie, *When a Man's Single*, 74.
46   Barrie, *When a Man's Single*, 75.
47   Barrie, *When a Man's Single*, 61, 68.
48   Barrie, *When a Man's Single*, 140.
49   Barrie, *When a Man's Single*, 142.
50   Barrie, *When a Man's Single*, 142.
51   Barrie, *When a Man's Single*, 75–6.
52   Barrie, *When a Man's Single*, 42.
53   Barrie, *When a Man's Single*, 78.
54   Barrie, *When a Man's Single*, 79.
55   Barrie, *When a Man's Single*, 168.
56   Barrie, *When a Man's Single*, 167.
57   Barrie, *Greenwood Hat*, 7.
58   Barrie, *When a Man's Single*, 151–2.
59   Barrie, *When a Man's Single*, 150.
60   Barrie, *When a Man's Single*, 152.
61   Barrie, *When a Man's Single*, 151.
62   'Miscellaneous Books', *Glasgow Herald*, 1 January 1889. *British Library Newspapers*.
63   Barrie, *When a Man's Single*, 171.
64   Hatton, *Club-Land*, 41.
65   Barrie, *When a Man's Single*, 208.
66   Barrie, *When a Man's Single*, 208.
67   Barrie, *When a Man's Single*, 252.
68   Zangwill, *Bachelors' Club*, in *Celibates' Club*, 70.
69   Sedgwick, *Between Men*, 179.
70   Barrie, *When a Man's Single*, 286.
71   Barrie, *When a Man's Single*, 284.
72   Barrie, *When a Man's Single*, 285–6.
73   Barrie, *When a Man's Single*, 287.
74   Birkin, *J. M. Barrie and the Lost Boys*, 37.
75   Barrie, *When a Man's Single*, 261.
76   'New Novels', *Graphic*, 19 January 1880.
77   'Literature', *Dundee Courier*, 26 October 1888: 6.
78   'A Tale of "Literary Life"', *Pall Mall Gazette*, 31 October 1888.
79   'Recent Novels', *Times*, 2 February 1889: 16.

80 Birkin, *J.M. Barrie and the Lost Boys*, 16.
81 Barrie, *Greenwood Hat*, 30.
82 Barrie, *Better Dead*, 1.
83 Barrie, *Better Dead*, 218.
84 Barrie, *Better Dead*, 220.
85 Barrie, *Better Dead*, 221.
86 Barrie, *Better Dead*, 216.
87 Barrie, *Better Dead*, 233, 229, 230.
88 Barrie, *Better Dead*, 234.
89 Barrie, *Better Dead*, 235.
90 Barrie, *Greenwood Hat*, 31.
91 Barrie, *Better Dead*, 254–5.
92 Barrie, *Better Dead*, 256.
93 Barrie, *When a Man's Single*, 166.
94 Barrie, *Better Dead*, 276.
95 Barrie, *My Lady Nicotine*, 99.
96 Wodehouse, *Summer Lightning*.
97 Mackail, *Barrie*, 164–5.
98 Barrie, *My Lady Nicotine*, 12.
99 Barrie, *My Lady Nicotine*, 12.
100 Barrie, *My Lady Nicotine*, 28.
101 Barrie, *My Lady Nicotine*, 28.
102 Barrie, *My Lady Nicotine*, 29.
103 Barrie, *My Lady Nicotine*, 36. Cf. Barrie, *When a Man's Single*, 162.
104 Barrie, *My Lady Nicotine*, 36–7.
105 Barrie, *My Lady Nicotine*, 37.
106 Barrie, *My Lady Nicotine*, 259.
107 Barrie, *My Lady Nicotine*, 260–1.
108 Byerly, *Are We There Yet*; Sullivan, 'Animating Flames'.
109 Barrie, *My Lady Nicotine*, 27.
110 Barrie, *My Lady Nicotine*, 27–8.
111 Barrie, *Greenwood Hat*, 198.
112 Doyle, *The Complete Sherlock Holmes*, 1: 411.
113 Carey Mickalites speaks of W—'s 'misogynistic jealousy of [David's] mother'. Mickalites, 'Fairies and a Flâneur', 18. Birkin, *Lost Boys*, 41–2.
114 Stevenson, *A Child's Garden of Verses*, 139.
115 Fiss, 'Pushing at the Boundaries of the Book', 269.
116 Stevenson, *A Child's Garden of Verses*, 139.
117 Milne-Smith, *London Clubland*, 24.

118 Milne-Smith, *London Clubland,* 176.
119 Black, *Room,* 12.
120 Wodehouse, *Leave it to Psmith,* 59.
121 Barrie, *Little White Bird,* 16.
122 Barrie, *Little White Bird,* 13.
123 Barrie, *Little White Bird,* 16, 17.
124 Barrie, *Little White Bird,* 18.
125 Barrie, *Little White Bird,* 110, 60.
126 Barrie, *Little White Bird,* 11.
127 Barrie, *Little White Bird,* 64–5.
128 Barrie, *Little White Bird,* 80.
129 Barrie, *Little White Bird,* 81.
130 Barrie, *Little White Bird,* 81.
131 Barrie, *Little White Bird,* 81.
132 Barrie, *Little White Bird,* 82.
133 Barrie, *Little White Bird,* 89, 88.
134 Barrie, *Little White Bird,* 90.
135 Barrie, *Little White Bird,* 136.
136 Barrie, *Little White Bird,* 129
137 Barrie, *When a Man's Single,* 171.
138 Barrie, *Little White Bird,* 143–4.
139 Barrie, *Little White Bird,* 1.
140 Barrie, *Little White Bird,* 10.
141 Barrie, *Little White Bird,* 11.
142 Barrie, *Little White Bird,* 12.
143 Barrie, *Little White Bird,* 13.
144 Doughan and Gordon, *Women, Clubs and Associations in Britain,* 52.
145 Barrie, *Little White Bird,* 141.
146 Barrie, *Little White Bird,* 14.

6

Idlers and Drones: P. G. Wodehouse and Twentieth-Century Class Confusion

In a sense, P. G. Wodehouse and J. M. Barrie represent opposite sides of the affective spectrum, particularly when it comes to clubs. Barrie focuses on unclubbable, unsociable and downright hostile clubmen who isolate themselves, whereas Wodehouse's principal characters radiate affability to readers and fellow clubmen alike. Yet the two share a focus on class. Wodehouse's most enduring character, Jeeves, embodies the type of ideal servant with which W—contrasts William in *The Little White Bird*. However, as we shall see, Jeeves is one extreme of Wodehouse's representations of valets, butlers, waiters and other servants. If Barrie chronicled class mobility, Wodehouse, who continued writing until his death in 1975, chronicled twentieth-century shifts in the meaning of class.

In some ways Wodehouse marks a departure from the other figures in this study, generally a generation older than him, but in other ways he intensifies and builds on the models they established. The Drones Club, his most well-known fictional club, provides a perfect example of both of these dynamics. Unlike the Bachelors' Club and its followers, the Drones lacks the fundamental joke at its premise and the self-defeating rules that drive plot. Yet in a sense the Drones is still a joke. Its name clearly plays on the upper classes' reliance on the worker bees of the lower classes and on club members' lack of intelligence. Rather than the exaggerated rules that characterise the Bachelors', Proposal, and similar clubs, the Drones has unwritten laws and habits, such as throwing dinner rolls, that generate humour in part due to their proximity to actual club antics. Furthermore, the Drones Club differs from the other clubs in this study in that it recurs over multiple books. In fact, it ties Wodehouse's large and disparate oeuvre together. In that sense, the Drones intensifies the work that the Idler's Club began:

it provides a cosy imagined space for readers. So, too, it intensifies the affects of belonging. Because it is fictional, anyone can join, but also if a reader does feel excluded, the club is so manifestly silly that it doesn't much matter.

Wodehouse also intensifies another dynamic we have seen swirling around other Idlers: the idea of humour as conservative or reactionary. In Jerome and Zangwill, this has manifested as posthumous accusations of misogyny: for Wodehouse, it had very real political implications during his lifetime. During the Second World War, Wodehouse was a prisoner of war in France and made five humorous radio programmes which were broadcast to the United States before the country had entered the war. At the time and since, many read these as Nazi propaganda because Wodehouse was making light of his experiences in the 'stiff upper lip' tradition.[1] The British response in particular prevented Wodehouse from returning to his home country and he became a dual citizen of the United States in 1955. Thanks in part to an MI5 investigation that cleared him (though it was not made public in his lifetime), he was knighted six weeks before his death. As with Zangwill and Jerome, the lightness and ambiguity of Wodehouse's humorous style lends itself to multiple political readings. He could also be accused of leaning excessively into the gender stereotypes of his day, without his predecessors' mitigating factors. Both of his 'sagas', as he ironically called them, follow upper-class or aristocratic, dim-witted men, plagued by domineering female relatives.[2] However, many of his early novels, especially the standalones, feature quick-witted, impecunious self-starters of both sexes, some of whom are American, such as *Uneasy Money* (1916), *A Damsel in Distress* (1919) and *Jill the Reckless* (1920).[3]

Wodehouse's representations of the British upper classes should be understood in relation to his popularity with the American market. His two major sagas feature an aristocrat, the Earl of Emsworth, and an upper-class gentleman, Bertie Wooster. Neither has to work for a living (fortunately, because both are humorously dim), and both are members of West End clubs. In his 1956 memoir, *America, I Like You*, Wodehouse stresses the pecuniary advantages of the American market. *Love among the Chickens* (1906) made its way into the hands of an American agent, who 'sold not only the book rights but also the serial rights and at a price which seemed to me fantastic. A thousand dollars it was, and to one who, like myself, had never gotten above fifty pounds for a serial and whose record royalties were £18.11.4, a thousand dollars was more than merely good.'[4] In a chapter entitled, 'Put Me among the Earls', Wodehouse implies that the Blandings saga grew out of the American market demands. Of the first Blandings book (1915), he writes, '*Something New* was bought as a serial by the *Saturday Evening Post*, and they paid me three thousand five hundred dollars for it, if you can believe there is that much money in the world.'[5] A focus on the peerage in particular, and the English upper classes in general, reaped great rewards in the American market. As Robert Hall Jr, has it, Bertie is something of a 'stage Englishman' – hardly coincidental considering Wodehouse's work for the stage, again largely in America.[6] In fact, Wodehouse himself famously called his novels 'musical comedies without the music', and some, such as *The Small Bachelor* (1927), overtly adapted his dramatic works.[7]

Looking at Wodehouse's oeuvre as a whole complicates several of the accepted narratives about his work. For instance, Hall claims that neither World War registers in Wodehouse's fictional world and cites 'the often observed fact that Wodehouse's mature stories take place in a world where time has basically stood still ever since ca. 1920'.[8] This is generally true, particularly in the sagas – although references to Hitler and Mussolini do pepper the interwar books. Yet the episodic novel *The Indiscretions of Archie* (1921) features a First World War veteran as the central character and talks clearly about the impacts of the war, including significant psychological effects on two secondary characters (one of whom is known, because this is still P. G. Wodehouse, as 'the Sausage Chappie').[9]

Fundamentally, Wodehouse's clubs carry on the joke established by the *Idler* circle: these are clubs for readerly enjoyment, warm enough to invite a sense of belonging yet simultaneously silly enough to make official belonging seem unnecessary. But the ease of the humour is the ease of privilege. That's what makes it work with a somewhat conservative politics of aspiration. Instead of being a wholesale socialist and trying to tear down the class system (even through overt, cutting satire), you can gently make fun of it in a way that holds open the possibility that one day you'll be sitting in those luxurious armchairs. In other words, whether or not these readers directly aspired to join clubs, they could see themselves there through reading these books. Like earlier Idlers,

Wodehouse makes the club accessible to readers by setting it up as something both to aspire to and to make fun of.

'Slip a ferret into any good club'

So associated with London Clubland was Wodehouse that he wrote a foreword for Richard Graves's 1963 book on London clubs, *Leather Armchairs*. Typically comic, Wodehouse's preface speaks of his disappointment that Graves does not discuss how to avoid being made a member of a club, a move similar to Dick's in Barrie's *When a Man's Single*, showing the status necessary to disavow the club. He also blurs the lines between these real clubs and his fictional ones:

> while the author speaks freely of the Travellers', Boodle's, White's and others, he makes no mention of the really interesting clubs such as the photographers' Negative and Solution, the debutantes' Junior Lipstick and the Senior Bloodstain, where the private investigators congregate. I shall never forget lunching with Adrian Mulliner, the private eye, at the Senior Bloodstain [. . .][10]

Of course, Mulliner is one of Wodehouse's own characters. In the Clubland imagined by Graves's and Wodehouse's readers, the fictional and non-fictional can rub elbows and socialise pleasantly together. Indeed, Graves's main text not only identifies the club on which Wodehouse based the Drones (he claims it was the Bachelors', creating an indirect link to Zangwill), but calls the non-fictional Constitutional 'The Earl of Emsworth's club'.[11] Wodehouse's list of his own fictional clubs serves as a reminder that the Drones is but the tip of his club iceberg, and also a rapid-fire reminder of his propensity, *Idler*-like, for humorous names, which include the Senior Buffers Club, a variation on Barrie's Junior Old Fogies' Club.[12]

Unlike Zangwill, Pain, Chesterton and Stevenson, Wodehouse rarely names novels after clubs, although he does have several short story collections linked through the frame of a club in which the stories are told. This extends to golf clubs and taverns, as in the Oldest Member's narration in *The Clicking of Cuthbert* (1922), linking to the larger tavern-tale genre.[13] In the Mulliner stories, minor characters in the frame narrative are referred to by their drinks. A posthumous collection names the club in its title, *Tales from the Drones Club* (1982), but collections published during his lifetime bore the titles *Young Men in Spats* (1936) and *Eggs, Beans and Crumpets* (1940) – the latter title similarly referring to the members of the Drones Club. Although the term 'crumpet' is now applied as a slang term to attractive women, at the time it was used similarly to 'egg' and 'bean' as a form of casual endearment, likewise often prefaced with 'old'.[14] *Young Men in Spats* combines tales told at the Drones with some Mulliner stories, which are told at the Angler's Rest. The Drones tales are narrated by a Crumpet in the Drones smoking room: 'It was the hour of the morning snifter, and a little group of Eggs and Beans and Crumpets had assembled in the smoking-room of the Drones Club to do a bit of inhaling.'[15] Club members, not the act of reading, are compared to food.

Over time, Wodehouse's characters practically form a club of their own – the interconnections between them, through various mentions and also various institutions, are legion. Hall includes with his book an amazing chart that connects the various characters to each other and to various institutions and locations, such as the Drones Club, Barribault's Hotel, Valley Fields and Roville-sur-Mer. But even this elaborate chart misses out a few connections, such as Psmith's membership of the Drones Club.[16] The Drones serves as a hub connecting the major series: the Blandings books, the Jeeves and Wooster 'saga', the Mulliner tales, the Psmith books, and even some otherwise standalones, such as *Big Money* and *Laughing Gas* (1936), which is highly unusual in Wodehouse's oeuvre in featuring a supernatural premise: the type of body switch made famous in *Vice Versa* (1882).

In that context, one surprising aspect of the Drones Club is its somewhat delayed initial appearance. It notably does not appear in *My Man Jeeves*, the first collection of Jeeves stories (some of which feature Reggie Pepper, not Bertie Wooster), published in 1919.[17] In 1920, the club appears incidentally in the one-off *Jill the Reckless*.[18] Freddie Rooke, friend of the eponymous Jill, is meeting a friend in the Drones, but because he's not a member he can't order a drink in the bar. And Freddie, with his upper-class background, his ineffectual good humour and his beautiful babble, is exactly the type of Englishman who would be a member of the fully fledged Drones Club. The club may have originally been simply a funny name.

The Drones really comes into prominence in the first full Bertie and Jeeves novel, *The Inimitable Jeeves* (1923), which weaves together previously published stories centring around Bingo Little. Bertie describes the Drones by contrast:

> Once a year the committee of the Drones decides that the old club could do with a wash and brush-up, so they shoo us out and dump us down for a few weeks at some other institution. This time we were roosting at the Senior Liberal, and personally I had found the strain pretty fearful. I mean, when you've got used to a club where everything's nice and cheery and where, if you want to attract a chappie's attention, you heave a piece of bread at him, it kind of damps you to come to a place where the youngest member is about eighty-seven and it isn't considered good form to talk to anyone unless you and he went through the Peninsular War together.[19]

The trope of chucking bread at fellow club members recurs as a mark of the Drones' irreverence and good nature. When a character minds being the recipient of a thrown roll, it is marked as a sign of age.[20] Here, as elsewhere, Wodehouse establishes two very different types of clubmen, couched in different kinds of clubs. Later, in *Very Good, Jeeves* (1930), Bertie (whose narration is a treat of his saga) describes his Uncle George: 'He is what they call a prominent London clubman – one of those birds in tight morning-coats and grey toppers whom you see toddling along St James's Street on fine afternoons, puffing a bit as they make the grade. Slip a ferret into any good club between Piccadilly and Pall Mall, and you would start half a dozen Uncle Georges.'[21] First of all, the humour of this quotation characterises Wodehouse, Bertie and the Drones. They are irreverent and prone to practical jokes and slapstick humour. In Bertie's case especially, the humour arises almost incidentally, often appearing in asides or rhetorical flourishes.

Two types of clubmen appear here: the Uncle Georges and the Drones. The Drones are those slipping the ferret: they have access to the 'good clubs', but they subvert them – through humorous chaos (rather than through socialist revolution, which forms another of Wodehouse's themes). The 'prominent London clubman' represents serious authority – the Victorian establishment, if you will. Notably, Bertie is a generation removed from this vision of the club establishment. In the half-century between *The Inimitable Jeeves* and *Aunts Aren't Gentlemen*, Bertie and the Drones don't seem to age much, although their youth remains somewhat vague. Bertie's calculation in the previous quotation doesn't add up: in 1923, an eighty-seven-year-old wouldn't have been in the Napoleonic Wars. Comic exaggeration meets an out-of-time quality. Much less seriously than Peter Wimsey, the Drones offer an alternative to an earlier generational model – even as the saga moves forward in time and the generation changes.

Bertie conscripts the reader by his use of the imperative.[22] 'Slip a ferret' implies that the reader is in a position not only to acquire a ferret but to enter 'any good club between Piccadilly and Pall Mall'. Clearly, this was not true of Wodehouse's audiences, mainly American and following the *Idler* market aimed at the large numbers of lower-middle and upper-lower-class readers (Wodehouse shared the *Strand* and *Saturday Evening Post* with other Idlers, sometimes in the same issue). This imperative is no anomaly. Bertie makes an even more explicit assertion in *The Mating Season* (1949): 'Look in at the Drones and ask the first fellow you meet "Can the fine spirit of the Woosters be crushed?" and he will offer you attractive odds against such a contingency.'[23] Not only does this clearly position the reader as one who is able to access the Drones, but it also shows the underlying affability of the Drones Club. They may play practical jokes on each other, such as when Tuppy Glossop wins a bet by nefariously looping back the final ring to cause Bertie to fall into the swimming pool, but in a pinch they'll back each other every time.

Yet Wodehouse's distinctive style, particularly in Bertie Wooster's narration, may be more typical of clerks than of clubmen. John Carey argues that 'The idiolect P. G. Wodehouse evolved for Bertie Wooster in the Jeeves books may be seen as an elaborate development of clerk's slang, in that it consists essentially of jaunty and defiantly un-highbrow circumlocutions. In Wodehouse's letters, where the idiolect is less fully worked out, the vestiges of clerk's slang ("old cake", "sound egg", "largely banana oil", etc.) can easily be spotted.'[24] Part of the fundamental humour of the Bertie Wooster books especially is their narration, its distinctive voice, and a sense of incongruity in that voice. The cleverness of the voice is incongruous: Bertie can pull off dexterous verbal tricks but cannot solve his way out of the myriad problems, mainly matrimonial, in which he finds himself – let alone tend to his own basic daily needs. He relies on Jeeves. But if we allow that Bertie speaks clerk's slang, or a recognisable variation thereof, it raises the possibility that part of the humour is meant to be a sense of class discrepancy. Wodehouse also followed the stylistic precedent of the New Humorists, who were also criticised for using clerk's slang, as we saw in Chapter 1.

Wodehouse's treatment of clubs distinctly follows the *Idler* circle's precedents. One of his early novels, *A Gentleman of Leisure* (1910), begins with a description of a club:

> The main smoking-room of the Strollers' Club had been filling for the last half-hour, and was now nearly full. In many ways the Strollers', though not the most magnificent, is the pleasantest club in New York. Its ideals are those of the Savage Club – comfort without pomp – and it is given over after eleven o'clock at night mainly to the Stage. Everybody is young, clean-shaven, and full of conversation – and the conversation strikes a purely professional note.[25]

'The pleasantest club in New York' echoes Barrie's reference to Kensington Gardens as 'the pleasantest club in London' in *The Little White Bird* (1903).[26] Moreover, the club as setting and the reference to real institutions such as the Savage Club recall other contemporaneous club stories.

The bee metaphor in the Drones Club's name implies that these upper-class men are idly profiting from the labour of others while waiting around to serve their only essential function: mating. This reads like quite stark political commentary, but the Drones' silliness makes the whole thing seem more like a joke. In the Drones Club, it seems members are always playing practical jokes and calling each other by absurd nicknames. These antics often appear as parenthetical asides leavening a moment that threatens to verge on the serious: 'Only once in my career had I experienced an emotion equally intense, on the occasion when Freddie Wigeon at the Drones, having possessed himself of a motor horn, stole up behind me as I crossed Dover Street in what is known as a reverie and suddenly tooted the apparatus in my immediate ear.'[27] They exaggerate some of the real qualities of West End clubs, such as absurd bets, including wagering on matrimonial prospects or playing golf through the streets of London.[28] An element of the 'superiority theory' of humour may be at play here, as Hobbes famously articulated, 'by comparison whereof [those who laugh] suddenly applaud themselves'.[29] Yet I doubt most readers feel unmitigated 'scorn', as Hobbes has it. The general affability, particularly of protagonists such as Bertie, Freddie Threepwood, Pongo Twistleton and Bingo Little, mitigates this effect. Bertie in particular goes to great lengths to help his friends and relations, frequently putting himself into ridiculous situations. Wodehouse sets up Bertie and his ilk as loveable and laughable characters, whom readers can laugh with as well as at.

The Drones is a club for readers. Long-time Wodehouse readers, fans of both the sagas and the one-offs, may find Drones Club membership an important credential when encountering a new character or novel. For instance, *Laughing Gas* (1936), an outlier in several ways, begins by invoking not one but two clubs:

> I had just begun to write this story, when a literary pal of mine who had just had a sticky night out with the P. E. N. Club blew in to borrow bicarbonate of soda, and I thought it would be as well to have him vet what I'd done, in case I might have foozled my tee-shot. Because, except for an occasional anecdote in the Drones smoking-room about Scotsmen, Irishmen, and Jews, and even then I generally leave out the point, I've never told a story in my life.[30]

This is the same kind of *in medias res* opening, in which the narrator questions his storytelling skills, that appears in many Bertie Wooster novels. Although this narrator and story are new to devoted readers of Wodehouse, we have the bona fides of the Drones, as well as the stylistic flair. The club serves as our introduction to Reggie, Earl of Havershot. In terms of content, the art of narration is immediately connected to the practice of telling jokes in the club smoking room. Furthermore, Reggie adopts a characteristic Wodehousian style, invoking the spontaneity and irrevocability of orality (for instance, when a narrator responds to a 'mistake' by adding an apology or correction rather than engaging in revision that would be invisible to a reader). However, the offhand reference to an ethnic joke also demonstrates the limits of the ability of the club to encompass all readers, or the elements readers must overlook in order to feel that sense of belonging. Even if Wodehouse occasionally toots a motor horn in our immediate ears, he still slips a ferret into the good clubs.

Calling clubs' bluff

As Wodehouse emerged from the school periodical to the mainstream fiction market, he used the club as a major setting for *Psmith in the City* (1910). Before Jeeves and Bertie, before

Emsworth and Blandings, there was Psmith. This early Wodehouse clubman embodies several class paradoxes: an avowed socialist who addresses everyone as 'Comrade', he is an upwardly mobile member of the nouveaux riches who tends to avoid doing actual work as much as possible. Like Dorothy Sayers's subsequent Lord Peter Wimsey, minus the title and the shell shock, Psmith is a friendly, easy-going, flippant dandy (complete with monocle) who uses excessive, flourishing talk to mask a keen intelligence and, when pressed, can produce physical strength. In *Psmith in the City*, the club marks Psmith and Wodehouse's transition out of school. Psmith takes advantage of the club's nominal democracy to annoy his new boss, in the process critiquing the club project of institutionalising friendship.

Over the course of two decades, Psmith bridged Wodehouse's early school stories with one of his 'sagas' – and even the Drones Club. His first two appearances were published, together and separately, under several different titles: as serials in *The Captain*, 'a magazine for boys and "old boys"',[31] under the titles *The Lost Lambs* and *Jackson Junior*; then combined as a book, *Mike: A Public School Story* (1909); and then divided again as *Enter Psmith* (1935), *Mike at Wrykyn* (1953) and *Mike and Psmith* (1953). Psmith's adventures continue in *Psmith in the City* (1910) and *Psmith, Journalist* (1915) before merging in with the Blandings series in *Leave it to Psmith* (1923), in which Psmith becomes the Earl of Emsworth's private secretary, reveals himself to be a member of the Drones Club, and falls in love with a girl he sees out the Drones Club window (not in that order).[32] He is never heard from again. His idiosyncratic name spelling parodies the trend of upwardly mobile middle-class families changing their last names to sound more aristocratic, the classic example being 'Smith' to 'Smythe'. As Psmith explains to Mike, who will become his best friend,

If you ever have occasion to write to me, would you mind sticking a P at the beginning of my name? P-s-m-i-t-h. See? There are too many Smiths, and I don't care for Smythe. My father's content to worry along in the old-fashioned way, but I've decided to strike out a fresh line. I shall found a new dynasty. The resolve came to me unexpectedly this morning, as I was buying a simple penn'orth of butterscotch out of the automatic machine at Paddington. I jotted it down on the back of an envelope. In conversation, you may address me as Rupert (though

I hope you won't), or simply Smith, the P not being sounded. Cp. the name Zbysco, in which the Z is given a similar miss-in-baulk. See?[33]

This attraction to the distinctive – and implicit class pretension – is never really reconciled with Psmith's socialism, which he presents as a fad, telling Mike soon after that he's 'just become a socialist';[34] however, he continues calling various characters 'Comrade' throughout his career. Stylistically, Psmith anticipates Bertie's narration, appearing more heightened and manic because it occurs in dialogue.

In *Psmith in the City*, Psmith and Mike leave public school not for the expected university, but for work in the City (in both the financial and geographic senses). Mirroring Wodehouse's own biography, Mike's family unexpectedly looses money and with it the chance to send Mike to university after preparatory school. Psmith joins Mike partially out of fellow feeling and partially because his wealthy but easily suggestible father is friends with the bank manager, Mr Bickersdyke, who promises he can knock the nonsense out of Psmith. Bickersdyke then becomes a direct substitute for their former teachers. Referring to their professorial nemesis from *Lost Lambs*, Psmith says, 'I wish Comrade Downing could see us now. . . . He always set us down as mere idlers. Triflers. Butterflies. It would be a wholesome corrective for him to watch us perspiring like this in the cause of Commerce.'[35] Indeed, 'idlers' is exactly what Bickersdyke pegs them as, admonishing, 'We do not encourage idling in this bank.'[36] However, the narrator reports that the actual demands of the bank are not pressing: 'They had leisure to think of other things besides their work. Indeed, they had so much leisure that it is a wonder they thought of their work at all.'[37] This is idling in the Jeromian sense of avoiding work, rather than the aristocratic loafing of Bertie Wooster.[38]

Nevertheless, Psmith insists on describing himself hyperbolically as a model of industry:

Psmith, the individual, ceases to exist, and there springs into being Psmith, the cog in the wheel of the New Asiatic Bank; Psmith, the link in the bank's chain; Psmith the Worker. I shall toil with all the accumulated energy of one who, up till now, has only known what work is like from hearsay. Whose is that form sitting on the steps of the bank in the morning, waiting eagerly for the place to open? It is the form of Psmith, the Worker. Whose is that haggard, drawn face which bends over a ledger long after the other toilers have sped blithely westwards to dine at Lyons' Popular Café? It is the face of Psmith, the Worker.[39]

Psmith paints a somewhat dismal picture, but with evident glee. The juxtaposition between style and content, as well as the reference slipped in that Psmith has hitherto been a stranger to work, indicates the mismatch between Psmith's class and his profession. This parody implies that generally those who laud work in flowery terms and those who perform repetitive labour remain distinct; hence the use of the third person.

Psmith exploits his position as Bickersdyke's social equal to hound his bank manager, using their mutual club as his vehicle. Due to his unusual reasons for being employed in the bank, Psmith explains that his father gives him

> just as large an allowance as he would have given me if I had gone to the 'Varsity. Moreover, while I was still at Eton he put my name up for his clubs, the Senior Conservative among others. My pater belongs to four clubs altogether, and in course of time, when my name comes up for election, I shall do the same. Meanwhile, I belong to one, the Senior Conservative. It is a bigger club than the others, and your name comes up for election sooner. About the middle of last month a great yell of joy made the West End of London shake like a jelly. The three thousand members of the Senior Conservative had just learned that I had been elected.[40]

The absurdity of the claim of his fellow members' elation highlights (through claiming to accept at face value) an assumption of friendship, or at least active fellowship, among its members. The fictional Senior Conservative indeed has a larger membership than many factual clubs. The historical Conservative Club had 1,200 members in 1890 according to Joseph Hatton (an 'Idler's Club' contributor), and the Carlton (which had a Junior branch) had 1,600.[41] Graves's contention that Wodehouse based the Senior Conservative on the Constitutional may stem from this number: Hatton lists the membership of the Constitutional as 3,700.[42] Wodehouse himself belonged to the Constitutional, listing it as his only club in the 1908 *Who's Who*.[43] The size of the club really is astounding, especially in relation to its fellows. As Wodehouse indicates here, the notion that a group of this size could be personally known to each other is indeed laughable.

Wodehouse plays on the balance between fellowship and anonymity in the fundamental assumptions of a club as he describes
Psmith's plan of attack:

> The club to which Psmith and Mr Bickersdyke belonged was cel-
> ebrated for the steadfastness of its political views, the excellence of its
> cuisine, and the curiously Gorgonzolaesque marble of its main stair-
> case. It takes all sorts to make a world. It took about four thousand
> of all sorts to make the Senior Conservative Club. To be absolutely
> accurate, there were three thousand and seven hundred and eighteen
> members.
>
> To Mr Bickersdyke for the next week it seemed as if there was only
> one.[44]

Again, Wodehouse emphasises the size of the club. A club of
almost four thousand members is a far cry from the cosy groups
of twelve celebrated in *The Problem Club* and (somewhat ambiv-
alently) *The Bachelors' Club*. Despite the notion of a club as
an institutionalised form of friendship or a rival domestic space,
some members, in the tendency humorously exaggerated in the
Diogenes Club, seek anonymity instead. The features for which
the Senior Conservative is 'celebrated' are largely ones that can be
enjoyed in solitude. Even the political views can be appreciated in
aggregate. More so than at the bank, Psmith here is a 'cog in the
wheel', helping make up the collective that builds other members'
social and political reputations. Of course, Psmith's own socialist
views are hardy 'steadfastly' conservative.

Psmith's campaign against Mr Bickersdyke consists of taking
the social assumptions of the club at face value. He occupies the
club at the same time as Bickersdyke and acts as if, in the space of
the club, the two are social equals:

> There was nothing crude or overdone about Psmith's methods.
> The ordinary man, having conceived the idea of haunting a fellow
> clubman, might have seized the first opportunity of engaging him in
> conversation. Not so Psmith. The first time he met Mr Bickersdyke
> in the club was on the stairs after dinner one night. The great man,
> having received practical proof of the excellence of cuisine referred
> to above, was coming down the main staircase at peace with all men,
> when he was aware of a tall young man in the 'faultless evening dress'
> of which the female novelist is so fond, who was regarding him with a

fixed stare through an eye-glass. The tall young man, having caught his eye, smiled faintly, nodded in a friendly but patronizing manner, and passed on up the staircase to the library.[45]

Psmith has committed no clear social foul, particularly from the context of club members. If there is anything incorrect in his manner, it is the combination of 'friendly' with 'patronizing' – but that is hardly something a member could bring up before the committee. Bickersdyke sends a waiter after Psmith to ascertain if he is a club member; he retorts, 'Will you tell Mr Bickersdyke that I am sorry, but that I have been elected, and have paid my entrance fee and subscription.'[46] Psmith leans on the specifics of the club's operations. If Bickersdyke wanted to blackball his election, he could have, but he has now missed his opportunity. Again, the club is so large that the fiction that members could all be known to each other is strained.

In fact, Psmith's irritating but correct actions provoke Bickersdyke into breaches of propriety: 'On the following day Mr Bickersdyke met Psmith in the club three times, and on the day after that seven. Each time the latter's smile was friendly, but patronizing. Mr Bickersdyke began to grow restless.'[47] The very presence of his new employee at his club irritates Bickersdyke. The notion that they could be social equals in this setting, even with Psmith allowed to patronise him in glance, is deeply irritating. On the fourth day, Psmith engages in a short conversation with Bickersdyke in the type of small talk entirely appropriate to acquaintances at the club. He comments on the weather, offers to order Bickersdyke a cup of coffee, and brings up a topic of potential mutual interest that does not involve the bank:

'I see from my morning paper,' said Psmith, affably, 'that you are to address a meeting at the Kenningford Town Hall next week. I shall come and hear you. Our politics differ in some respects, I fear – I incline to the Socialist view – but nevertheless I shall listen to your remarks with great interest, great interest.'[48]

Again, Psmith is quite correct: friendly, but still patronising – 'great interest' is more the type of remark one might expect to hear from an older man to a younger. Psmith seems to be taking the club's ideals at face value: the notion that as a clubman he is equal to his employer. In fact, he provokes Bickersdyke into rudeness. When he says 'I heard from father this morning,' Bickersdyke retorts, 'I don't wish to hear about your father.'[49] Psmith reacts with 'surprise and pain', affecting to understand that there has been a 'coolness' between the friends.[50] Bickersdyke, who has made a Diogenes-like effort to read his newspaper during this conversation, storms out. By purporting to accept another club assumption – that club members are social equals, at least within the space – Psmith reveals its practical limits.

Shortly thereafter, Psmith provokes Bickersdyke into behaving badly in front of other club members, merely by following him to the card-room and 'observ[ing] the play with silent interest'.[51] This 'unsettle[s]' Bickersdyke into making an error in his play, at which 'Psmith clicked his tongue sympathetically.'[52] Bickersdyke's bridge partner, meanwhile, upbraids his partner in a manner that is described as in keeping with the club habits: 'Dignified reticence is not a leading characteristic of the bridge-player's manner at the Senior Conservative Club on occasions like this.'[53] However, Bickersdyke's response, to blow up at Psmith, is framed as uncharacteristic: 'Mr Bickersdyke lost that control over himself which every member of a club should possess.'[54] While his partner's anger confirms club standards, Bickersdyke's anger at Psmith lacks a rationale that the club condones. He blames Psmith for 'staring at' him. Psmith then appeals to the observing club members:

> 'I am sorry,' said Psmith gravely, 'if my stare falls short in any way of your ideal of what a stare should be; but I appeal to these gentlemen. Could I have watched the game more quietly?'
>
> 'Of course not,' said the bereaved partner warmly. 'Nobody could have any earthly objection to your behaviour. It was absolute careless-ness. I should have thought that one might have expected one's partner at a club like this to exercise elementary—'[55]

Again the club's reputation is invoked, this time to criticise Bickersdyke's conduct in the game. And when he leaves, 'Psmith took his place at the table.'[56] Their club equality makes them interchangeable in this respect, and indeed the other members prefer Psmith.

The club even features in the cessation of Psmith's employment at the end of the story. A climactic scene in which Psmith black-mails Bickersdyke to allow Mike to remain at the bank occurs not at the club, but at a nearby Turkish bath. Finally, at the novel's end, Psmith and Mike both resign from the bank – knowing they would otherwise be fired – to go to Cambridge, both at Psmith's father's expense. As in all the Psmith and Mike stories up to this point, the moment that decides their fate occurs at a cricket game. At the end of the day, Psmith and Mike approach Bickersdyke 'in the lower smoking-room of the Senior Conservative Club' to share the news with him.[57] Bickersdyke tries to put them off, saying 'I shall speak to you tomorrow,'[58] but Psmith will not have it. Rather than conducting the interview in the office, where Bickersdyke will have the upper hand, he does so in the club, where they are social equals. Although this might be said to bend the unstated rules about discussing business in the club, it forms an appropriate bookend because Bickersdyke secured Psmith's employment when staying at his father's house for the weekend. Psmith leverages his social capital to secure a happy ending: a return to a life of comparative leisure and upper-class standing at the 'Varsity.

Joking about socialism

Psmith's socialism features as one of his many personality quirks, but Wodehouse went on to feature a variety of socialist and communist characters. A number of these are butlers and valets, including Meadows in 'Archibald and the Masses' (*Young Men in Spats*, 1936) and Augustus Robb in *Spring Fever* (1948).[59] *If I Were You* (1931) turns on a switched-at-birth story in which an earl discovers he is actually the son of his wet nurse and nephew to his butler, Slingsby. Syd, the rightful earl who's been raised in the servant's family, has his socialist principles tested when he has a chance to join the peerage. Not infrequently, Wodehouse jokes about a violent socialist uprising, as in when Syd 'ominously' refers to 'tumbrils in Piccadilly and blood running in rivers down Park Lane'.[60] One of the most extended jokes about violent class-based revolution comes in *The Inimitable Jeeves* (1923), a Jeeves and Bertie novel constructed out of several previously published stories, mainly featuring Bingo Little. Violent socialist revolution may not seem terribly funny, but through joking about it, Wodehouse allows for multiple readings of the upper classes' idleness.

Bingo's stint as a communist is more overtly fraught with tension than Psmith's socialism. A serial monogamist, Bingo falls head over heels for several women in quick succession over the course of this episodic novel, seeking Jeeves's counsel frequently. One such crush, on a member of the communist group 'Heralds of the Red Dawn' and daughter of its founder, prompts Bingo to join the group. He does so in disguise because part of his role is to make speeches in Hyde Park Corner, including one that attacks his own uncle – who controls his purse strings and keeps him on a tight allowance – and Bertie. His criticism hinges on their idleness: 'There you see two typical members of the class which has downtrodden the poor for centuries. Idlers! Non-producers!'[61] 'Idler' here becomes synonymous with 'drone' in the bee sense.

Indeed, Bertie seems to agree that he is, in fact, idle. A few chapters earlier, Bertie's theatrical friend George refers to him as a member of the 'Idle Rich'.[62] In this passage, Bertie echoes his language, though the context is quite embedded in his characteristic style, full of flourishes and several levels of irony. It comes at the end of a particularly long sentence that sets the scene, replete with various rhetorical flourishes and turns of phrase:

> On the edge of the mob farthest away from me a gang of top-hatted chappies were starting an open-air missionary service; nearer at hand an atheist was letting himself go with a good deal of vim, though handicapped a bit by having no roof to his mouth; while in front of me there stood a little group of serious thinkers with a banner labelled 'Heralds of the Red Dawn'; and as I came up, one of the heralds, a bearded egg in a slouch hat and a tweed suit, was slipping it into the Idle Rich with such breadth and vigour that I paused for a moment to get an earful.[63]

This passage exemplifies the style that characterises Wodehouse's prose, particularly Bertie's narration: the variation in register from 'chappies' to 'heralds' and back (this doesn't even include the more overt literary allusions to which Wodehouse/Bertie is prone). This sentence goes in and out of registers and in and out of degrees of seriousness in a supple way that casual readers of light literature might take for granted (or that critics wondering whether light literature deserves our attention might overlook). At several points in the sentence, readers have to decide how seriously to take the literal meaning of a phrase, such as the physical status of the atheist (that joke seems to be either ableist or classist, possibly both). Likewise, the socialist group is introduced with some irony:

it is quite possible to read 'serious thinkers' as implying the opposite. Likewise, before Bertie introduces the phrase 'Idle Rich' into
his own narration, he has engaged in a sort of ironic free indirect
discourse with their own language, picking up on their own use of
the phrase 'heralds', but applying it with, presumably, some level
of deadpan irony. This is partially effected through the contrast of
'herald' with 'egg', the Wodehousian clubman slang often applied
to Drones Club members. As it turns out, Bingo is both a herald
and an egg, an egg disguising himself as a herald, and, fundamentally, despite his faults, a good egg. The socialist rhetoric becomes
part of the mix here, and readers have some choice as to how seriously to take it.

As Bingo's storyline continues, so do humorous contrasts
between his heraldry and his eggishness, or between his socialist
rhetoric and his leisured lifestyle. After his tirade against Bertie
and his uncle, he reveals his dual identity to Bertie at the Drones
Club. He describes the political leanings of his prospective father-
in-law: 'You must meet old Rowbotham, Bertie. A delightful
chap. Wants to massacre the *bourgeoisie*, sack Park Lane and dis-
embowel the hereditary aristocracy. Well, nothing could be fairer
than that, what?'[64] This deadpan joke opens itself up to multiple readings, depending on one's sense of the extent of Bingo's
naivete. Clearly, the audience is invited to see the irony here, but
Bingo may have no sense of it at all – or might be attempting to
gesture towards a sense of fair play, acknowledging the injustice of class imbalance. The last statement could also be read as
sarcasm, but Bingo seems entirely unselfconscious as the scene
progresses. To raise enough money to marry Charlotte, Bingo
plans to make a large bet on his uncle's racehorse, Ocean Breeze.
He asks Bertie for advice:

> 'I say, you don't know how I could raise fifty quid somehow, do you?'
>   'Why don't you work?'
>   'Work?' said young Bingo, surprised. 'What, me? No, I shall have to
> think of some way. I must put at least fifty on Ocean Breeze.'[65]

Despite his familiarity, use, and possible sympathy with the socialist cause, Bingo seems entirely alienated from labour. He is completely confirmed in his eggishness. In fact, Bertie seems more alive
to the possibility of work, even for the eggish classes – although
for Bertie, still, work is something that happens to other people.

Reading Bingo's voice as naive, however, renders his commentary on the possibility of violent socialist revolution more chilling, despite its clear humour. Bingo tells Bertie that having tea with the revolutionaries will help him when they come down to murdering the aristocracy: 'Silly ass, don't you see that this is going to do you a bit of good when the Revolution breaks loose? When you see old Rowbotham sprinting up Piccadilly with a dripping knife in each hand, you'll be jolly thankful to be able to remind him that he once ate your tea and shrimps.'[66] This graphic image of the revolution depicts knives 'dripping' with the blood of clubmen. Piccadilly defines the border between St James's and Mayfair and appears on Amy Milne-Smith's map of Clubland.[67] Although no clubs actually face onto it, White's is just around the corner on St James's Street. Clubland did serve as a target of class-based violence in the Hyde Park Riot of 1886 during the build-up to the 1887 'Bloody Sunday' riot, probably the most significant moment of socialist violence in English history.[68] Thus Wodehouse's implied notion that clubs might be the focus of further socialist violence is not actually far-fetched. But Bingo's description is so graphic as to read as comic exaggeration, especially considering the juxtaposition between the 'dripping knife' and 'tea and shrimps'. Not to mention the fact that Bingo's whole premise seems unlikely: an ardent revolutionary with blood literally on his hands seems unlikely to be dissuaded by the memory of even a very pleasant tea. Bingo's enculturated notions of class-based propriety are comically inadequate when contemplating the possibility of violent revolution. Alternatively, tea could seriously become a way of heading off class destruction: to co-opt the revolutionaries with the attractions of moving up in, rather than dismantling, the class system.

Indeed, at the tea itself, revolutionaries and idlers discuss the ethics of consumption along similar terms. Comrade Butt, Bingo's rival in Charlotte's affections, points out that Bertie and Bingo profit from the exploitation of the proletariat: 'I wonder the food didn't turn to ashes in our mouths! Eggs! Muffins! Sardines! All wrung from the bleeding lips of the starving poor!'[69] Bertie replies, 'Oh I say! What a beastly idea!'[70] Yet there's a ring of truth. Neither Bingo nor Bertie tries to actively debate the socialists or argue with their rationales – perhaps because of the demands of upper-class politeness. The closest Bertie comes to engaging with the socialist rhetoric is when Rowbotham asks if he 'yearn[s] for the revolution'. Bertie replies, 'Well, I don't know that I exactly yearn. I mean to say, as far as I can make out, the whole hub of the scheme seems to be to massacre coves like me; and I don't mind owning I'm not frightfully keen on the idea.'[71] Comic understatement it may be, but one could imagine Bertie having a larger point: if the options are to carry on with life as he knows it or die on the point of a socialist knife, which seems easier or more pleasant? And the revolutionaries seem similarly attracted to the comforts they at least temporarily enjoy: 'It was all very well for Comrade Butt to knock the food, but he had pretty well finished the ham; and if you had shoved the remainder of the jam into the bleeding lips of the starving poor it would hardly have made them sticky.'[72] The socialists are negotiating a similar balance between comfort and principle – and, perhaps, so too are the readers of *The Inimitable Jeeves*. At least while they are immersed in the frothy world of Wodehouse's novels, readers are 'Idlers' and 'Non-producers' as well.

In addition to Drones, domestic servants come under fire from Wodehouse's socialists. In the course of their tea, Rowbotham criticises Jeeves's 'servility' in calling Bertie 'sir', saying, 'You're an obsolete relic of an exploded feudal system.'[73] Jeeves, typically, replies, 'Very good, sir.'[74] Rowbotham tries to engage further, but Bingo changes the subject 'and Jeeves drifted away'. Bertie says, 'I could see by the look of his back what he felt.'[75] Inexpressive as Jeeves appears, Bertie has learned literally to read his subtle clues, a running joke that begins in *My Man Jeeves*: 'For the first time in our long connection I observed Jeeves almost smile. The corner of his mouth curved quite a quarter of an inch, and for a moment his eye ceased to look like a meditative fish's.'[76] And indeed just as Bertie declares himself a member of the 'Idle Rich', so he refers to his relationship with Jeeves as 'feudal', as in the title *Jeeves and the Feudal Spirit* (1954). Their relationship is fundamentally unequal, yet each benefits and each repeatedly chooses the other. The communists, by contrast, seem out of touch with the subtleties of their relationship. Ultimately, the Heralds of the Red Dawn appear as ineffectual as many Wodehouse characters: the likelihood of their actually achieving a revolution seems remote. While the older generation and its tight control of the purse strings seems the common problem, Jeeves's elaborate machinations, which use Drones as pawns, appear the most effective and entertaining solution.

The butler and the earl

Jeeves may be Wodehouse's most famous servant character – indeed his most famous character *tout court* – but he represents only part of the textured picture of servants that Wodehouse paints. Again, most of Wodehouse's readers experienced the English country house life mainly through reading, which may have fuelled their interest in the Blandings saga in particular. Most of those books have the word 'Blandings' in the title, whereas most of the sagas narrated by Bertie mention Jeeves in their titles (many titles varied transatlantically). Conversely, many of the one-offs have titles that refer to money: *Money for Nothing* (1928), *Big Money* (1931), *Money in the Bank* (1942), *Frozen Assets* (1964), *Do Butlers Burgle Banks?* (1968) and even *The Little Nugget* (1913), whose title refers to a child's ransom value, and *Ice in the Bedroom* (1961), which refers to diamonds. As the twentieth century progressed, Wodehouse chronicled the real changes in the social order, less violent and more gradual than bloody revolution. The increasingly porous boundary between the servant class and the aristocracy manifests in comic plots of impersonation and identity confusion.

In his comic depictions of butlers, Wodehouse stresses their role as literal and figurative gatekeepers. The notion of the upper-class Drone cowed by the impressive butler becomes a running joke. Bertie has a particularly strong reaction to Jeeves's Uncle Charlie:

> the sudden impact of Charlie Silversmith had removed all the breath almost totally. He took me right back to the days when I was starting out as a *flâneur* and man about town and used to tremble beneath butlers' eyes and generally feel very young and bulbous.
>
> Older and tougher, I am able to take most of these fauna in my stride. When they open front doors to me, I shoot my cuffs nonchalantly. 'Aha, there, butler,' I say. 'How's tricks?' but Jeeves's Uncle Charlie was something special. He looked like one of those steel engravings of nineteenth-century statesmen[.][77]

The comparison to a nineteenth-century statesman indicates the paradox of butlers. Although technically lower-class, their position requires knowledge of etiquette and an immaculate demeanour. They cannot, in short, afford the antics of the Drones, who have the ease of privilege. Bertie explicitly distinguishes between

Uncle Charlie and the mainstream lower classes through a comic bit involving Corky's dog: 'A South London dog belonging to the lower middle classes or, rather, definitely of the people, I don't suppose he had ever seen a butler before, and it was a dashed shame that he should have drawn something like Uncle Charlie first crack out of the box.'[78] Outside of Jeeves and his relatives, Wodehouse uses this paradox as a source of humour, as in *If I Were You* when Slingsby the butler cannot bring himself to treat his nephew as a lord and works to undermine his case to the title.

Wodehouse frequently casts butlers as models of emotional restraint, and thus draws attentions to cracks in their customary reserve. This view permeates his fiction and also features in his memoir:

> A certain anemia of the exchequer caused me in those days to go about in the discarded clothes of relative, and it was this that once enabled me to see that rarest of all sights, a laughing butler. By the laws of their guild butlers of the Edwardian epoch were sometimes permitted a quick, short smile, provided it was sardonic, but never a guffaw.[79]

The idea of the butler as professionally compelled to maintain a façade of emotional impassivity operates along a similar logic to the plight of the sad clown, or the humorist forced to be merry and unable to make himself taken seriously, which Jerome frequently played on, although of course the trope is much older. Like that figure, the butler can become a figure of pathos:

> Among other things which contributed to make butlers gloomy was the fact that so many of their employers were sparkling raconteurs. Only a butler, my butler said, can realize what it means to a butler to be wedged against the sideboard and unable to escape and to watch his employer working the conversation around to the point where he will be able to tell that good story of his which he, the butler, has heard so often before. It was when my butler mentioned this, with a kindly word of commendation to me for never having said anything even remotely clever or entertaining since he had entered my service, that I at last found myself understanding the inwardness of a rather peculiar episode of my early manhood.[80]

The episode in question involves W. S. Gilbert, creator of a famous sad clown in *Yeomen of the Guard* (1888). When the young Wodehouse lunched with the elder humorist, Gilbert told a humorous story, but Wodehouse laughed before the punch line. When Wodehouse glanced at the butler, 'His eyes were shining with a doglike devotion.'[81] This metaphor prevents complete sympathy with the butler: he has gone from super- to sub-human.

Beach, Lord Emsworth's butler, is significantly more human than Jeeves. Rather than being the architect of the schemes surrounding Blandings Castle, he is usually caught up in them. The reader is granted more glimpses into his un-butler-like private moments:

> It is a fact not generally known, for a nice sense of the dignity of his position restrained him from exercising it, that Beach possessed a rather attractive singing-voice . . . we cannot advance a more striking proof of the lightness of heart which had now come upon him than by mentioning that, as he walked home through the wood, he broke his rigid rule and definitely warbled. [. . .] He felt more like a gay young second footman than a butler of years' standing.[82]

Beach's actions are played against the customary actions of a butler for comic effect. Keggs is perhaps the most actively benevolent of Wodehouse butlers; he appears in several Wodehouse novels and stories. In *Something Fishy* (1957), he is discovered supporting a former employer, Lord Uffenham, and his daughter, Jane, towards whom he assumes a godfatherly role. Keggs saves the day by thwarting a tontine (which itself is a bizarre kind of club).[83]

Although Jeeves may not manifest emotion strongly, he feels it nevertheless. Like Dr Watson scanning Sherlock Holmes for signs of emotion, Bertie learns to read Jeeves's emotional clues:

> 'I noticed, Jeeves, that when I started telling you the bad news just now, one of your eyebrows flickered.'
> 'Yes, sir. I was much exercised.'[84]

Jeeves's acknowledgement that Bertie successfully ascertains his emotional state typifies the intimacy of their homosocial relationship.[85] Bertie's affection for Jeeves is explicit. He introduces him in *The Inimitable Jeeves* in terms that elide their distinctions in rank: 'Right from the first day he came to me, I have looked on him as a sort of guide, philosopher, and friend.'[86] Yet the distance between the two is inescapable. When witnessing the fruits of

Jeeves's labour, Bertie reports, 'I came away from the window thrilled to the marrow; and when I met Jeeves on the stairs I was so moved that I nearly grasped his hand.'[87] Nearly, but never quite. The impulse towards intimate contact indicates Bertie's feelings towards Jeeves, but its impossibility shows the inevitable social distance between them. This from a man who performs all sorts of menial duties for Bertie, who in turn rewards him, in this case, with money that's literally lying around his apartment.

Thank You, Jeeves (1934) puts more emphasis on Bertie and Jeeves's relationship as Jeeves leaves Bertie's employ – temporarily, of course. Thus Bertie's feelings for Jeeves are more exposed. When Jeeves resigns because Bertie takes up the banjulele, Bertie registers as much dismay as his flippant style allows: 'This parting of the ways with Jeeves had made me feel a bit as if I had just stepped on a bomb and was trying to piece myself together again in a bleak world, but we Woosters can keep the stiff upper lip.'[88] Couched in Bertie's customary hedges lies an extreme metaphor of violent destruction. Later, when the two are reunited (temporarily), Bertie compares Jeeves to his mother:

'Jeeves,' I said, 'I feel like a lost child that has found its mother.'
'Indeed, sir?'
'If you don't mind me calling you a mother?'
'Not at all, sir.'
'Thank you, Jeeves.'[89]

Bertie uses his stylistic tendency to exaggeration to deliver an indication of his feelings for Jeeves without risking the 'awful' sense of disclosure Barrie describes.[90]

Beyond this metaphorical level, Wodehouse explores the real blurring of lines between the servant and upper classes. He picks up and expands themes of class impersonation introduced by the *Idler* circle in club stories and other writings.[91] Several club stories have characters who change from club servants to club members or vice versa, such as Leonard in *The Problem Club* or Willoughby in *The Bachelors' Club*. In several instances, the similarity of dress between club members in eveningwear and club servants (in similar dress) raises the possibility of confusing members with servants. Furthermore, J. M. Barrie's play *The Admirable Crichton* (1902) depicts a Radical earl and a Conservative butler who end up trading roles when members of the household and their social circle are shipwrecked on an island. When they are rescued, the eponymous butler is forced back into his subsidiary role, despite his clear 'natural' superiority. As with Wodehouse's jokes about violent revolution, this pokes fun at the Radical and Conservative sides alike, although Barrie characteristically has more of an edge, leaving the lingering impression that the earl's attempts at introducing equality into his household do not go nearly far enough.

Wodehouse's fiction is full of deliberate impersonation and mistaken identity, forming its own type of Pain's Impersonation Society. As Pongo's Uncle Fred declares, 'there is no more admirably educational experience for a young fellow starting out in life than going to stay at a country house under a false name'.[92] The impersonators tend to be Drones Club members and those of similar upper-class standing. While they often impersonate each other, sometimes the impersonation crosses class lines. For instance, in *The Mating Season* (1949), through a comically byzantine turn of events, Bertie and Gussie end up impersonating each other, while fellow Drones Club member Claude 'Catsmeat' Pirbright pretends to be a valet, serving Bertie as Gussie. In the one-off *Money in the Bank* (1942), an earl poses as 'Cakebread', the butler, as part of a plan to find jewels squirrelled away on his own property before a memory-damaging head injury. However, characters rarely impersonate across gender lines, which is almost surprising, given the long tradition of the pantomime dame and the prevalence of cross-dressing humour in works from the *Idler* circle, such as *Tommy and Co.* and *The Problem Club*. In fact, the television adaptation *Jeeves and Wooster*, starring Stephen Fry and Hugh Laurie, introduces cross-dressing into an adaptation of *Jeeves and the Feudal Spirit*.[93] Of course, this does not mean that gender is not implicated in Wodehouse's impersonations. As Uncle Fred's remark suggests, they are deeply implicated in masculine community formation, and they probably also reflect on the 'category crisis' of women's changing role.[94]

In addition to impersonation, marriage serves as a means of tracking relationships between servants and their employers – indeed, both serve as major driving forces of comic plot. Wodehouse often casts servants and upper-class employers as romantic partners and/or romantic rivals, with all the intimacy of Sedgwickian triangulation.[95] In *The Inimitable Jeeves*, not only does Bingo's uncle marry his cook, but Jeeves himself serves as a romantic rival to both Littles. It emerges, after Jeeves's plan has supposedly backfired, resulting in the senior Little marrying his cook rather than giving Bingo the money to marry a waitress, that Jeeves was engaged to both the cook and the waitress. He admits that he 'anticipated some such outcome' to his scheme, as he prefers the waitress to the cook.[96] In other words, Jeeves has his own ends in mind – and not truly to the detriment of Bingo, as Bertie quickly reassures readers: he quickly moves on to another flame.

In the one-off *Spring Fever* (1948), rivalry combines with a sense of interchangeability. Again, a cook forms the apex of a love triangle, in this case between Lord Shortlands and his butler, Mervyn Spink. The earl is down on his luck, entirely without funds of his own, and dependent on his married daughter for support. The cook declares that she will marry whichever of her suitors can muster two hundred pounds to set them up in a pub. And so the race is on.

Throughout the novel, Wodehouse stresses the interchangeable appearances of Spink and Lord Shortlands: 'Nature is a haphazard caster, and no better example of her sloppy methods could have been afforded than by the outer husks of the fifth Earl of Shortlands and Spink, his butler. Called upon to provide an Earl and a butler, she had produced an Earl who looked like a butler and a butler who looked like an Earl.'[97] The fact that the two are roughly financially equivalent adds to the potential for confusion between their position. The cook, their mutual love interest, says of Lord Shortlands, 'He isn't so much the gentleman as Mr Spink.'[98] Similarly, in *Full Moon*, published the previous year, Wodehouse emphasises in his narration that Lady Hermione, the Earl of Emsworth's sister, resembles a cook: 'Unlike the rest of the female members of her family, who were tall and stately, Lady Hermione Wedge was short and dumpy and looked like a cook – in her softer moods, a cook well satisfied with her latest soufflé; when stirred to anger, a cook about to give notice, but always a cook of strong character.'[99] Thus, when an impecunious suitor of the younger generation, attempting to gain access to Blandings, mistakes her for a cook, the reader might view it as a reasonable mistake – unlike Lady Hermione, who flies into a rage. Conversely, when his resemblance to a butler is pointed out to him, Shortlands views it as a fortuitous source of income. He plans to make 'a nice, steady living' playing butlers in Hollywood.[100]

Yet *Spring Fever* ends with a surprising instance of cross-class friendship. Despite the piling-up of invective against Spink, Lord

Shortlands does not best him in the affair of the cook. Rather, both parties are cut out by another colourful character in the book's Wodehousian pantheon: Augustus Robb, who (as the name suggests) used to be a burglar but found religion and is now a valet. Not at all in the model of Jeeves, he calls everyone, including his employer and social betters, 'cocky'. As it turns out, Robb and the cook had been engaged years previously but, due to a miscommunication about the name of the registry office where they were to wed, had each laboured for years under the misapprehension that the other had backed out at the eleventh hour without a word. This last-minute plot twist throws Shortlands and Spink together into an unlikely moment. Despite their open hostilities throughout the novel, which culminate in Spink's leaving Shortlands' employ, the novel's final scene shows a remarkable rapprochement:

> Mervyn Spink came silently in, and Lord Shortlands, seeing him in the mirror, turned. As these two strong men, linked by the bond of thwarted love, faced each other, there was a silence. Mervyn Spink was feeling that Lord Shortlands was not such a bad old buster, after all, and Lord Shortlands was feeling strangely softened towards Mervyn Spink.[101]

The use of the mirror clearly signals their resemblance and their mutual identification. The two have a short exchange in which Spink offers 'a drop of something' in the butler's pantry.

> 'Lead me to it, Spink.'
> 'This way, m'lord.'
> 'Don't call me "m'lord".'
> 'This way, Shortlands.'
> 'Don't call me "Shortlands",' said the fifth Earl. 'Call me Shorty.'
> He put his hand in his new friend's arm, and they went out.[102]

As in *Casablanca*, released five years prior, homosociability provides recompense for thwarted love, triumphing over differences between men. In this case, the difference includes not only interpersonal conflict, but class. A butler and an earl end this novel as unironic 'friends'.

The confusion between club members and club servants, between aristocrats and waiters, becomes less of an improbable joke as the twentieth century progresses. In later Wodehouse novels, waiters increasingly pass in and out of core groups of upper-class characters. In *French Leave* (1956), a French aristocrat becomes a waiter. In *Ice in the Bedroom* (1961), wealthy novelist Leila Yorke finds her lost husband because he's working as a waiter in a hotel restaurant, a descendant of the club restaurant. Several marriages between aristocrats and servants emerge. The butler marries the lady of the house in *Cocktail Time* (1958), aided by the Earl of Ickenham (Pongo's Uncle Fred), who served in the Home Guard with the butler. Even central cast member Gussie Fink-Nottle, who long seemed destined for Madeline Bassett, ends up eloping with the Bassetts' cook in *Stiff Upper Lip, Jeeves* (1962). Or rather, with Emerald Stoker, sister of Bertie's erstwhile fiancée Pauline and daughter of American millionaire J. Washburn Stoker, who has been moonlighting as a cook. Gussie's marriage to a cook in 1962 reads very differently to Bingo's uncle's marriage to a cook in the 1923 *Inimitable Jeeves*. Cross-class impersonation progressed in forty years from a humorous transgression of a firm line to an indication of the growing porousness of class boundaries.

Clubs for readers

From idleness to socialism, from masters to servants, the Drones is a club for readers. Wodehouse picks up on the notion of club-as-joke, but he does not alter the basic facts of West End clubs very far: the material almost parodies itself. And thus it affords a range of political readings. Wodehouse lends himself to a socially conservative reading – his treatment of gender and race doesn't help – but, like many of these humorists, his style allows for a multitude of potentially contradictory readings, and it is difficult to know which, if any, are primary. Wodehouse radically opens up the club – not, like his socialists, with a dripping knife, but by jovially throwing open the doors of the club and revealing it to be silly as well as fun. Although the antics of the Drones Club are generally enjoyable, its stakes are pretty low and its members often have problems familiar to readers of all classes: chiefly securing a regular income (ideally without doing too much arduous labour) or finding love – or, in the case of Bertie Wooster, avoiding matrimony. Even the timeless quality of Wodehouse (the extent of which can be debated) provides a sort of protected space: a club for readers, a space to shield them from the cares of everyday life. Yet through jokes about the fundamental changes to the social system, the Wodehouse canon also prepares its readers to face those social changes with the fundamental good will of Bertie Wooster. Following earlier traditions, Wodehouse uses exclusive sites to create a fictional space for all readers. In doing so, he continues the legacy of blurring boundaries between real and imagined clubs, making the fictional ones appear more real – and certainly more accessible – than their actual counterparts. Through the Drones and its comrades, he promotes affection for London's Clubland even while making it look ridiculous.

Complementing the Drones is the Junior Ganymede Club, the club for 'gentlemen's gentlemen'[103] to which Jeeves belongs, which in many ways follows the conventions of the Idlers' fictional clubs more closely than the Drones. Its premise is silly, but based on reality: Cecil Maxwell-Lyte wrote in 1919 that 'many Club servants have Clubs of their own, often mere coteries or public houses where they meet; still sufficiently Club-like for an *esprit de corps* to exist and Club gossip to circulate'.[104] Bertie describes the Ganymede as 'a rather posh club for butlers and valets called the Junior Ganymede, situated somewhere in Curzon Street'.[105] Curzon Street is in Mayfair, across Piccadilly from central Clubland (St James's and Pall Mall), yet, depending on where along the street the club is located, the Ganymede may be closer to central Clubland than the Bachelors' Club, the alleged model for the Drones, which was at 8 Hamilton Place W., in Mayfair near Hyde Park.[106] Like Zangwill exaggerating the real rules of the Bachelors' Club, Wodehouse envisions a servants' club far more conventional and respectable than that of their employers.

Indeed, the Ganymedes' higher standards create the plot driver of rule-based expulsion, generally not a concern in the roll-tossing Drones. The members of the Ganymede Club conduct themselves with far more decorum than the Drones; when Bertie asks Jeeves what members usually do, he replies, 'Well, sir, many of the members play a sound game of bridge. The conversation, too, rarely fails to touch a high level of interest. And should one desire more frivolous entertainment, there are the club books.'[107] These club books become a major plot engine of several books in the Jeeves saga – including Jeeves's attempts to wield them without running afoul of the Ganymede's rules. Each member of the Ganymede must write in the club book about his or her employer to serve as a guide – or warning – to others thinking of taking a situation in that household. Crossed with Bertie's absurd country house situations, the books end up being used for blackmail – to save Bertie's skin. The Drones and the Ganymedes complement each other, contributing to the impression of a social order in which the upper classes are steered by their much wiser servants. This may be read as carnivalesque joke or clear-eyed social commentary.

The Ganymede Club is the real club for readers. Closer in real class standing to the majority of Wodehouse readers, the Ganymedes enjoy reading about Bertie's antics in his ever-growing entry. Bertie objects: 'it was not pleasant to think that full details of episodes I would prefer to be buried in oblivion were giving a big laugh daily to a bunch of valets and butlers'.[108] However, Bertie often seems aware of his own audience, to whom he grants easy membership to the Drones. Readers who might gain entry to neither if either were real (by virtue of sex, for instance) can feel belonging to both. Or, because both are ridiculous in their own way, readers can feel that they aren't missing out on much by not having access to the portals of clubland. In book form, the clubs can be accessed at readers' own volition, time and time again – including at a historical remove.

Notes

1   Richardson, 'The Prison Camp as Public School'; Sproat, 'Wodehouse, Sir Pelham Grenville (1881–1975)'.
2   Wodehouse, *America, I Like You*, 69. Wodehouse thus puts his critic in the somewhat awkward position of adopting this term seriously.
3   Michael T. Williamson characterises these early stories as 'impudent'. Williamson, 'Before Jeeves'.
4   Wodehouse, *America, I Like You*, 43.
5   Wodehouse, *America, I Like You*, 69.
6   Hall, *The Comic Style of P.G. Wodehouse*, 26.
7   Wodehouse, *The Complete Lyrics of P.G. Wodehouse*, xvii; Wodehouse, *The Small Bachelor*. Serialised in *Liberty* magazine in 1926, based on 'a 1917 musical comedy script' PGW co-wrote with Guy Bolton (Overlook paratext). See Considine, 'P.G. Wodehouse and the American Musical Comedy'.
8   Hall, *Comic Style*, 51.
9   Wodehouse, *Indiscretions of Archie*, 187. See Simmers, 'P.G. Wodehouse and the First World War'.

10 Graves, *Leather Armchairs*, xiii.
11 Graves, *Leather Armchairs*, xvi.
12 Wodehouse, *Spring Fever*, 228.
13 First published in the US as *Golf Without Tears* in 1924.
14 The *OED* entry on 'crumpet' cites *The Inimitable Jeeves*. *OED Online*, s.v. 'crumpet', last modified December 2020.
15 Wodehouse, *Young Men in Spats*, 9.
16 Hall, *The Comic Style of P.G. Wodehouse*. The work was published during Wodehouse's lifetime and thus does not include some of his last works.
17 Wodehouse, *My Man Jeeves*. Search run on Project Gutenberg edition.
18 Wodehouse, *Jill the Reckless*, 157.
19 Wodehouse, *Inimitable Jeeves*, 204–5.
20 Wodehouse, *Big Money*, 130.
21 Wodehouse, *Very Good, Jeeves*, 207.
22 Stewart, *Dear Reader*.
23 Wodehouse, *The Mating Season*, 51.
24 Carey, *The Intellectuals and the Masses*, 59.
25 Wodehouse, *A Gentleman of Leisure*, 9.
26 Barrie, *Little White Bird*, 136.
27 Wodehouse, *The Mating Season*, 113.
28 Wodehouse, *Young Men in Spats*, 147. See Milne-Smith, *London Clubland*, 23; Graves, *Leather Armchairs*, 5.
29 Hobbes, *Leviathan*, 52.
30 Wodehouse, *Laughing Gas*, 7.
31 Masthead, *The Captain* 1, vol. 1 (London: George Newnes 1), accessed through North, *Waterloo Directory of English Newspapers and Periodicals*.
32 Wodehouse, *Leave it to Psmith*, 50–1.
33 Wodehouse, *Mike*, 166.
34 Wodehouse, *Mike*, 167.
35 Wodehouse, *Psmith in the City*, 43.
36 Wodehouse, *Psmith in the City*, 50.
37 Wodehouse, *Psmith in the City*, 130.
38 Humpherys, 'Putting Women in the Boat', 6.
39 Wodehouse, *Psmith in the City*, 40–1.
40 Wodehouse, *Psmith in the City*, 46.
41 Hatton, *Club-Land*, 35.
42 Hatton, *Club-Land*, 35.
43 *Who's Who* (1908), 2002.

44 Wodehouse, *Psmith in the City*, 64.

45 Wodehouse, *Psmith in the City*, 64.

46 Wodehouse, *Psmith in the City*, 65.

47 Wodehouse, *Psmith in the City*, 65.

48 Wodehouse, *Psmith in the City*, 66.

49 Wodehouse, *Psmith in the City*, 66.

50 Wodehouse, *Psmith in the City*, 66.

51 Wodehouse, *Psmith in the City*, 66.

52 Wodehouse, *Psmith in the City*, 66, 67.

53 Wodehouse, *Psmith in the City*, 67.

54 Wodehouse, *Psmith in the City*, 67.

55 Wodehouse, *Psmith in the City*, 67.

56 Wodehouse, *Psmith in the City*, 67.

57 Wodehouse, *Psmith in the City*, 198.

58 Wodehouse, *Psmith in the City*, 199.

59 Wodehouse, *Young Men in Spats*, 197; Wodehouse, *Spring Fever*, 182.

60 Wodehouse, *If I Were You*, 29.

61 Wodehouse, *Inimitable Jeeves*, 100.

62 Wodehouse, *Inimitable Jeeves*, 85.

63 Wodehouse, *Inimitable Jeeves*, 99–100.

64 Wodehouse, *Inimitable Jeeves*, 103.

65 Wodehouse, *Inimitable Jeeves*, 105.

66 Wodehouse, *Inimitable Jeeves*, 105.

67 Milne-Smith, *London Clubland*, 33.

68 Milne-Smith, *London Clubland*, 194. Her seventh chapter is devoted to the Hyde Park Riot and contains a detailed and sophisticated analysis of how the architecture of the club buildings, particularly their windows, contributed to the class feelings that bubbled up into the riots.

69 Wodehouse, *Inimitable Jeeves*, 109.

70 Wodehouse, *Inimitable Jeeves*, 109.

71 Wodehouse, *Inimitable Jeeves*, 108.

72 Wodehouse, *Inimitable Jeeves*, 109–10.

73 Wodehouse, *Inimitable Jeeves*, 109.

74 Wodehouse, *Inimitable Jeeves*, 109.

75 Wodehouse, *Inimitable Jeeves*, 109.

76 Wodehouse, *My Man Jeeves*, 162.

77 Wodehouse, *The Mating Season*, 50.

78 Wodehouse, *The Mating Season*, 51.

79 Wodehouse, *America, I Like You*, 104.

80   Wodehouse, *America, I Like You*, 107.

81   Wodehouse, *America, I like You*, 108.

82   Wodehouse, *Summer Lightning*, 233.

83   The novel refers to Stevenson's *The Wrong Box*, which also features a tontine. Wodehouse, *Something Fishy*, 9.

84   Wodehouse, *The Mating Season*, 228.

85   I stop short of reading this relationship as homoerotic, but Brian D. Holcomb speculates on the role of physical desire in it. Kate Macdonald, meanwhile, reads Jeeves's interest in Bertie's dress as crucially professional. Holcomb, 'The Queer Domesticity of Bertie and Jeeves', 222–3; Macdonald, 'Problematic Menswear', 248.

86   Wodehouse, *Inimitable Jeeves*, 2.

87   Wodehouse, *Inimitable Jeeves*, 147.

88   Wodehouse, *Thank You, Jeeves*, 21.

89   Wodehouse, *Thank You, Jeeves*, 173.

90   Barrie, *When a Man's Single*, 252.

91   My thinking about class impersonation relies on Marjorie Garber and Marah Gubar, although I have decided not to continue using the term 'transvestism'. Gubar, 'Who Watched *The Children's Pinafore?*', 411. Garber, *Vested Interests*, 16, 22.

92   Wodehouse, *Service with a Smile*, 40.

93   'Arrested in a Night Club (or, the Delayed Arrival)', *Jeeves and Wooster* (1993).

94   Garber, *Vested Interests*, 16.

95   Sedgwick, *Between Men*.

96   Wodehouse, *Inimitable Jeeves*, 20.

97   Wodehouse, *Spring Fever*, 36.

98   Wodehouse, *Spring Fever*, 45.

99   Wodehouse, *Full Moon*, 12–13.

100   Wodehouse, *Spring Fever*, 272.

101   Wodehouse, *Spring Fever*, 272–3.

102   Wodehouse, *Spring Fever*, 273.

103   Wodehouse, *Stiff Upper Lip, Jeeves*, 8.

104   Cecil Maxwell-Lyte, 'A Club Secretary on Clubs', *The Nineteenth Century and After* (New York ed. of a London paper) 86, no. 1 (July 1919): 149.

105   Wodehouse, *Jeeves and the Feudal Spirit*, 9.

106   Bachelors' Club address from Sladen, *Who's Who* (1897), 30.

107   Wodehouse, *Jeeves and the Feudal Spirit* 37–8.

108   Wodehouse, *Jeeves and the Feudal Spirit*, 38.

Conclusion: Mass Readership, Then and Now

This book opened, like many of the stories studied within its pages, with the formation of a club from a motley group of individuals. As in many of the stories, the eventual dissolution of the club was a foregone conclusion. Jerome went bankrupt (although he kept writing); Doyle went to war (although the cricket team played in his name); Wodehouse moved to America. They married and had children, not necessarily biological (a surprising number were step-parents or guardians). By the time they published their memoirs in the 1920s and '30s, the *Idler* group loomed large for some – Jerome and Doyle, especially – and less so for others, such as the deliberately antisocial Barrie. And of course they all died. Even after death, their works rarely socialise in academic institutions such as syllabi and monographs – unless one counts the shelving of Barr next to Barrie, which provided early inspiration for this book. By reuniting the Idlers, this book celebrates the biographical and stylistic connections between them as well as the theme of the club.

The dissolution of the club does not overshadow the power of its affiliation. As Caroline Levine and Mario Oritz-Robles have argued, endings can be given too much weight.[1] There's a reason we talk about fiction in the perpetual present, and it's not just to tie ourselves into difficult grammatical knots. Zangwill's Bachelors' Club never existed, because it's fictional, and even within the fictional realm, it ceased to exist. Yet we can all visit it whenever we want to by picking up the book. Even though Zangwill had an existence and is now gone, we can today experience contact with him in the same way that contemporary 'common' readers could – minus the possibility of attending a lecture of his or the fantasy of bumping into him in a crowded street. By creating the Idler's Club, Barr, Jerome, Zangwill and Pain, as well as the others who contributed to its early solidification, created fictionalised versions of themselves in a space accessible to newly literate readers. The metaphor of the club for mass readership is a joke, but the kernel of truth is that a magazine or book can function like a club. It can foster a sense of belonging, both to itself and to larger imagined and imaginary communities, and it can be exclusive. Some of those excluded may never even know or care. But some readers may feel a kind of cognitive dissonance: included by virtue of some of their identities but excluded by others. And one response to cognitive dissonance is laughter.

The subtitle of this book pairs Jerome and Wodehouse, in a way that might be misleading because the two have few direct biographical links. But some of the distinctions between the two are telling. Wodehouse succeeded where Jerome failed: financially, in gaining a knighthood, and in class standing (both were from families faltering on the social ladder, although from different rungs). Yet Wodehouse's success carries the significant caveat that he was nearly an exile from his home country as a result of a miscalculated bout of humour. Jerome often complained of being trapped in his role as a humorist. In the preface to *John Ingerfield and Other Stories* (1894), he addressed 'the Gentle Reader' and 'the Gentle Critic', specifying that several stories 'are not intended to be amusing'.[2] In *Paul Kelver* (1902), a comic actor complains, 'It makes me very angry sometimes. . . . If I were to enter a room full of people . . . and tell them that my mother had been run over by an omnibus, they would think it the funniest story they had heard in years.'[3] With many of these figures, their chief tragedies seem to be either being taken too seriously or not seriously enough. Insofar as they appear in the Victorian canon – Stevenson and Doyle consistently, strengthening interest in Barrie and Zangwill, and of course Chesterton, although he plays a minor role in the biographical picture – their humour does not figure in the conventional narrative about them. Yet I would argue that all are funny, if not all the time – like humorists, as Jerome reminds us.

The Idlers were not, of course, the only ones to make jokes about the club during this period. Humour set in clubs or involving clubmen range from H. G. Wells's short story 'The Truth about Pylecraft', first published in the *Strand* in 1903, to T. S. Eliot's 'Bustopher Jones: The Cat about Town' from *Old Possum's Book of Practical Cats* (1939). Even in texts far flung from the *Idler* social circle, the club can be a shorthand for belonging and exclusivity.

The vantage point of the clubroom can create a ready-made implied community for readers and authors. When Wells's story opens in the club, the reader is positioned within the exclusive community with the first-person narrator and eponymous Pylecraft. That sense of belonging cannot always be taken for granted, however: Wells's narrator fears that Pylecraft will expose his Hindu ancestry, just as Pylecraft relies on the narrator to keep his secret in turn. The club may be a place of nominal belonging, yet it clearly also serves as a stage for performance of that belonging – and its precarity is perpetually reinforced by fears, spoken or unspoken, of losing one's membership. Perhaps the Idlers' most radical notion is that the club itself can be the subject of mirth, that perhaps belonging doesn't matter because the club itself is so silly. Clubs with ridiculous premises, such as the Failure Club and the Society for Doing Without Some People, make this gesture overtly. The Drones, which never dissolves and lasts much longer over narrative time, presents the club as silly in a different way. The Drones accentuates the Idler's Club's invitation to middle-class readers to think of themselves as putting their feet on the club's mantelpiece and chucking a roll at a nearby aristocrat. When belonging is less in question, one can laugh at the club from within.

Ambivalence about the club as an institution was baked into the form of the club novel from *The Bachelors' Club* onwards. In fact, the earlier *Suicide Club* presents it as an outright evil. Even Jerome sees the ultimate expression of the cosiness of the club as the domestic periodical office. The often-antisocial Barrie similarly lauds the newspaper office as a semi-domestic space, connecting it to the shared stairways and corridors of his bachelor newspapermen. Yet print sociability has its limits. Barrie stresses the illusion of its imagined landscape in *When a Man's Single* and also exaggerates the consequences of readership in *Better Dead*. Chesterton and Pain exaggerate readership in a different way through the Adventure and Romance Agency and Impersonation Society. Both show the desire to live out the actions of a book, but also the joke turns on the absurdity of what happens when one does. Elsewhere I have said that humour pushes at the boundaries of the book.[4] A good joke can create a sense of affiliation across the page. A joke that misfires can throw a reader out of an immersive state.

Humour is a slippery object of study: is it a genre, a mode, a style, an emotion? All shade into each other, and the combination of texts in this book shows that moments of humour in an otherwise serious text can participate in a conversation with texts that fall more squarely into the 'humour' genre. Precisely because humour relies so fundamentally on double meanings, it can be difficult to pin down critically. As I hope I have shown, humour can be deeply related to other emotions, from pathos to anger to contented belonging. Doyle's Diogenes Club clearly draws on the fictional clubs created by his friends and colleagues. Conversely, Pain took some of the humour – and some of the pathos – of Stevenson's Suicide Club and amped it up in his Proposal Club. This example also shows how thin the razor edge of humour can be: the topic of the Suicide Club or the Proposal Club can be either funny or deadly serious, depending on one's perspective. In that sense, humour can be a genre that depends entirely on interpretation for its definition. As Jerome shows so clearly, work can be identified as humour that misfires, and work can be incorrectly identified as humour when it's meant to be serious. But humour may also be missed, as in the case of Doyle or Stevenson, if a reader is predisposed to take it too seriously.

Rather than arguing that we should take humour seriously, I'd like to propose that we take more literature humorously. In other words, I advocate that critics of the Victorian period open themselves up to the possibility of laughing with the Victorians. Laughing at the Victorians is undoubtedly easier, and titters at conference talks about sentimentality are a commonplace way of providing an outlet for our discomfort at the topic and at times a form of bonding as a critical community, perhaps predicated on a sense of superiority to our object of study. It can indeed be uncomfortable when a book asks you to feel something, or even makes you feel something without your full consent. Pleasant feelings can be as uncomfortable as 'ugly feelings'.[5] If, as I hope I have shown, humour can create a sense of belonging or affiliation, it can be uncomfortable to associate too closely with the Victorians.

Embracing the enjoyment of literature entails viewing literary escapism as social action, an idea still nearly as radical as when Janice Radway proposed it in the 1980s.[6] Of course, we don't want enjoyment to serve as a substitute for adequate compensation of our labour or form its own set of requirements, as Deidre Lynch rightly cautions.[7] But neither do we want to become the Diogenes Club, shushing any voice that interrupts our perusal of 'the latest periodicals' – in this case, perhaps the scholarly journals.[8] Many of the humorous texts treated here remain understudied by scholars of the British nineteenth and twentieth centuries, even as they remain beloved by erudite pleasure readers.[9] Thinking of these texts as enacting important social action through their light and pleasant affect may help scholars integrate these works into their syllabi and their research. While we can certainly take these works seriously, it is perhaps even more radical to embrace the pleasure they can afford us and our students. Laughing with these texts does not necessarily mean swallowing their worldview whole, any more than laughing with Bertie Wooster means accepting him as an exemplar of the legitimate ruling classes. Even though some of their jokes are far from subtle, the social meaning of these texts, in their moment and in ours, is far from straightforward.

In the 'Idler's Club' headpiece, the members assert their power and their right to belong through their visible comfort and irreverence. Outsiders like Jerome and Zangwill not only entered the portals reserved for the upper classes, but they put their feet up on the mantelpiece. Even though many of these jokes turn on the arbitrary nature of belonging, through their jokes, the Idlers asserted their presence. Zangwill, who really started the joke, knew well what it was like to be excluded, formally or informally, from clubs and clublike structures. The informal clubs seem the most compelling, from Jerome's newspaper office to Barrie's staircase, but even these communities operate under rules whose transgression can signal exile, as the nostalgic cast of *My Lady Nicotine* and *Novel Notes* underscores. But although anxiety about exclusion, social missteps and failure certainly appear in these texts, those affects do not dominate. Rather, they serve as fuel for the humour which predominates. Perhaps we might imitate this comfortable audacity in our own critical communities, similarly built on texts, grappling with issues of inclusivity, and working at the intersection of labour and idleness. As the ground shifts under us, we might take a lesson from the Idlers and make our own clubs as welcoming and attractive as we can.

Notes

1 Levine and Oritz-Robles, eds, *Narrative Middles*.
2 Jerome, *John Ingerfield and Other Stories*, vi.
3 Jerome, *Paul Kelver*, 338.
4 Fiss, 'Pushing at the Boundaries of the Book', 19.
5 Ngai, *Ugly Feelings*.

6 Radway, *Reading the Romance*, 55.
7 Lynch, *Loving Literature*, 5.
8 Doyle, 'The Greek Interpreter', 297.
9 A large display of Wodehouse books at the Brookline Booksmith inspired his inclusion in this project.

Appendix: The Numbers on Women in the 'Idler's Club'

In order to approach the question of how much the 'Idler's Club' column incorporated women, I undertook a small quantitative study of the collaborative column.

Methodology

I manually recorded the named contributors in all the collaboratively authored 'Idler's Club' columns, from its origins in February 1892 until Robert Barr's single-authored column in October 1902, using ProQuest's digitised run. There were some lacunae in 1901 and 1902 – completely missing issues – which could have been the result of editorial changes (the magazine was changing hands fast) or a problem with the ProQuest run itself. In any case, the final collaboratively authored column appears to have been January 1901 (vol. 18, no. 6, 'Should Professional Men Work?'). The spot at the end of the magazine briefly carried a 'Cornish Mystery' with a prize offered for its continuation (June–September 1901). I only included in my data set the collaboratively authored columns with the title 'The Idler's Club'.

I correlated the number of contributions per contributor, and I coded the contributors for gender. Not all contributors were named. Some went by initials, difficult to code for gender. Other contributors were obviously fictional, such as 'a lady' and 'Angelina', a stock name used in *Punch* and elsewhere. I did not code fictional characters for gender, even in a whimsical column from October 1895 supposedly in the voices of club members' children. When I knew pseudonyms, as in John Strange Winter for Henrietta Stannard, I coded them by the gender of the person (in this case, female). My complete data set is available on EUP's website (see 'Idler's Club' Contributors https://edinburghuniversitypress.com/book-the-idler-s-club.html).

Discussion

It is undeniable that women were in the minority as 'Idler's Club' contributors during the collaborative period from February 1892 to January 1901. They made up 17 per cent of the total authors (48 out of 280, with 27 not coded) and contributed 14 per cent of the entries (99 out of 716, with 29 not coded). Novel authorship, as recorded in *At the Circulating Library*, shows men-authored titles and women-authored titles vying for the majority throughout the Victorian period, with men-authored titles claiming the majority in 1895 and holding it for the remainder of the century.[1] The overall percentage of women in the 'Idler's Club' column falls far short of this benchmark. However, this overall statistic only begins to tell the story.

Two-thirds of the overall contributors contributed only once: 188 of 280 contributors.[2] Of these 188 one-time contributors, 31 were women. This also means that of the 48 total female contributors, over a third contributed more than once. Conversely, slightly less than a quarter of the total male contributors (48) contributed more than once. The difference may not be hugely significant, but it might suggest that Barr and Jerome actively cultivated relationships with some female journalists. The number of contributions by women also rose during Jerome's involvement with the paper (Fig. A.1). It could only go up because it started at zero in the first volume, but it jumped when Jerome was sole editor, peaking in the last full year he owned the paper. At the same time, Jerome expanded the total contributors per 'Idler's Club' column. Still, the percentage of female contributors by year also rose, peaking at 35 per cent in 1897 (Fig. A.2). During the period from 1893 to 1898, women comprised 20 per cent of contributors and 20 per cent of contributions. After Jerome, the number of women fell off dramatically from almost thirty per year to below five. Although 14 per cent is not very much, 35 per cent starts to look like more active representation, especially considering that women were still underrepresented in journalism at the time.

Of the twenty most frequent contributors to the 'Idler's Club' column (Table A.1), two were women. Eliza Lynn Linton ties for twelfth place with ten contributions and Evelyn Sharp ties for seventeenth with eight. Linton died in 1898, making it impossible for her to pen any new contributions after that point. In terms of feminism, Linton and Sharp were almost diametrically opposed.

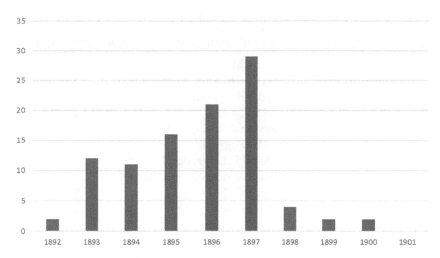

Figure A.1 Contributions by women by year.

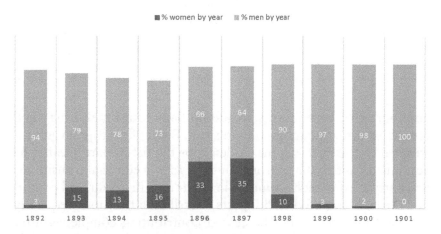

Figure A.2 Gender percentages by year. Some contributions not coded for gender.

Although she broke barriers in the literary world as the first salaried woman on an English national newspaper, Linton vocally opposed women's suffrage and has been dubbed an antifeminist.[3] Sharp, by contrast, was a militant feminist, although she really became involved in the twentieth century.[4] Table A.2 shows the contributors to the 'Idler's Club' column in the first issue. Israel Zangwill contributed to each issue, Jerome and Eden Phillpotts five times,

Table A.1 Twenty most frequent contributors

Rank by Frequency	Name of contributor	Total contributions
1	W. L. Alden	35
2	George Brown Burgin	31
3	Jerome K. Jerome	21
4	Robert Barr	19
5	Barry Pain	19
6	Israel Zangwill	17
7	Arthur H. Lawrence	17
8	Eden Phillpotts	15
9	George R. Sims	13
10	Arnold Golsworthy	13
11	Joseph Hatton	11
12	Eliza Lynn Linton	10
13	W. Pett Ridge	10
14	Inglis Allen	10
15	Conrad Weguilin	10
16	F. Frankfort Moore	9
17	Miss Evelyn Sharp	8
18	The Rev. Bennett Coll	8
19	Percy Kent	8
20	Louis Tracy	7

and four other contributors, including Barr, four times. This trend continued throughout the column's run. Eight of the top eleven contributed to this first volume. Alden tops the list in part because he continued contributing throughout the *Idler*'s editorial transitions: he contributed to eight columns in the *Idler*'s first year and continued through 1900. Eden Phillpotts contributed the most frequently in 1892, nine times, but he ceased contributing completely after 1895. He ties Conrad Weguilin for most contributions in a single year; the latter kept the column aloft in 1900. These eight contributors alone account for 24 per cent of the column's contributions. The five most frequent contributors – who include both founding editors and subeditor George Brown Burgin – contributed a total of 17 per cent of the entries. Thus these five men contributed more than all the women combined, even though Barr stopped contributing when he sold the paper (although he returned for two entries in 1899), as did Jerome. Despite its size and number of contributions, the 'Idler's Club' retained some of the insularity – and demographic uniformity – of a club.

Table A.2 Contributors to the first volume

Name of contributor	Feb 1892	Mar 1892	April 1892	May 1892	June 1892	July 1892	Aug 1892	Total
Robert Barr	1	1	1			1		4
Barry Pain	1	1			1			3
Israel Zangwill	1	1	1	1	1	1	1	7
Kennedy	1		1					2
Jerome K. Jerome	1	1		1	1		1	5
George Brown Burgin		1					1	2
Eden Phillpotts	1	1	1	1	1			5
George R. Sims		1	1	1			1	4
Joseph Hatton		1	1	1			1	4
W. L. Alden				1	1	1	1	4
J. F. Sullivan				1	1			2
Coulson Kernahan					1			1
Captain David Gray						1		1
Clement R. Markham						1		1
Admiral Markham						1		1
Frank Mathew							1	1
Total	5	6	6	7	9	7	7	47

Conclusion

The 'Idler's Club' column's community may be conceptualised as a series of concentric rings, from an inner circle of extremely frequent, interrelated contributors, many of whom were involved in the magazine in a variety of capacities, out to a large array of one-time contributors. Women do not appear in the inner circle, although some occupy prominent places in the second-largest circle, as identified by the top twenty contributors. Jerome seems to have made a concerted effort to recruit and retain women as contributors to the column. In his absence, the number and percentage of women both fell off considerably.

Further studies might include more quantitative studies of women in different periodicals, so that we can get a better sense of how many women were working in the profession at this time. The 'Idler's Club' column still has a lot to tell us about journalism in this period, and I hope others will use the data I have gathered to continue the conversation.

Notes

1 Bassett, *At the Circulating Library*, Data: Authorship. http://www.victorianresearch.org/atcl/graphs_auth.php (consulted 9 September 2021).

2 For context, Patrick Leary notes that in *Fraser's*, known as a very close-knit group, 'more than half of the magazine was written by persons with no close, continuing connection to it'. Leary, '"Fraser's Magazine" and the Literary Life, 113.

3 Barbara Onslow, 'Eliza Lynn Linton', *Dictionary of Nineteenth-Century Journalism* (online ed, accessed 3 February 2014.) Andrea L. Broomfield, 'Much More than an Antifeminist: Eliza Lynn Linton's Contributions to the Rise of Victorian Popular Journalism', *Victorian Literature and Culture* 29, no. 2 (2001): 267–83.

4 Angela V. John, *Evelyn Sharp: Rebel Woman, 1869–1955* (Manchester: Manchester University Press, 2009).

Bibliography

'A Chat with Robert Louis Stevenson'. *To-Day* 1, no. 4 (2 December 1893): 6–7.

Ablow, Rachel, ed. *The Feeling of Reading: Affective Experience and Victorian Literature.* Ann Arbor: University of Michigan Press, 2010.

Adams, James Eli. *Dandies and Desert Saints: Styles of Victorian Manhood.* Ithaca: Cornell University Press, 1995.

Alden, William Livingston, George R. Sims, J. F. Sullivan, Eden Phillpotts, Jerome K. Jerome, Israel Zangwill and Joseph Hatton. 'The Idler's Club'. *Idler* 1 (May 1892): 474–84.

Altick, Richard D. *The English Common Reader: A Social History of the Mass Reading Public 1800–1900.* Chicago: University of Chicago Press, 1957.

American Resident in the United Kingdom. *'Good Form' in England.* New York: D. Appleton, 1888.

Anderson, Benedict. *Imagined Communities: Reflections on the Origin and Spread of Nationalism*, rev. ed. London: Verso, 2006.

Arata, Stephen D. 'The Occidental Tourist: "Dracula" and the Anxiety of Reverse Colonization'. *Victorian Studies* 22, no. 4 (1990): 621–45.

Arnold, Edwin, William Sharp, F. W. Robinson, Oscar Wilde, Coulson Kernahan, George Gissing, Norman Gale, Aaron Watson, Joseph Knight, Israel Zangwill, Grant Allen, George Manville Fenn, William Archer, John Strange Winter, Clement Scott, Barry Pain, Richard Le Gallienne, [W.] Clark Russell, G. B. Burgin, George Bernard Shaw, John Davidson, E. Nesbit. 'The Idler's Club: Who Shall Be Laureate?' *Idler* 7, no. 3 (April 1895): 401–13.

Ashton, Owen R. 'Stannard [née Palmer], Henrietta Eliza Vaughan [pseuds Violet Whyte, John Strange Winter]'. *Oxford Dictionary of*

National Biography. Oxford: Oxford University Press, 2004. <https://doi.org/10.1093/ref:odnb/36251> (accessed 13 February 2018).

Atkinson, Damian. 'Jerome, Jerome Klapka (1859–1927)'. *Oxford Dictionary of National Biography*. Oxford: Oxford University Press, 2004. <https://doi.org/10.1093/ref:odnb/34183> (accessed 16 September 2013).

Baker, William. 'Zangwill, Israel (1864–1926)'. *Oxford Dictionary of National Biography*. Oxford: Oxford University Press, 2004. <https://doi.org/10.1093/ref:odnb/37087> (accessed 20 May 2022).

Barr, Robert [published under Luke Sharp]. 'Detective Stories Gone Wrong: The Adventures of Sherlaw Komes'. *Idler* 1, no. 4 (May 1892): 413–24.

——. *Jennie Baxter, Journalist*. 1888. New York: Frederick A. Stokes, 1899.

——, Isabel Burton, G. R. Sims, Lady Henry Somerset, Joseph Hatton, Edna Lyall, Forbes Winslow, Justin McCarthy and G. B. Burgin. 'The Idler's Club: Some Literary Typewriters'. *Idler* 5, no. 3 (April 1894): 321–36.

——, David Gray, Clement R. Markham, Admiral Markham, W. L. Alden, Israel Zangwill and Eden Phillpotts. 'The Idler's Club'. *Idler* 1 (July 1892): 712–24.

——, Barry Pain, Israel Zangwill, Kennedy and Jerome K. Jerome. 'The Idler's Club'. *Idler* 1 (February 1892): 106–18.

——, Dr Percival, The Captain of HMS training ship 'St Vincent', The Colonial College staff, J. Gordon, The Head Master of Berkhamsted School, The Head Master of Denstone College, The Head Master of Bradfield College, The Head Master of Dover College, The Rev. Bennett Coll and Dr Joseph Parker. 'The Idler's Club: A Substitute for Swearing'. *Idler* 5, no. 6 (July 1894).

Barrie, J. M. *Better Dead*. 1888. In *The Novels, Tales and Sketches of J. M. Barrie*, vol. 1. New York: Charles Scribner's Sons, 1917.

——. *My Lady Nicotine*. New York: Cassell, [1890].

——. *The Greenwood Hat, Being a Memoir of James Anon 1855–1887*. London: Peter Davies, 1937.

——. *The Little White Bird: or Adventures in Kensington Gardens*. Toronto: Copp, Clark, 1902.

——. *When a Man's Single*. 1902. In *The Novels, Tales and Sketches of J. M. Barrie*. New York: Charles Scribner's Sons, 1912.

Bassett, Troy J. *At the Circulating Library: A Database of Victorian Fiction, 1837–1901*, <http://www.victorianresearch.org/atcl/> (accessed 20 May 2022).

————. 'Robert Barr's Life at *The Idler*: Four Unpublished Letters'. *English Literature in Transition, 1880–1920* 59, no. 4 (2016): 510–24.

Batts, John S. 'American Humor: The Mark of Twain on Jerome K. Jerome'. In Jennifer A. Wagner-Lawlor (ed.), *The Victorian Comic Spirit: New Perspectives*. Aldershot: Ashgate, 2000, pp. 91–113.

Beaumont, Matthew and Matthew Ingleby, eds. *G. K. Chesterton, London, and Modernity*. London: Bloomsbury, 2013.

Benfey, Christopher. *If: The Untold Story of Kipling's American Years*. Penguin, 2019.

Bergson, Henri. *Laughter*. In Wylie Sypher (ed.), *Comedy*. New York: Doubleday, 1956: 61–193.

Beringer, Vera, W. Alden, Elsie Jerome, Grant Allen Junior, Miss Alden, Freda Hawtrey, Miss Helen Fenwick Miller, 'Bootles' Stannard, Gertrude Warden, Miss Beerbohm Tree, W. S. Penley [pseuds]. 'How I Bring Up My Parents'. *Idler* 8, no. 3 (October 1895): 292–9.

Betensky, Carolyn. 'Casual Racism in Victorian Literature'. *Victorian Literature and Culture* 47, no. 4 (2019): 723–51.

Birkin, Andrew. *J. M. Barrie and the Lost Boys: The Love Story that Gave Birth to Peter Pan*. New York: Clarkson N. Potter, 1979.

Black, Barbara. *A Room of His Own: A Literary-Cultural Study of Victorian Clubland*. Athens: Ohio University Press, 2012.

Bold, Valentina and Andrew Nash, eds. *Gateway to the Modern: Resituating J. M. Barrie*. Occasional Papers series No. 18. Glasgow: Scottish Literature International, 2014.

Boos, Florence S. 'The Education Act of 1870: Before and After'. In Dino Franco Felluga (ed.), *BRANCH: Britain, Representation and Nineteenth-Century History*, <http://www.branchcollective.org> (accessed 20 May 2022).

Bown, Nicola, ed. 'Rethinking Victorian Sentimentality'. Special issue, *19: Interdisciplinary Studies in the Long Nineteenth Century* 4 (2007).

Brake, Laurel and Marysa Demoor, eds. *The Dictionary of Nineteenth-Century Journalism*. Ghent and London: Academia Press and the British Library, 2009.

Brantlinger, Patrick. *Rule of Darkness: British Literature and Imperialism, 1830–1914*. Ithaca: Cornel University Press, 1988.

————. *The Reading Lesson*. Bloomington: Indiana University Press, 1998.

Byerly, Alison. *Are We There Yet?: Virtual Travel and Victorian Realism*. Ann Arbor: University of Michigan Press, 2013.

Carey, John. *The Intellectuals and the Masses: Pride and Prejudice among the Literary Intelligentsia 1880–1939*. New York: St Martin's, 1992.

Carlson, Richard S. *The Benign Humorists*. [North Haven, CT]: Archon Books, 1975.

Chatterjee, Ronjaunee, Alicia Mireles Christoff and Amy R. Wong, 'Introduction: Undisciplining Victorian Studies'. *Victorian Studies* 62, no. 3 (2020): 369–91.

Chesterton, Gilbert K. *The Club of Queer Trades*. New York: Harper & Brothers, 1905. Google Books.

Christie, William. '"Where Personation Ends and Imposture Begins": John Wilson, *Noctes Ambrosiane*, and the Tory Populism of *Blackwood's Edinburgh Magazine*'. In Jock Macleod, William Christie and Peter Denney (eds), *Politics and Emotions in Romantic Periodicals*. London: Palgrave Macmillan, 2019: 175–94.

Cloy, John D. *Muscular Mirth: Barry Pain and the New Humor*. Victoria: English Literary Studies, 2003.

Connolly, Joseph. *Jerome K. Jerome: A Critical Biography*. London: Orbis, 1982.

Considine, Basil. 'P. G. Wodehouse and the American Musical Comedy: Innovations in Writing'. In Ann Rea (ed.), *Middlebrow Wodehouse: P. G. Wodehouse's Work in Context*. London: Routledge, 2016: 123–52.

Cox, Alison Janice McNabb. 'Robert Barr'. In Bernard Benstock and Thomas F. Staley (eds), *British Mystery Writers, 1860–1919*. *Dictionary of Literary Biography* vol. 70. Detroit: Gale Research, 1988: 14–22.

Dames, Nicholas. *The Physiology of the Novel*. Oxford: Oxford University Press, 2007.

Damkjær, Maria. 'Awkward Appendages: Comic Umbrellas in Nineteenth-Century Print Culture'. *Victorian Literature and Culture* 45 (2017): 475–92.

Daniels, Harold G. 'An Afternoon with Mr Bernard Partridge'. *Idler* 11 (1897): 358–74.

Day, Charles William [published under Αγωγός]. *Hints on Etiquette*. 1836. London: Turnstile, 1947.

Dickens, Charles. *The Pickwick Papers*. Oxford: Oxford World's Classics, 2008.

Dixon, Ella Hepworth. *The Story of a Modern Woman*. New York: Cassell, 1894. Google Books.

Donaldson, Frances, ed. *Yours, Plum: The Letters of P. G. Wodehouse*. London: Hutchinson, 1990.

Doughan, David and Peter Gordon, *Women, Clubs and Associations in Britain*. Abington: Routledge, 2006.

Doyle, Arthur Conan. *Memories and Adventures*. London: Hodder and Stoughton, 1924. Facsimile edition. Cambridge: Cambridge University Press, 2012.

———. 'The Adventures of Sherlock Holmes II: The Red-Headed League'. *Strand* 2 (August 1891): 190–204.

———. 'The Adventures of Sherlock Holmes XXII: The Adventure of the Greek Interpreter'. *Strand* 6 (October 1893): 296–307.

———. 'The Adventures of Sherlock Holmes XXIV: The Adventure of the Final Problem'. *Strand* 6, no. 12 (1893): 558–70.

———. *The Complete Sherlock Holmes*, 2 vols. New York: Doubleday, 1930.

———. 'The Return of Sherlock Holmes I: The Adventure of the Empty House', *Strand* 26, no. 154 (October 1903): 363–76.

Dudgeon, Piers. *Neverland: J. M. Barrie, the Du Mauriers, and the Dark Side of* Peter Pan. New York: Pegasus, 2009.

East London Editor. *The Habits of Good Society*. New York: Carleton, 1867.

Eliot, T. S. *The Waste Land*. 1922. New York: W. W. Norton, 2001.

Faurot, Ruth Marie. *Jerome K. Jerome*. Twayne's English Authors Ser. 164. New York: Twayne, 1974.

Findon, B. W. *The Playgoers' Club 1884 to 1905: Its History and Memories*. London: Playgoers' Club, 1905.

Fiss, Laura Kasson. 'Out With It, as the Subeditor Said to the Novel: Wellerisms and the Humor of Excerption'. *Victorian Periodicals Review* 40, no. 1 (2017): 228–37.

———. 'Pushing at the Boundaries of the Book: Humor, Mediation, and Distance in Carroll, Thackeray, and Stevenson'. *The Lion and the Unicorn* 38, no. 3 (2014): 258–78.

———. '*The Idler*'s Club: Humor and Sociability in the Age of New Journalism'. *Victorian Periodicals Review* 49, no. 3 (2016): 415–30.

Flint, Kate. *The Woman Reader 1837–1914*. Oxford: Clarendon Press, 1993.

———. 'Women, Men, and the Reading of *Vanity Fair*'. In James Raven et al. (eds), *The Practice and Representation of Reading in England*. Cambridge: Cambridge University Press, 1996.

Forrest, Denys. *Foursome in St James's: The Story of the East India, Devonshire, Sports and Public Schools Club*. Published by the club, 1982.

Freud, Sigmund. *The Joke and Its Relation to the Unconscious*. Original German edition pub. 1905. Trans. Joyce Crick. New York: Penguin, 2003.

Garber, Marjorie. *Vested Interests: Cross-Dressing and Cultural Anxiety*. 1992. New York: Routledge, 1997.

Gilbert, Sandra M. and Susan Gubar. *The Madwoman in the Attic: The Woman Writer and the Nineteenth-Century Literary Imagination*, 2nd ed. New Haven: Yale University Press, 2000.

Gilbert, W. S. *The Complete Annotated Gilbert and Sullivan*. Edited by Ian Bradley. Oxford: Oxford University Press, 1996.

Gillooly, Eileen. *Smile of Discontent: Humor, Gender, and Nineteenth-Century British Fiction*. Chicago: University of Chicago Press, 1999.

Graves, Charles. *Leather Armchairs: The Book of London Clubs*. New York: Coward-McCann, 1963.

Gray, Donald J. 'The Uses of Victorian Laughter'. *Victorian Studies* 10, no. 2 (1966): 145–76, and 'Victorian Verse Humor, 1830–70'. PhD diss., Ohio State University, 1956.

Gubar, Marah. *Artful Dodgers: Reconceiving the Golden Age of Children's Literature*. Oxford: Oxford University Press, 2009.

——. 'Who Watched *The Children's Pinafore*? Age Transvestism on the Nineteenth-Century Stage'. *Victorian Studies* 54, no. 3 (2012): 410–26.

Habermas, Jürgen. *The Structural Transformation of the Public Sphere: An Inquiry into a Category of Bourgeois Society*. Trans. Thomas Burger. Cambridge: MIT Press, 1992.

Halberstam, Jack [published under Judith]. *Female Masculinity*. Durham, NC: Duke University Press, 1998.

Hall, Robert A. Jr, *The Comic Style of P. G. Wodehouse*. Hamden, CT: Archon, 1974.

Han, Carrie Sickmann. 'Pickwick's Other Papers: Continually Reading Dickens'. *Victorian Literature and Culture* 44 (2016): 19–41.

Hatton, Joseph. *Club-Land: London and Provincial*. London: J. S. Virtue, 1890. Google Books.

Hatton, Joseph, Giuseppe of the Café Doney at Florence, The Head Waiter at the *——, A Commissionaire, and Robert Barr. 'The Idler's Club', *Idler* 15, no. 5 (June 1899).

Henkle, Roger B. *Comedy and Culture: England 1820–1900*. Princeton: Princeton University Press, 1980.

Hilton, Matthew. *Smoking in British Popular Culture 1800–2000: Perfect Pleasures*. Manchester: Manchester University Press, 2000.

Hobbes, Thomas. *Leviathan*. Edited by Michael Oakeshott. New York: Simon & Schuster, 1962.

Holcomb, Brian D. 'The Queer Domesticity of Bertie and Jeeves'. In Ann Rea (ed.), *Middlebrow Wodehouse: P. G. Wodehouse's Work in Context*. London: Routledge, 2016: 209–27.

Holt, Jim. *Stop Me if You've Heard This: A History and Philosophy of Jokes*. New York: W. W. Norton, 2008.

Howes, Craig. 'Comic/Satiric Periodicals', in Andrew King, Alexis Easley and John Morton (eds), *The Routledge Handbook to Nineteenth-Century British Periodicals and Newspapers*. London: Routledge, 2016: 318–27.

Hughes, Linda K. 'Anti-Elitist Elitist Verse Forms: Comic Ballades and Rondeaus in *Punch* and *Fun*'. In Lee Behlman and Olive Loksing Moy (eds), *Victorian Verse in Everyday Life* (London: Palgrave Macmillan, 2022 [forthcoming]).

———. Review of Valerie Fehlbaum, *Ella Hepworth Dixon: The Story of a Modern Woman. Nineteenth-Century Gender Studies* 2.2 (2006): 1.

Humble, Nicola. 'From Holmes to the Drones: Fantasies of Men without Women in the Masculine Middlebrow'. In Kate Macdonald (ed.), *The Masculine Middlebrow, 1880–1915: What Mr Miniver Read*. New York: Palgrave Macmillan, 2011: 90–103.

Humpherys, Anne. '*Idler* (1892–1898)'. In Laurel Brake and Marysa Demoor (eds), *Dictionary of Nineteenth-Century Journalism*, online ed. (accessed 13 October 2009).

———. 'Putting Women in the Boat in *The Idler* (1892–1898) and TO-DAY (1893–1897)'. *19: Interdisciplinary Studies in the Long Nineteenth Century*, 1 (2005), <https://doi.org/10.16995/ntn.438> (accessed 20 May 2022).

Hunt, Leigh. 'On the Combination of Grave and Gay'. *The Musical Times and Singing Class Circular* 6, no. 126 (1854): 91–3.

'Introduction'. *Strand* 1 (January 1891): 1.

J. M. Barrie's Allahakbarries C.C. 1899. London: James Barrie Publishers Ltd, 1950.

Jack, R. D. S. 'Barrie, Sir James Matthew, baronet (1860–1937)'. *Oxford Dictionary of National Biography*. Oxford: Oxford University Press, 2004. <https://doi.org/10.1093/ref:odnb/30617> (accessed 26 March 2013).

Jerome, Jerome K. 'Gossips' Corner'. *Home Chimes* 4, no. 2 (1886): 155–60.

———. *John Ingerfield and Other Stories*. New York: Henry Holt, 1894.

———., ed. *My First Book*. London: Chatto & Windus, 1897.

———. *My Life and Times*. New York: Harper, 1926.

———. *Novel Notes*. London: Leadenhall Press, 1893.

———. *Paul Kelver*. New York: Dodd, Mead & Co., 1902.

———. *The Angel and the Author – and Others*. London: Hurst and Blackett, 1908.

──────. *Three Men in a Boat (To Say Nothing of the Dog)*. London: Arrowsmith, 1889.

──────. 'To the Readers of "*The Idler.*"' *Idler* 8, no. 43 (August 1895): 97–100.

──────. *Tommy and Co.* London: Hutchinson, 1904.

Jerome K. Jerome Collection, Walsall Archives, Walsall Local History Centre.

Jerome K. Jerome Society, 'Periodical contributions by Jerome'. <https://www.jeromekjerome.com/bibliography/periodical-contributions-by-jerome/> (accessed 17 September 2021).

Johnson, Samuel. 'The Preface to Shakespeare'. In Stephen Greenblatt (ed.), *The Norton Anthology of English Literature: The Major Authors*, 6th ed. (New York: W. W. Norton, 1996): 1224.

Kasson, John F. *Rudeness and Civility: Manners in Nineteenth-Century Urban America*. New York: Hill and Wang, 1990.

Kincaid, James R. *Child-Loving: The Erotic Child and Victorian Culture*. New York: Routledge, 1992.

──────. *Dickens and the Rhetoric of Laughter*. Oxford: Oxford University Press, 1971.

Langbauer, Laurie. *Novels of Everyday Life: The Series in English Fiction, 1850–1930*. Ithaca: Cornell University Press, 1999.

Leary, Patrick. '"Fraser's Magazine" and the Literary Life, 1830–1847'. *Victorian Periodicals Review* 27, no. 2 (1994): 105–26.

──────. *The* Punch *Brotherhood: Table Talk and Print Culture in Mid-Victorian London*. London: British Library, 2010.

Lecercle, Jean-Jacques. *Philosophy of Nonsense: The Intuitions of Victorian Nonsense Literature*. London and New York: Routledge, 1994.

Ledbetter, Kathryn. 'The Delicate Task of Sub-Editing: Edmund Yates, Charles Thomas, and *The World*', *Victorian Periodicals Review* 54, no. 2 (2021): 258–78.

Lee, Louise, ed. *Victorian Comedy and Laughter: Conviviality, Jokes and Dissent*. London: Palgrave Macmillan, 2020.

Lellenberg, Jon, Daniel Stashower and Charles Foley, eds. *Arthur Conan Doyle: A Life in Letters*. New York: Penguin, 2007.

Levine, Caroline and Mario Oritz-Robles, eds. *Narrative Middles: Navigating the Nineteenth-Century British Novel*. Columbus: Ohio State University Press, 2011.

Levine, Lawrence W. *Highbrow Lowbrow: The Emergence of Cultural Hierarchy in America*. Cambridge, MA: Harvard University Press, 1988.

Lubenow, William C. *'Only Connect': Learned Societies in Nineteenth-Century Britain.* Woodbridge: Boydell, 2015.

Lynch, Deidre Shauna. *Loving Literature: A Cultural History.* Chicago: University of Chicago Press, 2015.

Macdonald, Kate. 'Problematic Menswear in P. G. Wodehouse and Dornford Yates'. In Ann Rea (ed.), *Middlebrow Wodehouse: P. G. Wodehouse's Work in Context.* London: Routledge, 2016: 229–48.

Mackail, Denis. *Barrie: The Story of J. M. B.* New York: Charles Scribner's Sons, 1941.

'Magazines for January'. *Bury and Norwich Post, and Suffolk Herald.* 15 January 1884, 8.

Maidment, Brian. *Comedy, Caricature and the Social Order, 1820–50.* Manchester: Manchester University Press, 2013.

Marcus, Sharon. *Between Women: Friendship, Desire, and Marriage in Victorian England.* Princeton: Princeton University Press, 2007.

Martin, Robert Bernard. *The Triumph of Wit: A Study of Victorian Comic Theory.* London: Oxford University Press, 1974.

Mehew, Ernest. 'Henley, William Ernest (1849–1903)'. In *Oxford Dictionary of National Biography.* Oxford: Oxford University Press, 2004.

Meredith, George. 'An Essay on Comedy'. In Wylie Sypher (ed.), *Comedy.* New York: Doubleday, 1956: 43.

Mickalites, Carey. 'Fairies and a Flâneur: J. M. Barrie's Commercial Figure of the Child'. *Criticism* 54, no. 1 (2012): 1–27.

Milne-Smith, Amy. *London Clubland: A Cultural History of Gender and Class in Victorian Britain.* New York: Palgrave Macmillan, 2011.

Moss, Alfred. *Jerome K. Jerome: His Life and Work (From Poverty to the Knighthood of the People).* London: Selwyn & Blount: 1928.

Murphy, N. T. P. 'Pain, Barry Eric Odell (1864–1928)'. *Oxford Dictionary of National Biography.* Oxford: Oxford University Press, 2004. <https://doi.org/10.1093/ref:odnb/35362> (accessed 16 September 2013).

Mussell, James. 'New Journalism'. In Laurel Brake and Marysa Demoor (eds), *Dictionary of Nineteenth-Century Journalism.* Ghent and London: Academia Press and the British Library, 2009: 443.

Ngai, Sianne. *Ugly Feelings.* Cambridge, MA: Harvard University Press, 2005.

Nicholas, Jeremy, ed. *Idle Thoughts on Jerome K. Jerome: A 150th Anniversary Celebration.* Great Bardfield: The Jerome K. Jerome Society, 2009.

Nicholson, Bob. '"You Kick the Bucket; We Do the Rest!": Jokes and the Culture of Reprinting in the Transatlantic Press'. *Journal of Victorian Culture* 17, no. 3 (2012): 273–86.

North, John, ed. *Waterloo Directory of English Newspapers and Periodicals*. <https://www.victorianperiodicals.com/series3/index.asp> (accessed 20 May 2022).

'Note'. *Idler* 17 (April 1900): 201.

Observer of Men and Things. *Blunders in Behaviour Corrected: A Concise Code of Deportment for Both Sexes*. London: Groombridge & Sons, 1855.

Oulton, Carolyn W. de la L. *Below the Fairy City: A Life of Jerome K. Jerome*. Brighton: Victorian Secrets, 2012.

Pain, Barry. *One Kind and Another*. London: Martin Secker, 1914.

———. *Stories Without Tears*. New York: Frederick A. Stokes, 1914. Google Books.

———. *The Problem Club*. London: W. Collins Sons, 1919. Google Books.

Parker, Rev. Dr, G. B. Burgin, F. W. Robinson, Gribble, Frank Mathew, W. L. Alden and Israel Zangwill, 'The Idler's Club: Awkward Predicaments'. *Idler* 3, no. 2 (March 1893).

Parker, Rev. Dr, G. R. Sims, G. B. Burgin, 'A lady', Eden Phillpotts, Joseph Hatton, W. L. Alden, 'James I', Israel Zangwill, 'Angelina', Robert Barr and Benjamin Ward Richardson. 'The Idler's Club'. *Idler* 2 (November 1892).

Pearsall, Ronald. *Collapse of Stout Party: Victorian Wit and Humor*. London: Weidenfeld and Nicolson, 1975.

Phillpotts, Eden. *One Thing and Another*. London: Hutchinson, 1954.

Pinch, Adela. *Strange Fits of Passion: Epistemologies of Emotion, Hume to Austen*. Stanford: Stanford University Press, 1996.

Polhemus, Robert M. *Comic Faith: The Great Tradition from Austen to Joyce*. Chicago: University of Chicago Press, 1980.

Price, Leah. *How to Do Things with Books in Victorian Britain*. Princeton: Princeton University Press, 2012.

Puckett, Kent. *Bad Form: Social Mistakes and the Nineteenth-Century Novel*. Oxford: Oxford University Press, 2008.

Radway, Janice A. *A Feeling for Books: The Book-of-the-Month Club, Literary Taste, and Middle-Class Desire*. Chapel Hill: University of North Carolina Press, 1997.

———. 'Reading Is Not Eating: Mass-Produced Literature and the Theoretical, Methodological, and Political Consequences of a Metaphor'. *Book Research Quarterly* 2, no. 2 (Fall 1986): 7–29.

———. *Reading the Romance: Women, Patriarchy, and Popular Literature.* Chapel Hill: University of North Carolina Press, 1984.

Ramkin, Scott. 'People I Have Never Met – Jerome K. Jerome'. *Idler* 4 (1893): 100.

Ratcliffe, Sophie, ed. *P.G. Wodehouse: A Life in Letters.* New York: W.W. Norton, 2011.

Rea, Ann. *Middlebrow Wodehouse: P. G. Wodehouse's Work in Context.* London: Routledge, 2016.

Rich, Adrienne. 'Compulsory Heterosexuality and Lesbian Existence'. *Signs* 5, no. 4 (1980): 631–60.

Richardson, Caleb. 'The Prison Camp as Public School: Wodehouse, School Stories and the Second World War'. In Ann Rea (ed.), *Middlebrow Wodehouse: P. G. Wodehouse's Work in Context.* London: Routledge, 2016: 87–103.

Ring, Tony. 'P. G. Wodehouse: A Broadway Centenary'. *Plumtopia*, April 2017. <https://honoriaplum.com/2017/04/30/p-g-wodehouse-a-broadway-centenary-by-tony-ring/> (accessed 20 May 2022).

Roberts, S. C. 'Introduction'. In Arthur Conan Doyle, *Sherlock Holmes: Selected Stories.* 1950. Oxford: Oxford World's Classics, 1998.

Rochelson, Meri-Jane. *A Jew in the Public Arena: The Career of Israel Zangwill.* Detroit: Wayne State University Press, 2008.

Rogin, Michael. 'Blackface, White Noise: The Jewish Jazz Singer Finds His Voice'. *Critical Inquiry* 18, no. 3 (1992): 417–53.

Rose, Jonathan. *The Intellectual Life of the British Working Classes.* New Haven: Yale University Press, 2001.

Rubin, Gayle. 'The Traffic in Women: Notes on the "Political Economy" of Sex' [1975]. In Sandra M. Gilbert and Susan Gubar (eds), *Feminist Literary Theory and Criticism: A Norton Reader.* New York: W. W. Norton, 2007: 392–413.

Sayers, Dorothy L. *Murder Must Advertise.* 1933. New York: Avon, 1967.

———. 'The Man with the Copper Fingers'. Originally published as 'The Abominable History of the Man with Copper Fingers' in *Lord Peter Views the Body* (1928). In *Alfred Hitchcock Presents Stories Not for the Nervous.* New York: Random House, 1965.

———. *The Unpleasantness at the Bellona Club.* 1928. New York: Avon, 1963.

———. *Unnatural Death.* 1927. New York: Avon, 1964.

———. *Unpopular Opinions.* London: Victor Gollancz, 1946.

———. *Whose Body?* 1923. New York: Harper-Bourbon Street Books, 2014.

Scott, Clement, Eden Phillpotts, Robert Barr, W. L. Alden, Frank Mathew, G. B. Burgin and Joseph Hatton, 'The Idler's Club'. *Idler* 2, no. 2 (September 1892).

Sedgwick, Eve Kosofsky. *Between Men: English Literature and Male Homosocial Desire*. 1985. New York: Columbia University Press, 1992.

——. 'Paranoid Reading and Reparative Reading, or, You're So Paranoid, You Probably Think This Essay Is About You', in Eve Kosofsky Sedgwick, *Touching Feeling*. Durham: Duke University Press, 2003: 123–51.

Shannon, Mary L. *Dickens, Reynolds and Mayhew on Wellington Street: The Print Culture of a Victorian Street*. Farnham: Ashgate, 2015.

Sharp, Evelyn. *The Making of a Prig*. New York: John Lane, the Bodley Head, 1897. Internet Archive.

Shattock, Joanne. 'Professional Networking, Masculine and Feminine'. *Victorian Periodicals Review* 44, no. 2 (2011): 128–40.

Showalter, Elaine. *Sexual Anarchy: Gender and Culture at the Fin de Siècle*. New York: Viking, 1990.

Simmers, George. 'P. G. Wodehouse and the First World War'. In Ann Rea (ed.), *Middlebrow Wodehouse: P. G. Wodehouse's Work in Context*. London: Routledge, 2016: 73–86.

Sladen, Douglas, ed. *Who's Who*, vol. 49. London: A. & C. Black, 1897. Google Books.

Spacks, Patricia Meyer. *Gossip*. New York: Alfred A. Knopf, 1985.

Sproat, Iain. 'Wodehouse, Sir Pelham Grenville (1881–1975)'. *Oxford Dictionary of National Biography*. Oxford: Oxford University Press, 2004. <https://doi.org/10.1093/ref:odnb/31851> (accessed 30 May 2013).

Stedman, Jane W. 'Gilbert, Sir William Schwenck (1836–1911)'. *Oxford Dictionary of National Biography*. Oxford: Oxford University Press, 2004. <https://doi.org/10.1093/ref:odnb/33400> (accessed 8 September 2013).

Stetz, Margaret. *British Women's Comic Fiction, 1890–1990: Not Drowning, But Laughing*. Burlington, VT: Ashgate, 2001.

——. 'The Laugh of the New Woman'. In Jennifer A. Wagner-Lawlor (ed.), *The Victorian Comic Spirit: New Perspectives*. Aldershot: Ashgate, 2000, pp. 219–42.

Stevenson, Robert Louis. *A Child's Garden of Verses*. 1885. Ware, Hertfordshire: Wordsworth Editions, 1993.

——. 'An Apology for Idlers'. *Cornhill* 36 (July 1877): 83.

——. 'My First Book'. *Idler* 6, no. 1 (January 1895): 5–11.

———. *New Arabian Nights*, Biographical Edition. New York: Charles Scribner's Sons, 1922. Google Books.

——— and Lloyd Osbourne. *The Ebb Tide*. 1893. In *The Novels and Tales of Robert Louis Stevenson*, vol. 11. New York: Charles Scribner's Sons, 1902: 221–399.

——— and Lloyd Osbourne. *The Wrong Box*. 1889. In *The Novels and Tales of Robert Louis Stevenson*, vol. 11. New York: Charles Scribner's Sons, 1902: 1–220.

Stewart, Garrett. *Dear Reader: The Conscripted Audience in Nineteenth-Century British Fiction*. Baltimore: Johns Hopkins University Press, 1996.

Sullivan, Anne. 'Animating Flames: Recovering Fire-Gazing as a Moving-Image Technology'. *19: Interdisciplinary Studies in the Long Nineteenth Century*, 25 (2017), <https://doi.org/10.16995/ntn.792> (accessed 20 May 2022).

Taunton, Matthew. '*Puck*'. In Laurel Brake and Marysa Demoor (eds), *Dictionary of Nineteenth-Century Journalism*, online ed. (accessed 26 February 2013).

Tave, Stuart M. *The Amiable Humorist: A Study in the Comic Theory and Criticism of the Eighteenth and Early Nineteenth Centuries*. Chicago: University of Chicago Press, 1960.

Telfer, Kevin. *Peter Pan's First XI: The Extraordinary Story of J. M. Barrie's Cricket Team*. London: Sceptre, 2010.

Thackeray, W. M. *Pendennis*. 1848–50. Oxford: Oxford World's Classics, 1994.

[Thackeray, William Makepeace]. 'Roundabout Papers. – No. I: On a Lazy Idle Boy'. *Cornhill Magazine* 1, no. 1 (January 1860): 124–8.

'The Case of the Resurrected Detective: "The Empty House"'. *Discovering Sherlock Holmes*, Stanford University, <http://sherlockholmes.stanford.edu/issue12_8.html> (accessed 20 May 2022).

'The Chronicles of the Strand Club – No. 1'. *Strand* 30, no. 175 (July 1905): 66–71.

The Club of Odd Volumes Year Book for 1922. Boston: Printed for the club at the Riverside Press, 1922. Google Books.

The Curran Index. Edited by Lara Atkin and Emily Bell. 2017–present, <curranindex.org> (accessed 20 May 2022).

Thévoz, Seth Alexander. *Club Government: How the Early Victorian World was Ruled from London Clubs*. London: I. B. Tauris, 2018.

Thwaite, Ann. *A. A. Milne: The Man behind Winnie-the-Pooh*. New York: Random House, 1990.

Valverde, Mariana. 'The Love of Finery: Fashion and the Fallen Woman in Nineteenth-Century Social Discourse'. *Victorian Studies* 32 (1989): 169–88.

Varga, Zsuzsana. 'St James's Gazette'. In Laurel Brake and Marysa Demoor (eds), *Dictionary of Nineteenth-Century Journalism*, online ed. (accessed 5 June 2013).

Wagner-Lawlor, Jennifer A., ed. *The Victorian Comic Spirit: New Perspectives*. Aldershot: Ashgate, 2000.

Warne, Vanessa and Colette Colligan, 'The Man Who Wrote a New Woman Novel: Grant Allen's "The Woman Who Did" and the Gendering of New Woman Authorship'. *Victorian Literature and Culture* 33, no. 1 (2005): 21–46.

Weiner, Joel H., ed. *Papers for the Millions: The New Journalism in Britain, 1850s to 1914*. New York: Greenwood, 1988.

Who Was Who. London: Adam and Charles Black, 1929–40.

Who's Who. London: Adam and Charles Black, 1908.

Who's Who, vol. 56. London: Adam and Charles Black, 1904.

Wild, Jonathan. *The Rise of the Office Clerk in Literary Culture, 1880–1939*. Houndmills: Palgrave Macmillan, 2006.

———. 'What was *New* about the "New Humour"? Barry Pain's "Divine Carelessness"'. In Louise Lee (ed.), *Victorian Comedy and Laughter: Conviviality, Jokes and Dissent*. London: Palgrave Macmillan, 2020: 291–308.

Wilkie, Laurie A. *The Lost Boys of Zeta Psi*. Berkeley: University of California Press, 2010.

Williams, Carolyn. *Gilbert and Sullivan: Gender, Genre, Parody*. New York: Columbia University Press, 2011.

Williams, Raymond. *The Long Revolution*. 1961. New York: Broadview, 2001.

Williamson, Michael T. 'Before Jeeves: Impudence in P. G. Wodehouse's Novels, 1909–23'. In Ann Rea (ed.), *Middlebrow Wodehouse: P. G. Wodehouse's Work in Context*. London: Routledge, 2016: 51–72.

Winehouse, Bernard. 'Israel Zangwill's *Children of the Ghetto*: A Literary History of the First Anglo-Jewish Best-Seller'. *ELT: English Literature in Transition, 1880–1920* 16, no. 197: 93–117.

Wodehouse, P. G. *A Gentleman of Leisure*. London: Herbert Jenkins, [1935?].

———. *America, I Like You*. New York: Simon & Schuster, 1956.

———. *Big Money*. 1931. Woodstock: Overlook, 2007.

———. *Full Moon*. 1947. New York: Overlook, 2006.

———. *If I Were You*. 1931. New York: Overlook, 2013.

———. *Indiscretions of Archie*. New York: George H. Doran, 1921. Hathi Trust.

———. *Jeeves and the Feudal Spirit*. 1954. New York: Overlook, 2001.

———. *Jill the Reckless*. 1920. Woodstock: Overlook, 2005.

———. *Laughing Gas*. 1936. Woodstock: Overlook, 2001.

———. *Leave It to Psmith*. 1923. London: Herbert Jenkins [1927?].

———. *Mike: A Public School Story*. 1909. Rockville: Ark Manor, 2008.

———. *My Man Jeeves*. 1919. Woodstock: Overlook, 2006.

———. *Psmith in the City*. 1910. New York: Overlook, 2003.

———. *Service with a Smile*. 1961. New York: Norton, 2013.

———. *Something Fishy*. 1957. New York: Overlook, 2008.

———. *Spring Fever*. 1948. Woodstock: Overlook, 2004.

———. *Stiff Upper Lip, Jeeves*. 1962. New York: Overlook, 2012.

———. *Summer Lightning*. 1929. New York: Overlook, 2003.

———. *Thank You, Jeeves*. 1934. New York: Overlook, 2003.

———. *The Complete Lyrics of P.G. Wodehouse*, edited by Barry Day. Lanham, MD: Scarecrow Press, 2004.

———. *The Inimitable Jeeves*. 1923. New York: W.W. Norton, 2011.

———. *The Mating Season*. 1949. New York: Overlook, 2001.

———. *The Small Bachelor*. 1927. New York: Overlook, 2013.

———. *Uncle Fred in the Springtime*. 1939. Woodstock: Overlook, 2004.

———. *Very Good, Jeeves*. 1930. Harmondsworth: Penguin, 1959.

———. *Young Men in Spats*. 1936. Woodstock: Overlook Press, 2002.

——— and Guy Bolton, *Bring on the Girls! The Improbable Story of Our Life in Musical Comedy, with Pictures to Prove It*. New York: Simon and Schuster, 1953.

'Wodehouse Works and Research Resources'. P. G. Wodehouse Society (UK), <www.pgwodehousesociety.org.uk> (accessed 30 May 2013).

Zangwill, Israel. *The Bachelors' Club*. New York: Brentano's, 1891.

———. *The Celibates' Club: Being the United Stories of The Bachelors' Club and The Old Maids' Club*. New York: Macmillan, 1905.

———. *The Melting Pot*. Edited by Meri-Jane Rochelson. Peterborough: Broadview, 2018.

Zieger, Susan. 'Holmes's Pipe, Tobacco Papers and the Nineteenth-Century Origins of Media Addiction'. *Journal of Victorian Culture* 19, no. 1 (2014): 24–42.

Index